1, 2, 3 JOHN

BHGNT

Baylor Handbook on the Greek New Testament
Martin M. Culy
General Editor

1, 2, 3 JOHN
A Handbook on the Greek Text

Martin M. Culy

BAYLOR UNIVERSITY PRESS

Scripture translations are the author's.

Cover Design by Pamela Poll Graphic Design

The 13-digit ISBN is 978-1-932792-08-9.

Library of Congress Cataloging-in-Publication Data

Culy, Martin M.
 1, 2, 3 John : a handbook on the Greek text / Martin M. Culy.
    p. cm.
 Includes bibliographical references.
 ISBN 1-932792-08-2 (pbk. : alk. paper)
 1. Bible. N.T. Epistles of John--Commentaries. 2. Bible. N.T. Epistles of John--Language, style. I. Title: First, second, third John. II. Title: 1st, 2nd, 3rd John. III. Title.

 BS2805.53.C85 2004
 227'.94077--dc22
                              2004018681

Printed in the United States of America on acid-free paper with 30% PCW content.

CONTENTS

Contents

SERIES INTRODUCTION

The Baylor Handbook on the Greek New Testament (BHGNT) is designed to guide new readers and seasoned scholars alike through the intricacies of the Greek text. Each handbook provides a verse-by-verse treatment of the biblical text. Unlike traditional commentaries, however, the BHGNT makes little attempt to expound on the theological meaning or significance of the document under consideration. Instead, the handbooks serve as "prequels" to commentary proper. They provide readers of the New Testament with a foundational analysis of the Greek text upon which interpretation may then be established. Readers of traditional commentaries are sometimes dismayed by the fact that even those that are labeled "exegetical" or "critical" frequently have little to say about the mechanics of the Greek text and all too often completely ignore the more perplexing grammatical issues. In contrast, the BHGNT offers an accessible and comprehensive, though not exhaustive, treatment of the Greek New Testament, with particular attention given to the grammar of the text. In order to make the handbooks more user-friendly, authors have only selectively interacted with secondary literature. Where there is significant debate on an issue, the handbooks provide a representative sample of scholars espousing each position; when authors adopt a less known stance on the text, they generally list any other scholars who have embraced that position.

The BHGNT, however, is more than a reliable guide to the Greek text of the New Testament. Each author brings unique strengths to the task of preparing the handbook. As a result, students and scholars alike will at times be introduced to ways of looking at the Greek language that they have not encountered before. This feature makes the handbooks valuable not only for intermediate and advanced Greek courses but also for students and scholars who no longer have the luxury of increasing their Greek proficiency within a classroom context. While handbook authors do not consider modern linguistic theory to be a panacea for all questions exegetical, the BHGNT does aim both to help move linguistic insights into the mainstream of New Testament reference works and, at the same time, to help weed out some of the myths about the Greek language that continue to appear in both scholarly and popular treatments of the New Testament.

Using the Baylor Handbook on the Greek New Testament

Each handbook consists of the following features. The introduction draws readers' attention to some of the distinctive features of the biblical text and treats some of the broader issues relating to the text as a whole in a more thorough fashion. In the handbook proper, the biblical text is divided into sections, each of which is introduced with a translation that illustrates how the insights gleaned from the analysis that follows may be expressed in modern English. Following the translation is the heart of the handbook, an extensive analysis of the Greek text. Here, the Greek text of each verse is followed by comments on grammatical, lexical, and text-critical issues. Handbook authors may also make use of other features, such as passage overviews between the translation and notes.

Each page of the handbook includes a header to direct readers to the beginning of the section where the translation is found (left page header) or to identify the range of verses covered on the two facing pages (right hand header). Terminology used in the comments that is potentially unfamiliar is included in a glossary in the back of the handbook and/or cross-referenced with the first occurrence of the expression, where an explanation may be found. Each volume also includes an index that provides a list of grammatical phenomena occurring in the biblical text. This feature provides a valuable resource for students of Greek wanting to study a particular construction more carefully or Greek instructors needing to develop illustrations, exercises, or exams. The handbooks conclude with a bibliography of works cited, providing helpful guidance in identifying resources for further research on the Greek text.

The handbooks assume that users will possess a minimal level of competence with Greek morphology and syntax. Series authors generally utilize traditional labels such as those found in Daniel Wallace's *Greek Grammar Beyond the Basics*. Labels that are drawn from the broader field of modern linguistics are explained at their first occurrence and included in the glossary. Common labels that users may be unfamiliar with are also included in the glossary.

The primary exception to the broad adoption of traditional syntactic labels relates to verb tenses. Most New Testament Greek grammars describe the tense system as being formally fairly simple (only 6 tenses) but functionally complex. The aorist tense, it is frequently said, can function in a wide variety of ways that are associated with labels such as "ingressive," "gnomic," "constative," "epistolary," "proleptic," and so forth. Similar functional complexity is posited for the other tenses. Positing such "functions," however, typically stems not from a careful analysis of Greek syntax but rather from grappling with the challenges of translating Greek verbs into English. When we carefully examine the Greek verb tenses themselves, we find that the tense forms do not themselves denote semantic features such as ingressive, iterative, or conative; they certainly do not emphasize such notions; at best they may allow for ingressive, iterative, or conative translations. Although many of the other traditional labels are susceptible to similar critique, the tense labels have frequently led to exegetical claims that go beyond the syntax, e.g., that a particular aorist verb *emphasizes* the beginning of an action. For this reason, we have chosen not to utilize these labels.

Instead, where the context points to an ingressive nuance for the action of the verb, this will be incorporated into the translation.

Deponency

Although series authors will vary in the theoretical approaches they bring to the text, the BHGNT has adopted the same general approach on one important issue: deponency. Traditionally, the label "deponent" has been applied to verbs with middle, passive, or middle/passive morphology that are thought to be "active" in meaning. Introductory grammars tend to put a significant number of middle verbs in the New Testament in this category, despite the fact that some of the standard reference grammars have questioned the validity of the label. Robertson (332), for example, argues that the label "should not be used at all."

In recent years, a number of scholars have taken up Robertson's quiet call to abandon this label. Carl Conrad's posts on the B-Greek Internet discussion list (beginning in 1997) and his subsequent formalization of those concerns in unpublished papers available on his website have helped flesh out the concerns raised by earlier scholars. In a recent article, Jonathan Pennington (61–64) helpfully summarizes the rationale for dispensing with the label, maintaining that widespread use of the term "deponent" stems from two key factors: (1) the tendency to attempt to analyze Greek syntax through reference to English translation—if a workable translation of a middle form appears "active" in English, we conclude that the verb must be active in meaning even though it is middle in form; and (2) the imposition of Latin categories on Greek grammar. Pennington (61) concludes that "most if not all verbs that are considered 'deponent' are in fact truly middle in meaning." The questions that have been raised regarding deponency as a syntactic category, then, are not simply issues that interest a few Greek scholars and linguists but have no bearing on how one understands the text. Rather, if these scholars are correct, the notion of deponency has, at least in some cases, effectively obscured the semantic significance of the middle voice, leading to imprecise readings of the text (see also Bakker and Taylor).

It is not only middle voice verbs, however, that are the focus of attention in this debate. Conrad, Pennington, and others also maintain that deponency is an invalid category for passive verbs that have traditionally been placed in this category. To account for putative passive deponent verbs, these scholars have turned to the evolution of voice morphology in the Greek language. They draw attention to the fact that middle morphology was being replaced by passive morphology (the -θη- morpheme) during the Koine period (see esp. Conrad, 3, 5–6; cf. Pennington, 68; Taylor, 175; Caragounis, 153). Consequently, in the Common Era we find "an increasing number of passive forms without a distinctive passive idea ... replacing older middle forms" (Pennington, 68). This diachronic argument leads Conrad (5) to conclude that the -θη- morpheme should be treated as a middle/passive rather than a passive morpheme. Such arguments have a sound linguistic foundation and raise serious questions about the legitimacy of the notion "passive deponent."

Should, then, the label "deponent" be abandoned altogether? While more research needs to be done to account for middle/passive morphology in Koine Greek fully, the arguments, which are very briefly summarized above, are both compelling and exegetically significant. "The middle voice needs to be understood in its own status and function as indicating that the subject of a verb is the focus of the verb's action or state" (Conrad, 3; cf. Taylor, 174). Consequently, users of the BHGNT will discover that verbs that are typically labeled "deponent," including some with -θη- morphology, tend to be listed as "middle."

In recognizing that so-called deponent verbs should be viewed as true middles, users of the BHGNT should not fall into the trap of concluding that the middle form emphasizes the subject's involvement in the action of the verb. At times, the middle voice appears simply to be a morphological flag indicating that the verb is intransitive. More frequently, the middle morphology tends to be driven by the "middle" semantics of the verb itself. In other words, the middle voice is sometimes used with the verb not in order to place a focus on the subject's involvement in the action but precisely because the sense of the lexical form itself involves subject focus.

It is the hope of Baylor University Press, the series editor, and each of the authors that these handbooks will help advance our understanding of the Greek New Testament, be used to further equip the saints for the work of ministry, and fan into flame a love for the Greek New Testament among a new generation of students and scholars.

Martin M. Culy

PREFACE

As I have wrestled with the text of 1, 2, and 3 John in preparing this handbook, I have once again not only been challenged by its frank message, which leaves little room for a complacent faith, but have also been reminded that there remains much to learn about the language of the New Testament. After more than 20 years of working with Koine Greek, I still frequently discover something that I had overlooked in the past. Only a fellow linguist or Greek scholar can appreciate the excitement of such a discovery! My hope is that this handbook will both provide a reliable guide through the intricacies of the biblical text and occasionally shed fresh light on how the Greek language works.

Completion of this handbook in a timely fashion would not have been possible without the support of Dr. Paul Magnus, past President of Briercrest Family of Schools, Dr. Dwayne Uglem, Executive Vice President of Briercrest Family of Schools, and Dr. David Shepherd, Dean of Briercrest Seminary. I am privileged to work in an environment where both ministry and scholarship are held in high esteem.

Throughout the writing process I have greatly benefited from the input of others. Four of my current students—David Atmore, Joshua Drake, Bernd Heyde, and Josh Stigall—carefully worked through an early draft of the handbook, section by section, and then met with me to discuss the biblical text and critique the manuscript. Their helpful comments and words of encouragement were greatly appreciated and our time together was spiritually enriching. Susan Wendel, a former student and future New Testament scholar herself, offered many helpful suggestions for how the handbook could be improved and graciously raised questions where my argument was weak. Dr. Wes Olmstead, my Briercrest colleague and friend, was always ready to give immediate feedback on issues I was struggling to resolve in spite of his heavy responsibilities. Dr. Mikeal Parsons, friend and mentor, offered encouragement throughout the process. Two individuals deserve special thanks for the time and energy they invested in this project. Jim Stewart, a former student and faculty assistant, saved me from many misplaced or incorrect accents and other typographical errors through his incredible eye for detail and saved readers from potential confusion by identifying numerous places where my explanations were not as clear as they should have been. Dr. Carl Conrad graciously and thoroughly reviewed a late draft of the manuscript, noted a significant number of problems, and offered numerous helpful suggestions for improving the handbook. Our ongoing dialogue on various issues not only saved me from many careless mistakes but also frequently led my wife to ask what was giving me so much pleasure. This handbook would have been far weaker without the generous input of these friends, students, and colleagues, and I offer them my sincere gratitude.

I also owe a debt of gratitude to the staff at Baylor University Press. Dr. Carey Newman, Director, not only encouraged me to take on this project but also provided the support and guidance needed to bring it to completion. Diane Smith, Production Editor, once again made the process of moving from manuscript to publication almost painless through the competence and dedication that she brings to the task. Finally, to my wife Jo-Anna, and my children, Chris, Calvin, and Charissa, I am grateful for your graciousness as I often took time and energy away from you to complete this project, and for your patience as we struggle together to "walk as Jesus did."

Martin Culy
Briercrest Seminary

ABBREVIATIONS

act   active
aor   aorist
BAGD   W. Bauer, *A Greek-English Lexicon of the NT*, 1979
BDAG   F. Danker, *A Greek-English Lexicon of the NT*, 2000
BDF   F. W. Blass, A. Debrunner, and R. W. Funk, *A Greek Grammar of the NT*
CEV   Contemporary English Version
dat   dative
fem   feminine
fut   future
gen   genitive
GW   God's Word (version)
impf   imperfect
impv   imperative
ind   indicative
inf   infinitive
KJV   King James Version
LN   Louw and Nida, *Greek-English Lexicon*
LXX   Septuagint
masc   masculine
mid   middle
NASB   New American Standard Bible
NCV   New Century Version
NEB   New English Bible
NET   New English Translation
neut   neuter

NIV	New International Version
NJB	New Jerusalem Bible
NLT	New Living Translation
nom	nominative
NRSV	New Revised Standard Version
NT	New Testament
opt	optative
pass	passive
pl	plural
plprf	pluperfect
pres	present
prf	perfect
ptc	participle
REB	Revised English Bible
RSV	Revised Standard Version
sg	singular
subj	subjunctive
TEV	Today's English Version

INTRODUCTION

The letter known as 1 John has long been a favorite among beginning and intermediate students of Koine Greek. The "almost elementary character" (Brown, x) of the writer's Greek makes it a suitable introduction to the literature of the New Testament. In the first chapter of the letter, for example, readers encounter only three words that occur less than ten times in the New Testament. The fact that the author continues to use common vocabulary throughout the letter and has an affinity for repeating himself helps emerging readers gain confidence quickly. In this short letter, εἰμί is used 99 times; θεός 62 times; ἔχω 28 times; ἀγαπάω 28 times; γινώσκω 25 times; μένω 23 times; κόσμος 23 times; ἀγάπη 18 times; ἁμαρτία 17 times; ἀδελφός 15 times; ἐντολή 14 times; πατήρ 14 times; ἀκούω 14 times; γράφω 13 times; ποιέω 13 times; ζωή 13 times; πνεῦμα 12 times; and γεννάω 10 times. Such lexical simplicity, however, is not always matched by grammatical simplicity. Readers attempting to grapple with the subtleties of the argument and the complexities of the syntactic structure will soon discover that analysis of the text of 1 John can be as challenging as its in-your-face message. Indeed, quite frequently it has been theological discomfort with the superficial sense of the text that has precipitated debate regarding the syntax of 1 John. For example, when modern readers, especially of the Western variety, encounter statements like, "Everyone who remains in him does not sin," they tend to turn quickly to their Greek grammars to determine what the author really meant by what, on the surface, is a patently false statement.

The verse-by-verse treatment of 1, 2, and 3 John that follows attempts to guide new readers and seasoned scholars alike through the intricacies of the Greek text. Although this handbook does not endeavor to label exhaustively every feature of the syntax, discuss every textual problem, or provide analysis of all lexical forms, it does attempt to address all significant questions arising from the Greek text itself. While users of this handbook will no doubt encounter questions that they deem significant but are nevertheless overlooked, the intention has been to anticipate where students of Greek with at least a basic knowledge of the language may encounter difficulties and thus need guidance. What distinguishes this work from other analytical guides to the Greek New Testament (most of which are single volumes covering the entire New Testament) is the detailed and comprehensive attention paid to the text of 1, 2, and 3 John. Some of the more complex issues related to Greek syntax, in particular, tend to be ignored by the standard commentaries.

Although at certain points, commentary on the text cannot be avoided, this handbook does not aim to elucidate the theological meaning of the text. Nor does it attempt to address introductory issues such as authorship, date, provenance, or the nature and history of the "Johannine community." Rather, this volume provides a guide to understanding the linguistic characteristics of the text from which the message of the text may then be derived. Consequently, no attempt has been made to interact thoroughly with the secondary literature on the Johannine Letters, as one would expect in a critical commentary. Those interested in bibliography on a particular passage or fuller lists of scholars espousing particular views may consult Brown's commentary and the *Exegetical Summary* by Anderson.

Although traditional introductory topics go beyond the goals of this handbook, there are a number of broad issues relating to the Greek text of the letters of John that are worth introducing prior to the verse-by-verse treatment in the handbook proper.

These include questions of genre and structure, the significance of the writer's choices of verb tense, the writer's use of mitigated exhortations, and the writer's propensity for Trinitarian ambiguity.

Genre and Structure

The fact that 1 John lacks many of the features of contemporary letters, such as a greeting from the author, a thanksgiving section, and a conclusion, has led to some debate over the years regarding its genre. Although most scholars, in the end, are content to label the work a letter or epistle, the text reads more like a sermon than a letter. For our purposes, recognizing that 1 John represents hortatory discourse is more important than settling the question of whether or not it represents an actual letter. The primary purpose of this "letter" is to exhort, not to inform (cf. Miehle, ix). Although the entire letter contains only 11 imperative verbs, with the first not occurring until 2:15, when the full range of forms used for exhortation are considered (including imperatives, ἵνα clauses that are introduced as an ἐντολή, the use of the verb ὀφείλω, the construction πᾶς plus a participle, and the frequent ἐάν clauses), the hortatory character of the text becomes readily apparent. I agree with Miehle that "1 John was written primarily to persuade its readers to act consistently with what they say they believed, rather than to inform them about what was desirable to believe" (quoted in Olsson, 178).

In two articles (1983, 1992) that complement analysis done by his doctoral student (see Miehle), R. Longacre notes that although "the brute statistics of the book (as far as the type of verbs that occur) are misleading" (1992, 277), with only 9 percent of the verbs being imperative in nature (1992, 278), "the command forms are central . . . [and] the book moves from mitigated (almost disguised) commands to overt commands at the structures which we call the peaks of the book" (1992, 277). Indeed, Longacre (1992, 271) notes that with hortatory discourse, the various forms of command will constitute "the basic material around which the rest of the book nucleates."

These peaks, or most prominent portions of the discourse, provide the clearest direction for determining the overall message of the letter. Longacre (1983, 1992) argues that 1:1–2:29 contains two peaks, an ethical peak (2:12-17) and a dogmatic peak (2:18-27). The same types of peaks occur in reverse order in 4:1-6 (dogmatic peak) and 4:7-21 (ethical peaks). In a hortatory letter like 1 John, the peaks are the places where explicit imperative verbs (contrast mitigated exhortations) and verbs like ὀφείλω are characteristically found (Longacre 1992, 279). Such discourse peaks "develop the main message of the book," while the material surrounding them provides overt statements concerning the text's macrostructure, i.e., what the work is about (Longacre 1992, 272). Indeed, Longacre argues that the paragraphs preceding the peaks in chapter 4 clearly lay out the central thrust of the whole letter. In 4:1-6, the author of 1 John argues that "What God has commanded of us, what He wants of us is that we should believe on the name of His Son Jesus Christ and love one another" (Longacre 1992, 283). This "macrostructure" is reiterated in the paragraph that follows the second peak of chapter 4, which begins with 5:1 ("Everyone who believes that Jesus is the Christ has been born of God, and everyone who loves the parent [also] loves the one who has been born of him"). The same may be argued for the relationship between 1 John 2:28-29 and the two peaks of chapter 2 (see 2:28 on Καὶ νῦν, τεκνία). Discourse peaks may also be readily identified in 2 and 3 John through reference to the location of imperative verbs. In 2 John, a cluster of three imperative forms helps mark verses 8-11 as the peak of the letter. In 3 John, the sole imperative verb (verse 11), along with other command forms, marks verses 9-12 as the letter's peak.

While identifying such peaks may be relatively straightforward, broader questions relating to the structure of 1 John are quite complex. Nearly 100 years ago, Brooke's (xxxii) careful examination of the structure of 1 John and his review of scholarly analyses led him to conclude that "perhaps the attempt to analyse the [structure of the] Epistle should be abandoned"! Seventy years later, Brown (x) expressed essential agreement with Brooke's assessment, conceding that "it is virtually impossible to detect a structured sequence of thought" in 1 John. The structural puzzle, however, has not deterred scholars in the last century from attempting to unlock its secrets. Unfortunately, few or none of the "distressingly many" (Olsson, 370) analyses agree on all points.

In his excellent summary of recent analyses, Olsson (372) points out that the letter is commonly agreed to contain a prologue (1:1-4) and epilogue (5:13-21). Broad consensus on the structure of the letter, however, comes to a screeching halt at that point, with scholars positing anywhere from two to seven sections for the central portion of the letter. Although this handbook does not attempt to resolve all questions of structure, it does highlight features of the text that suggest a structural boundary, and offers words of caution against basing structural decisions on perceived changes of theme or topic, without considering the syntax of the text itself. Although such an approach may sound obvious, most analyses to date have been predominantly content-oriented, relying almost exclusively on thematic analysis to determine the structure of the letter (see Olsson for an excellent summary). In other words, they have focused more on identifying "semantic paragraphs" than grammatical paragraphs (cf. Larson, 353–56). Indeed, while Longacre (1992, 270) points out that beginning with an outline of a book "enables us to grasp the fundamental thrust of the whole and to understand better what the book is saying," scholars have often worked in reverse order, using what they perceive the book to be saying to determine the outline of the book. To avoid this, interpreters must attempt to detect "the reading instructions to be found in the text itself" (Olsson, 371).

Unfortunately, much work needs to be done to determine what constitutes "reading instructions" (see Brown and Yule, 95–100). Consequently, even analyses that are based on both grammatical and thematic analysis of the letter vary considerably. Longacre (1992), for example, appears to be the only scholar to argue that 1:1–2:29 forms the rather oversized introduction to the letter, an introduction that contains most of the themes of the letter. He bases his argument on the fact that the performative verb γράφω is ubiquitous in this section (1:4; 2:1, 7, 8, 26; and six times in 2:12-14) and does not reappear until the beginning of the closing of the letter in 5:13. Although the distribution of γράφω within the letter is likely significant, such an analysis is not consistent with what is known of typical ancient letters, regardless of their subgenre.

Longacre is on firmer ground in identifying boundary markers within the text. He gives special attention to the role of vocatives in marking new paragraphs (1992, 272–76). Such an analysis is consistent with conventional thinking concerning how vocatives typically function in hortatory discourse (cf. Larson, 341; Floor, 6; Levinsohn 1992, 198). In addition to vocatives, typical markers of boundaries in this and other genres include: changes of time, scene, or participant in narrative texts, changes of tense or mood, the use of conjunctions (esp. οὖν, τότε, διό, etc.), special phrases (like καὶ ἐγένετο in narrative), performative verbs, back reference, and rhetorical questions (see Beekman and Callow, 279–80; Larsen 1991b, 49–50; Levinsohn 1992, 191–203). Larsen (1991b), however, building on the work of Rogers, has raised serious questions regarding the role of the vocative as a boundary marker. Basing her study on the Pauline corpus, Rogers (26) concluded that "In many places where vocatives seem to signal boundaries, other forms or factors are decisive. In itself, the vocative form cannot be said to signal change of theme." Larsen goes further and maintains that "there are seldom any grammatical criteria which clearly signal a new paragraph or section. Such breaks function in the deep structure of a text more than in the surface structure" (1991b, 48). Although he concedes that "there are various grammatical features which may lend support to such boundaries" (1991b, 48), he rejects the vocative as a boundary marker and argues that it serves as a rhetorical device, used to develop rapport with the hearers, rather than a structural device (1991b, 50–51). Following Beekman and Callow's claim that "The basic criterion is that a section, or a paragraph, deals with one theme," Larsen (1991b, 51) places particular emphasis on the use of introductory and summary statements as boundary markers. In his own analysis, however, which divides the main body of 1 John into two sections made up of a total of 11 sub-units, seven of those units have a vocative in the first verse of the unit. There seems to be a similar correlation between vocatives and boundaries in 3 John. Given this distribution of vocatives, it is not inappropriate to recognize that this particular writer frequently uses vocatives to help mark boundaries. Such an observation does not require that vocatives were always used in this way. It simply recognizes that while vocatives function primarily as a literary device, this particular literary device may, at least in certain authors, provide corroborative evidence of a structural boundary.

Verbal Aspect and Prominence

In recent years, a number of scholars (see esp. Porter 1989, 1994) have argued for a correlation between verbal aspect and the notion of prominence. "Prominence is the feature of discourse structure which makes one part more important, i.e. more significant or prominent than another" (Larson, 405). Theoretically, an interpreter can look to verbal aspect to help identify material that the writer wants to highlight. While there is certainly not a one-to-one correlation between verbal aspect and prominence in Koine Greek, there do appear to be some patterns in the Letters of John. In main clauses, the writer generally uses the aorist tense (which occurs 68 times total) with information that is already assumed and thus serves as the foundation for his exhortations and supporting arguments. When carrying the argument or "mainline" of the hortatory discourse forward, the writer tends to utilize the present tense (which occurs 284 times total). These correlations between perfective aspect (aorist tense) and background material, and between imperfective aspect (especially present tense) and mainline material may shed important light on the otherwise perplexing shift in tense in 1 John 2:12-14. We should not, however, overlook the fact that mainline material in the Letters of John tends to be introduced primarily through the use of the imperative mood, the hortatory subjunctive, a verb of obligation (such as ὀφείλω), or by identifying the information as a command (ἐντολή). In 1 John, it is worth noting that nearly all of the imperative verbs and the only two examples of hortatory subjunctives (3:18; 4:7) occur in the present tense. The passages where the only two examples of aorist imperative verbs occur (3:1; 5:21) do not serve to carry the argument forward. In 3:1, the aorist imperative ἴδετε serves as more of an exclamation than a command, while in 5:21, the aorist imperative φυλάξατε serves to summarize what precedes rather than advance the argument.

The imperfect tense, which is also imperfective aspect, is used just seven times in 1 John, always with the verb εἰμί, except in 2:7, where it is used with εἴχετε to refer to something that has been true over the course of time in the past. Although the perfect tense (stative aspect according to Porter) is used 69 times, it is used with a limited number of verbs: οἶδα (15 times), γινώσκω (8 times), γεννάω (8 times), ὁράω (7 times), ἀκούω (4 times), τελειόω (4 times), νικάω (3 times), δίδωμι (3 times), ἀποστέλλω (twice), θεάομαι (twice), πιστεύω (twice), μαρτυρέω (twice), ἐξέρχομαι (once), ἔρχομαι (once), ἀγαπάω (once), μεταβαίνω (once), ἀφίημι (once), πληρόω (once), ἁμαρτάνω (once), γίνομαι (once), and αἰτέω (once). While it may help lend prominence to the clauses in which it occurs, as Porter's theory predicts, it is not clear that it typically marks information as prominent on the discourse level.

In the end, this handbook takes a cautious approach to identifying the semantic or discourse significance of verb tenses within the letter. It is likely accurate to maintain that there is some correlation between prominence and verbal aspect in Greek, as in many other languages, but verbal aspect remains only one among many markers of prominence in the Greek language and is insufficient grounds on its own for determining the relative prominence of a portion of text, as most scholars would readily concede.

Mitigated Exhortations

When analyzing a hortatory discourse one must be careful not to overlook the more subtle forms of persuasion that are utilized by most writers. R. Longacre has argued that a significant number of the non-imperative propositions in 1 John function as mitigated commands. Mitigation is a way of softening a command so as to make it more palatable to the listener/reader. It serves to urge a particular course of action gently rather than demand it. Thus, according to Longacre (1983, 7), the author's statement in 1:6 (Ἐὰν εἴπωμεν ὅτι κοινωνίαν ἔχομεν μετ' αὐτοῦ καὶ ἐν τῷ σκότει περιπατῶμεν, ψευδόμεθα καὶ οὐ ποιοῦμεν τὴν ἀλήθειαν) serves as a mitigated command meaning, "Do not claim to have fellowship with him and continue to walk in the darkness." Indeed, he maintains that although 1 John 1:5-10 is superficially a paragraph of exposition, i.e., it is expository in its surface structure, it is full of "covert exhortations" (Longacre 1992, 272).

Although it is helpful to recognize that non-imperative forms frequently carry an implied exhortation, it may be preferable to reserve the label "mitigated command" for a specific type of implied exhortation. I might, for example, ask my son on a Saskatchewan winter day when it is minus 40° outside, "Did you leave the front door open?" The question, in such a case, truly functions as a mitigated command. I am intentionally asking him to go back and close the door because I can feel the cold air coming in. Similarly, I might say to my daughter, "The stove is hot." In this case, a statement functions as a mitigated command. I am gently telling her to be careful not to touch the stove. Such mitigated commands, however, tend to stand on their own, rather than serving as part of an extended exhortation.

In 1 John, statements such as the one cited from 1:6 clearly have a hortatory function, i.e., they urge a particular course of action. They are, however, more of the "you should not" type than the "do not" type. As such, they help build a picture of a larger command rather than serving as a command in and of themselves. This becomes clear as we consider Longacre's analysis of 1 John 2:15—Μὴ ἀγαπᾶτε τὸν κόσμον μηδὲ τὰ ἐν τῷ κόσμῳ. ἐάν τις ἀγαπᾷ τὸν κόσμον, οὐκ ἔστιν ἡ ἀγάπη τοῦ πατρὸς ἐν αὐτῷ. Longacre (1983, 13) identifies the second sentence as a mitigated command meaning, "Don't love the world." Such an analysis, however, raises the question of why a conditional clause that follows a direct command should be viewed as a miti-gated command (in its own right) rather than simply a supporting reason for the command, which already explicitly says, "Don't love the world." Why add a second version of an imperative command that is softer than the first version? Instead of labeling such constructions mitigated commands, then, it is preferable to note that rhetorically they carry hortatory force and support the overall hortatory goals of the letter or section. This handbook thus labels such phenomena "mitigated exhortations" except in cases like 1 John 3:3, where the mitigated construction stands on its own and serves more as an implicit command.

Finally, we should note that the same types of mitigated exhor-tations are found in 2 John and 3 John. In 2 John, the mitigated exhortations are achieved, for example, through the use of the language of command (ἐντολή is used four times in verses 4-6) or the characterization of those who do not follow the writer's wishes as not "having God" (verse 9). In 3 John, the writer uses an imperative verb only once in the main body of the letter (verse 11; the other imperative is in verse 15). Nevertheless, the letter is full of mitigated exhortations that urge Gaius to embrace a particular course of action. For example, the way the writer frames his statement in verse 4 ("my greatest joy comes from hearing that my children are living in the truth") sends the subtle message that pleasing the Elder will require continued adherence to the truth (Floór, 5, 9). Less subtle exhortations follow in verse 6 (καλῶς ποιήσεις plus a participle of means), verse 8 (where the verb ὀφείλω is used), and in verse 11 (where we find the only explicit command/imperative). Interestingly, rhetorical devices that mark foregrounding tend to occur along with the mitigated exhortations (see comments on 3 John).

Trinitarian Ambiguity

Finally, one of the most difficult challenges of the letters of John relates to the writer's use of the pronoun αὐτός and third person verbs without an explicit subject. In 1 John in particular, it is frequently difficult to determine whether he intended to refer to the Father or the Son.

Where there is some basis for arguing one way or the other, I have presented the evidence or simply identified the referent, if the solution is obvious. In many cases, however, it is important to recognize that the ambiguity is indicative of both the writer's disregard for modern conceptions of precision and, more importantly, his Trinitarian theology. Assuming common authorship for the Fourth Gospel and 1 John, we can conjecture that the writer's emphasis on the absolute unity, mutuality, and equality of the Father and the Son evidenced in the Fourth Gospel (see Culy 2010, 118–24) has led him to feel under no compulsion always to distinguish between members of the Godhead within his letter.

A HANDBOOK ON THE GREEK TEXT
OF 1, 2, 3 JOHN

1 John

1 John 1:1-4

[1](Here is what we announce to you) concerning the word of life: that which was from the beginning, that which we have heard, that which we have seen with our own eyes, that which we have scrutinized and our own hands have handled. [2]Now, Life was revealed and we have seen it and testify and announce to you the Eternal Life that was with the Father and was revealed to us. [3]Yes, that which we have seen and heard we announce to you also in order that you too might have fellowship with us; and indeed our fellowship is with the Father and with his Son, Jesus Christ. [4]So then, we are writing these things in order that your joy might be complete.

1:1 Ὁ ἦν ἀπ᾽ ἀρχῆς, ὃ ἀκηκόαμεν, ὃ ἑωράκαμεν τοῖς ὀφθαλμοῖς ἡμῶν, ὃ ἐθεασάμεθα καὶ αἱ χεῖρες ἡμῶν ἐψηλάφησαν, περὶ τοῦ λόγου τῆς ζωῆς

The Prologue of John's first letter (vv. 1-4) functions as the epistolary counterpart of the Prologue of the Fourth Gospel. As in the Fourth Gospel, the writer of 1 John does not immediately identify Jesus as the topic. The structure here does not imply a lack of stylistic concern on the part of the author (cf. Strecker, 8), nor does it "lapse into grammatical impossibilities" (Houlden, 45). On the contrary, the structure serves as a powerful literary device. In the Fourth Gospel, the fact that "Jesus is not actually named until the end of the Prologue (1:17), he does not come onto the stage until 1:29, and he does not speak until 1:38. . . . helps build both interest and tension" (Culy 2010, 96). The same is true here. The

1

writer's coyness in not directly naming the incarnate Jesus as the topic draws the reader into his discourse that follows.

In order to untangle the seemingly tortured syntax of the first three verses, the reader must recognize that the writer has used a topic (or "cleft") construction as a literary strategy. The series of appositional relative clauses in verse 1 introduces the topic, though in a referentially oblique manner. In a topic construction, the referent that is in focus is placed at the beginning of the sentence. If the topic has a syntactic relationship to a clause that follows, it is generally placed in the case it would bear in that clause, even though it is typically picked up with a demonstrative pronoun within that clause (see, e.g., Ἰησοῦν τὸν Ναζωραῖον in Acts 2:22). At times, however, it appears in the nominative case (as a "hanging," or pendent nominative). Here, the relative clauses function as direct objects of the main verb ἀπαγγέλλομεν, which does not appear until verse 3.

Ὅ . . . ὅ. The neuter relative pronouns introduce a series of "headless" relative clauses (relative clauses with no expressed antecedent: "that which . . .") that stand in apposition to each other. The first relative pronoun is the nominative subject of ἦν, while the subsequent ones are accusative direct objects of ἀκηκόαμεν, ἑωράκαμεν, and ἐθεασάμεθα καὶ . . . ἐψηλάφησαν. The neuter gender may be explained by the fact that the writer is talking about his and other eyewitnesses' broad experience of the incarnate Jesus (cf. Harris 2003, 49).

ἦν. Impf ind 3rd sg εἰμί. On the significance of the verb tense, see below on ἀκηκόαμεν.

ἀπ᾽ ἀρχῆς. Given the thematic and linguistic links to the Fourth Gospel's Prologue, ἀρχή could be understood here as a pre-creation "beginning" (so Strecker, 9; cf. Smalley, 7), particularly given the expression ἦν πρὸς τὸν πατέρα in verse 2. The later use of the expression τὸν ἀπ᾽ ἀρχῆς in 2:13 as a title for Jesus supports this view. The immediate context, however, and the use of the preposition ἀπό rather than ἐν may point to the beginning of Jesus' ministry (see esp. Brown, 155–58). It is probably best to affirm intertextual links between the two passages (see below on περὶ τοῦ λόγου τῆς ζωῆς) without positing a referential link between ἀπ᾽ ἀρχῆς and Ἐν ἀρχῇ (John 1:1).

ἀκηκόαμεν. Prf act ind 1st pl ἀκούω. The first person plural verbs in verses 1-4 probably both (1) highlight the writer's

1 John 1:1 3

status as one of a limited group of eyewitnesses, and (2) bolster the authority of the letter by linking it to that group. There is movement between present, imperfect, aorist, and perfect tenses in verses 1-4. Although verbal aspect is certainly not the sole indicator of prominence, there does appear to be some correlation between a verb's tense and the role or status of the information in this section and the rest of the letter (see also "Verbal Aspect and Prominence" in the Introduction). In verses 1-4, the foundational actions of God, which serve as the basis for what follows, are placed in the aorist tense, or perfective aspect (ἐφανερώθη, 1:2a; ἐφανερώθη, 1:2b). The main hortatory line of thought is carried forward with present tense (imperfective aspect) verbs of communication (μαρτυροῦμεν, 1:2; ἀπαγγέλλομεν, 1:2; ἀπαγγέλλομεν, 1:3; γράφομεν, 1:4). The perfect tense (stative aspect) is used with ἀκούω and ὁράω to help highlight the author's status as an eyewitness authority (ἀκηκόαμεν, 1:1; ἑωράκαμεν, 1:1; ἑωράκαμεν, 1:2; ἑωράκαμεν, 1:3; ἀκηκόαμεν, 1:3). We are then left with two finite aorist verbs (ἐθεασάμεθα, 1:1; and ἐψηλάφησαν, 1:1) that must be accounted for (ἦν is "aspectually vague," since the writer only had present and imperfect tenses to choose from; see Porter, 1989). Given the limited correlations between verbal aspect and prominence outlined in the Introduction (see "Verbal Aspect and Prominence"), the relative prominence of the events described by these verbs is downgraded, suggesting that they clarify the two verbs that precede and provide supporting information (see further below). Such an analysis recognizes that the author made a conscious choice (he uses perfect forms of θεάομαι in 4:12, 14; cf. John 1:32) to portray the events using the aorist tense (contra Louw, 101; and Smalley, 7, who argue that the perfects and aorists in v. 1 carry the same semantic value).

ἑωράκαμεν. Prf act ind 1st pl ὁράω. On the significance of the tense and number, see above on ἀκηκόαμεν.

τοῖς ὀφθαλμοῖς ἡμῶν. Used with ὁράω, the seemingly redundant information emphasizes the eyewitness nature of the writer's testimony (cf. αἱ χεῖρες ἡμῶν below).

τοῖς ὀφθαλμοῖς. Dative of instrument. The expression should be understood as the literal instrument of ἑωράκαμεν not as an example of synecdoche (see below on αἱ χεῖρες ἡμῶν; contra Sherman and Tuggy, 21).

ἡμῶν. Possessive genitive.

ἐθεασάμεθα. A or mid ind 1st pl θεάομαι. On the significance of
the tense and number, see above on ἀκηκόαμεν. The voice should
probably be viewed as a true middle, indicating that the subject
is "the center of emphasis, the receiver of sensory perception"
(Miller, 429). For more on the voice, see "Deponency" in the
Series Introduction. According to Louw and Nida (24.14), θεάομαι
differs from ὁράω (used above) in that it carries the nuance of
"continuity and attention, often with the implication that what
is observed is something unusual." If the tense analysis above is
correct, θεάομαι is probably not simply being used as a stylistic
near synonym of ὁράω. It will not do simply to maintain that the
writer preferred one verb of seeing when he wrote in the aorist and
another one when he used the perfect tense, since he uses θεάομαι
in the perfect later in the letter (4:12, 14; contra Brown, 162, whose
argument follows the earlier work of Tarelli and Freed).
  αἱ χεῖρες ἡμῶν. Synecdoche for "we." Synecdoche is a figure of speech in which one term is used in place of another with
which it is associated. Unlike metonymy (see 2:2 on τοῦ κόσμου),
synecdoche specifically involves a part-whole relationship. Here,
a part of the writer(s), i.e., "our hands," is used to refer to the
whole. Used with ψηλαφάω, the seemingly redundant information
emphasizes the eyewitness nature of the writer's testimony (cf.
τοῖς ὀφθαλμοῖς ἡμῶν above).
  ἐψηλάφησαν. Aor act ind 3rd pl ψηλαφάω. On the significance
of the tense and number, see above on ἀκηκόαμεν. Strecker (14,
n. 27) notes, "The combination of verbs of seeing with ψηλαφάω
is striking. This 'touching' is to be found only at this point in
the Johannine writings. In Luke 24:39 and Ignatius *Smyrn.* 2.2,
in combination with forms of εἶδον, it appears in this concrete,
sensory meaning as a proof of the bodily resurrection (cf. John
20:25)."
  περὶ τοῦ λόγου τῆς ζωῆς. Reference. The prepositional phrase
clarifies what the writer intends to talk about and syntactically
anticipates the main verb (ἀπαγγέλλομεν), which is eventually
introduced in verse 3. Given the intertextual links to the Prologue
of the Fourth Gospel—the reference to the "beginning" (ἀπ' ἀρχῆς
versus Ἐν ἀρχῇ; v. 1; John 1:1); the use of πρὸς τὸν πατέρα versus
πρὸς τὸν θεόν (v. 2; John 1:1); the use of θεάομαι with reference to
the λόγος (v. 1; John 1:14); the connection between the λόγος and ἡ

ζωή (v. 2; John 1:4); and the revelation (ἐφανερώθη) of the λόγος in the flesh (v. 2; John 1:14)—a reference to the "(living) Logos" (cf. Burdick, 100–101; Bultmann, 8) here is conceivable, with τῆς ζωῆς then serving as an attributive genitive. Such a reference, however, is probably ruled out by the fact that (1) it is ἡ ζωή that is picked up, explained, and personified in the following verse (cf. Harris 2003, 48); (2) λόγος is used elsewhere in 1 John (1:10; 2:5, 7, 14; 3:18), but not to refer to Jesus (Harris 2003, 52); (3) there are no clear examples of a personified λόγος modified by an attributive genitive elsewhere in the NT; and (4) there are no clear contextual markers pointing to personification here.

τῆς ζωῆς. Objective genitive (but see above). Genitive modifiers of verbal nouns, i.e., nouns with an implicit event idea, will frequently provide either the "subject" or "object" of the implied event. It is highly unlikely that τῆς ζωῆς could be taken as a genitive in apposition to τοῦ λόγου, and thus a second title for Jesus (contra Burdick, 101). It is only in the following verse that ἡ ζωή is personified through its use with ἐφανερώθη.

1:2 καὶ ἡ ζωὴ ἐφανερώθη, καὶ ἑωράκαμεν καὶ μαρτυροῦμεν καὶ ἀπαγγέλλομεν ὑμῖν τὴν ζωὴν τὴν αἰώνιον ἥτις ἦν πρὸς τὸν πατέρα καὶ ἐφανερώθη ἡμῖν

καὶ. The resumptive relative clause that follows (1:3) strongly suggests that verse 2 is parenthetical (contra Francis, 122). As Titrud (247) notes, "καὶ is used as a function word to express the general relation of connection or addition, especially accompaniment, participation, combination, contiguity, continuance, simultaneity, and sequence." While the specific semantic relationship between clauses or sentences linked by καὶ will vary, clause-initial conjunctive uses of καὶ generally highlight both thematic continuity and progression of thought, i.e., they "signal that the following clause is still closely related semantically to the preceding one" (Titrud, 251). They thus tend to introduce additional comments regarding a theme or idea that has just been introduced (cf. 1:3b; 2:1b, 2, 17; 3:5, 12, 15, 16, 24; 4:21; 5:6, 14, 17, 20). When καὶ introduces a new sentence or paragraph it indicates a close thematic relation to the preceding sentence or paragraph. Although such continuity is usually made clear through the repetition of theme words, in some cases the thematic linkage is made explicit through an anaphoric demonstrative pronoun (3:3), while in a number of cases no lexical linkage is used (1:4, 5; 2:24; 4:3, 14, 16). In this first example of a clause-initial καί, the conjunction introduces a further comment on τῆς ζωῆς (v. 1). At times, sentence-initial καίs are used with common Johannine expressions. The use of the conjunction in the expression, καὶ αὕτη ἐστὶν (2:25; 3:23; 4:3; 5:4, 11, 14; 2 John 6), for example, appears to highlight thematic continuity, whereas the same construction without the conjunction is used with parenthetical or supplementary comments (cf. 2:22; 5:6, 20). The contrast between καὶ ἐν τούτῳ γινώσκομεν (2:3; 3:19, 24) and ἐν τούτῳ γινώσκομεν (2:5; 3:16; 3:19 variant; 4:2; 4:13; 5:2) is less clear. The lack of clarity may relate to the fact that the construction itself always points forward (with the cataphoric demonstrative pronoun). If the above analysis is correct, καὶ ἐν τούτῳ serves as a cataphoric expression that closely links what follows to what precedes.

ἡ ζωή. Nominative subject of ἐφανερώθη. Personification (a figure of speech in which an abstract idea, or something not human, is treated as though it were a person).

ἐφανερώθη. Aor ind 3rd sg φανερόω. In light of the personified subject, the verb could be viewed as either middle or passive voice (see "Deponency" in the Series Introduction; cf. BDAG, 1048). On the significance of the tense, see v. 1 on ἀκηκόαμεν.

ἑωράκαμεν. Prf act ind 1st pl ὁράω. On the significance of the tense and number of the verb, see v. 1 on ἀκηκόαμεν.

μαρτυροῦμεν καὶ ἀπαγγέλλομεν. Although there is overlap in the semantics of these two verbs, given the fact that they are conjoined with ἑωράκαμεν, they should not be viewed as a doublet (see 3:18 on ἐν ἔργῳ καὶ ἀληθείᾳ). The first verb probably highlights, once more, the speaker's direct knowledge of the subject matter (cf. LN 33.262), while the second verb points to more generic "informing" or "announcing."

μαρτυροῦμεν. Pres act ind 1st pl μαρτυρέω. On the significance of the tense and number of the verb, see v. 1 on ἀκηκόαμεν.

ἀπαγγέλλομεν. Pres act ind 1st pl ἀπαγγέλλω. On the significance of the tense and number of the verb, see v. 1 on ἀκηκόαμεν.

ὑμῖν. Dative indirect object of μαρτυροῦμεν καὶ ἀπαγγέλλομεν.

τὴν ζωὴν τὴν αἰώνιον. Accusative direct object of μαρτυροῦμεν καὶ ἀπαγγέλλομεν. Given its use with πρὸς τὸν πατέρα, this phrase should be viewed as personification (see above on ἡ ζωὴ).

ἥτις. Nominative subject of ἦν.

πρὸς τὸν πατέρα. When followed by a familial term or human referent, the preposition frequently carries a relational nuance, as here (cf. LN 89.112).

ἐφανερώθη. Aor ind 3rd sg φανερόω. On the voice, see above on ἐφανερώθη. The repetition of this verb with the specific target of the revelation emphasizes (even more) the reliability of the writer and the teaching he is going to convey.

ἡμῖν. Dative indirect object of ἐφανερώθη.

1:3 ὃ ἑωράκαμεν καὶ ἀκηκόαμεν ἀπαγγέλλομεν καὶ ὑμῖν, ἵνα καὶ ὑμεῖς κοινωνίαν ἔχητε μεθ᾽ ἡμῶν. καὶ ἡ κοινωνία δὲ ἡ ἡμετέρα μετὰ τοῦ πατρὸς καὶ μετὰ τοῦ υἱοῦ αὐτοῦ Ἰησοῦ Χριστοῦ.

ὃ ἑωράκαμεν καὶ ἀκηκόαμεν. Topic constructions (see 1:1) typically require a resumptive demonstrative pronoun near the main verb. Here, however, in light of the lengthy parenthetical statement in verse 2, the topic is repeated in summary form with a "headless" relative clause (see 1:1), which serves as the direct object of ἀπαγγέλλομεν. The reiteration of this material, along with ἀπαγγέλλομεν . . . ὑμῖν (cf. v. 2), makes it clear that the focus is on providing eyewitness testimony. Rhetorically, the language bolsters the reliability of the message that follows. The shift in order of verbs (verse 1 has ἀκηκόαμεν preceding ἑωράκαμεν) is probably simply stylistically motivated, perhaps because ἐφανερώθη (v. 2) naturally results in ἑωράκαμεν, while ἀκηκόαμεν naturally leads to ἀπαγγέλλομεν.

ὅ. Accusative direct object of ἑωράκαμεν καὶ ἀκηκόαμεν.

ἑωράκαμεν. Prf act ind 1st pl ὁράω. On the significance of the tense and number of the verbs in this verse, see v. 1 on ἀκηκόαμεν.

ἀκηκόαμεν. Prf act ind 1st pl ἀκούω.

ἀπαγγέλλομεν. Pres act ind 1st pl ἀπαγγέλλω.

ὑμῖν. Dative indirect object of ἀπαγγέλλομεν.

ἵνα. Introduces a purpose clause.

καὶ ὑμεῖς. The use of the conjunction with the explicit nominative subject pronoun is emphatic.

κοινωνίαν. Accusative direct object of ἔχητε. Louw and Nida (34.5) define κοινωνία as "an association involving close mutual relations and involvement." The focus is not simply on enjoying one another's company or social interaction, but rather entering into a relationship of joint participation in the work and life of God (see also Campbell).

ἔχητε. Pres act subj 2nd pl ἔχω. Subjunctive with ἵνα.

καὶ. The sentence-initial καὶ marks thematic continuity (see 1:2 on καὶ) and introduces a further comment on κοινωνίαν. Westcott (12) points out that the combination of καὶ with δὲ, as here, "occurs sparingly in the N.T. The δὲ serves as the conjunction, while καὶ emphasizes the words to which it is attached" (cf. Moule, 165).

ἡ κοινωνία. The use of the adjective rather than ἡμῶν is probably stylistic (cf. 2:2, where ἡμῶν and ἡμετέρων appear to be used interchangeably).

μετὰ τοῦ πατρὸς. Association. The construction μετὰ . . . καὶ μετὰ should not be pressed to indicate the equality of the Father and Son (contra Smalley, 13).

αὐτοῦ. Genitive of relationship.

Ἰησοῦ Χριστοῦ. Genitive in apposition to τοῦ υἱοῦ.

1:4 καὶ ταῦτα γράφομεν ἡμεῖς ἵνα ἡ χαρὰ ἡμῶν ᾖ πεπληρωμένη.

καὶ. As a clausal conjunction the καὶ marks thematic continuity (see 1:2 on καὶ). Although such continuity is not as obvious as elsewhere in the letter, the presence of the conjunction would suggest that the writer's goal was for the readers (and/or themselves; see the textual issue relating to ἡμῶν below) to experience the full measure of joy through experiencing the full benefit of their κοινωνία with the Father and the Son (1:3). Brown (151, 172) appears to treat the καὶ as adverbial: "Indeed, we are writing these things" (on the distinction between conjunctive and adverbial uses of καὶ, see Titrud, 242–45).

ταῦτα. Neuter accusative plural direct object of γράφομεν. The demonstrative pronoun could be anaphoric (Burdick, 106), and thus refer to what precedes, but more likely refers to the entire letter

(Brown, 172–73; Smalley, 14), particularly the body of the letter that follows (cf. Brooke, 9). If the pronoun is viewed as cataphoric, then the overall stated purpose of the letter is to help the readers experience the full measure of joy in their relationship with the Father and the Son.

γράφομεν. Pres act ind 1st pl γράφω. On the significance of the tense and number, see v. 1 on ἀκηκόαμεν.

ἡμεῖς. The explicit nominative subject pronoun is probably stylistic rather than emphatic, given its unmarked position following the verb (cf. 1:5 on σκοτία). As Metzger (639) notes, scribes would have been far more likely to change ἡμεῖς (ℵ A*vid B P Y 33 itᶻ copˢᵃᵐˢˢ) to the expected and well attested ὑμῖν (Aᶜ C 81 322 323 436 945 1067 1175 1241 1243 1292 1409 1505 1611 1735 1739 1844 1852 1881 2138 2298 2344 2464 Byz [K P] Lect itᵃʳ, ᵗ vg syrᵖ, ʰ, ᵖᵃˡ copˢᵃ(ᵐˢ), ᵇᵒ arm eth geo slav Augustine) than vice versa.

ἵνα ἡ χαρὰ ἡμῶν ᾖ πεπληρωμένη. The same clause appears in 2 John 12, with the participle preceding the verb ᾖ (but note the textual issue relating to ἡμῶν).

ἵνα. Introduces a purpose clause.

ἡ χαρά. Nominative subject of ᾖ.

ἡμῶν. Subjective genitive (see 1:1 on τῆς ζωῆς). The editors of the UBS⁴ gave ἡμῶν an "A" rating (an upgrade from the third edition's "B" rating). This is a good example of the "textual optimism" of the fourth edition (see Clarke). The external evidence is not heavily weighted in either direction. The first plural form ἡμῶν occurs in ℵ B L Ψ 322 436 1067 1175 1241 1409 Lect itᵃʳ, ᶻ vgʷʷ, ˢᵗ copˢᵃ geo, while the second plural form ὑμῶν occurs in A C 33 81 945 1243 1292 1505 1611 1735 1739 1844 1852 1881 2138 2298 2344 2464 Byz [K P] *l* 422 *l* 598 *l* 938 *l* 1021 vgᶜˡ syrʰ, ᵖᵃˡ copᵇᵒ arm eth slav Augustine Bede. Metzger (639) argues that the change to second person may be based on scribes' recollection of John 16:24—ἵνα ἡ χαρὰ ὑμῶν ᾖ πεπληρωμένη. Although this is plausible, faulty hearing could have led to unintentional changes in either direction. Moreover, the preceding first person plural pronoun could have influenced a scribal change to first person here. The fact that the purpose of the letter is clearly to benefit the readers (cf. the explicit purpose clause in 1:3) suggests that ὑμῶν may well have been the original reading, which was accidentally changed early in the text's transmission history (see also the discussion of the analogous textual variant in 2 John 12).

ᾖ. Pres act subj 3rd sg εἰμί. Subjunctive with ἵνα.

πεπληρωμένη. Prf ptc fem nom sg πληρόω (perfect periphrastic; the present tense form of εἰμί used with a perfect participle forms a periphrastic construction equivalent to a finite perfect verb). The verb could be viewed as either middle or passive voice. Porter (1989, 486) *may* be correct in arguing that "the periphrasis [here] draws attention to the state of completeness of such a joy."

1 John 1:5–2:2

⁵And this is the message that we have heard from him and announce to you: God is light and there is no darkness in him at all. ⁶If we say that we have fellowship with him and live in the darkness, we lie and are not living by the truth. ⁷If, though, we live in the light, as he is in the light, we have fellowship with one another, and the blood of Jesus, his Son, washes us clean from all sin. ⁸If we claim to be free of sin, we deceive ourselves and the truth is not in us. ⁹If, on the other hand, we confess our sins, he is faithful and just and thus will forgive our sins and wash us clean from all unrighteousness. ¹⁰If we say that we have not sinned, (in effect) we brand him a liar and his message is not in us.

²:¹My dear children, I am writing these things to you so that you do not sin. Now, if anyone *does* sin, we have an advocate before the Father, Jesus Christ, the righteous one. ²*He* is the means by which our sins are dealt with; and not our sins alone, but also the sins of the entire world.

1:5 Καὶ ἔστιν αὕτη ἡ ἀγγελία ἣν ἀκηκόαμεν ἀπ᾽ αὐτοῦ καὶ ἀναγγέλλομεν ὑμῖν, ὅτι ὁ θεὸς φῶς ἐστιν καὶ σκοτία ἐν αὐτῷ οὐκ ἔστιν οὐδεμία.

Καὶ ἔστιν αὕτη. Brown (192) points out that this formula occurs at 2:25; 3:23; 5:4, 11, 14; and 2 John 6, though in these passages the word order is always καὶ αὕτη ἔστιν. The demonstrative pronoun always points forward to an epexegetical construction. Moreover, in every case, the cataphoric demonstrative pronoun points forward to a noun that expresses an event idea and introduces one of the main themes of 1 John. It thus serves as a powerful "highlighting device" in the letter (Anderson and Anderson, 43). The alteration in word order here may suggest a slightly different discourse function, perhaps helping to mark the beginning of the letter proper (cf.

John 1:19, where the transition from the Prologue to the Gospel proper is marked with a καί; Harris 2003, 59), or may mark the καί as resumptive ("picking up the theme of proclamation or announcement . . . from the prologue, as indicated by the phrases 'heard from him and announce to you' in 1:5, which echo the similar statements in 1:3"; so Harris 2003, 59). Where the order καὶ αὕτη ἔστιν is used, the conjunction carries its usual sentence-initial function of marking thematic continuity (see 1:2 on καί). If the same is true here, this would provide further evidence that the letter is all about having fellowship with the Father and Son (see 1:4 on καί), which can only take place within "the light."

ἔστιν. Pres act ind 3rd sg εἰμί. On the movement of the accent, see below.

αὕτη. Predicate nominative. In equative clauses (X = Y) with a nominative personal pronoun and nominative noun (articular or not), the pronoun will be the subject (see Wallace 1996, 42–44). Demonstratives in such constructions, on the other hand, will tend to function as the predicate when they are cataphoric and as the subject when they are anaphoric (see, e.g., οὗτός in 2:22). Here, the demonstrative is cataphoric, i.e., it points forward to the ὅτι clause.

ἡ ἀγγελία. Nominative subject of ἔστιν. This term occurs only here and in 3:11 in the NT. Louw and Nida (33.193) define it as "the content of what has been announced," while Harris (2003, 59) views it as a synonym of εὐαγγέλιον (cf. BDAG, 8), which occurs 76 times in the NT, but only once in Johannine literature (Rev 14:6). With no clear data indicating the more specific nuance "*gospel* message," however, it is better to view ἀγγελία as a more generic term.

ἦν. Accusative direct object of ἀκηκόαμεν.

ἀκηκόαμεν. Prf act ind 1st pl ἀκούω. Pointing to the use of first person plural inclusive verbs, and the choice of the verbs ἀκηκόαμεν and ἀναγγέλλομεν (as a synonym for ἀπαγγέλλομεν), Talbert (14) argues that verse 5 should be taken with verses 1-4, with the whole unit forming an A B A' B' pattern. Verse 4, however, with its summary character (cf. 3:24), appears to provide closure to verses 1-4.

ἀπ᾽ αὐτοῦ. Source. The antecedent is Ἰησοῦ Χριστοῦ (1:3).

ἀναγγέλλομεν. Pres act ind 1st pl ἀναγγέλλω. Westcott (15) has argued that this verb, which is a near synonym of ἀπαγγέλλω (1:2, 3), focuses on the recipient, while ἀπαγγέλλω focuses on the origin of the message. It is unlikely, however, that a different meaning, however slight, is intended. Westcott's etymological analysis of the terms, which emphasizes the meaning of ἀνά and ἀπό, is not supported by usage. In John 16:25, for example, where ἀπαγγέλλω is used, the context points to emphasis on the recipients, while in 16:13, where ἀναγγέλλω is used, the contextual emphasis is on the source. The shift to the synonym here may have been motivated by a stylistic desire to avoid repeating the morpheme ἀπ- on the heels of the preposition ἀπ᾽ three words earlier.

ὑμῖν. Dative indirect object of ἀναγγέλλομεν.

ὅτι. Introduces a clause that is epexegetical to αὕτη. BDF §394 points out that cataphoric demonstrative pronouns can be followed by epexegetical clauses introduced by ἵνα, ὅτι, or even ἐάν. They go on to argue that "If . . . the epexegetical phrase refers to an actual fact, John uses ὅτι rather than ἵνα . . . and if the fact is only assumed, ἐάν or ὅταν" (cf. Larsen 1990a, 29). They cite 1 John 3:16 as an example of the former, and 1 John 2:3 and 5:2 as examples of the latter.

ὁ θεὸς. In equative clauses (X = Y) with two nominative nouns, the articular one will be the subject (see Wallace 1996, 42–44).

φῶς. Predicate nominative (see 1:5 on αὕτη). Given the following context, which speaks of "walking" in the light or "walking" in darkness, the metaphor φῶς almost certainly focuses on moral purity, while σκοτία points to the opposite. It is likely that the lack of article is not intended to point to "light" as a quality (contra most scholars), something that is already clear from the fact that it functions as a metaphor here, but rather simply serves syntactically to mark φῶς as the predicate of the equative clause (see above on ὁ θεὸς).

ἐστιν. In the present indicative (except εἶ), the verb εἰμί is an enclitic. A clitic is a word that appears as a discreet word in the syntax but is pronounced as if it were part of another word. In linguistic jargon, it is syntactically free but phonologically bound. Enclitics "give" their accent to the *preceding* word (cf. 1:5b, 7, 9; 2:2, 5, 7, 8, 14, 22a, 22c, 27a, 29; 3:2a, 2b, 3, 7a, 7b, 10a; 4:1, 2, 3b, 4a, 6a, 7, 15, 17a, 17b; 5:1, 3a, 5a, 5b, 7, 8, 11b, 19, 20b). The accent simply shifts to the first syllable when the third singular ἐστίν follows οὐκ (cf. 1:5c, 8, 10; 2:4b, 10, 15, 16a, 21, 22b, 27b; 3:5, 10b; 4:3a, 6b, 18) or καὶ (cf. 1:5a; 5:17b), or when the verb begins a clause or sentence (5:16). The accent is unaffected when a disyllabic enclitic follows a word that has an acute accent on the penult (cf. ψεύστης ἐστίν, 2:4; see also 2:9, 11, 16b, 18a, 18b, 25; 3:4, 8, 11, 15, 19, 20, 23; 4:3c, 4b, 5, 8, 10, 12, 16, 20; 5:4, 9a, 9b, 11a, 17a), though some argue that accent retention marks emphasis.

The problem with the view that accent retention marks emphasis in 3:1 (καὶ ἐσμέν), for example, is the fact that the constructions καὶ ἐσμέν (also 5:20 and Acts 17:28) and καὶ εἰσίν (Matt 19:12a, 12b; Luke 13:30) *always* retain their accent in the NT. It is unclear why the accent of the third singular form shifts to the penult, while the first and third plural forms remain *in situ*. For a fuller discussion of Greek clitics (proclitics and enclitics) and their accents, see Carson (1985, 47–50).

σκοτία. Nominative subject of ἔστιν. The fronting of σκοτία without its modifying adjective, οὐδεμία, makes the statement more prominent. Following Levinsohn (1987, 3; cf. Friberg; BDF §472), the unmarked, or "normal" order of the major constituents of the Greek clause should be viewed as verb-subject-object. Anything that precedes the verb is "fronted," in order to highlight the information in some way (cf. 1:6 on κοινωνίαν). The main exception to this general rule will be with "BE" verbs like εἰμί, which "carry very little semantic content," and thus frequently follow their subject (cf. Larsen 2001, 25). Larsen (2001, 14) suggests a more general principle: "The more to the left an item occurs, the more prominent it is." This principle has the advantage of potentially being applicable to other constituents within the clause, including constituents within phrases (e.g., the position of an adjective with respect to the noun it modifies). The fact that ordering within a phrase is often conditioned by the writer's "idiolect," as Larsen recognizes (2001, 15), however, makes the application of his rule more problematic.

ἐν αὐτῷ. Locative, in a metaphorical sense.

οὐκ . . . οὐδεμία. The double negative is emphatic (Young, 203).

1:6 Ἐὰν εἴπωμεν ὅτι κοινωνίαν ἔχομεν μετ᾿ αὐτοῦ καὶ ἐν τῷ σκότει περιπατῶμεν, ψευδόμεθα καὶ οὐ ποιοῦμεν τὴν ἀλήθειαν·

Verses 6-10 are set off by an *inclusio* (an envelope structure in which the same theme or wording appears at both the beginning and end of a unit of text): Ἐὰν εἴπωμεν ὅτι . . . ψευδόμεθα (v. 6) is reiterated by ἐὰν εἴπωμεν ὅτι . . . ψεύστην ποιοῦμεν αὐτὸν in verse 10. On the relationship of 2:1-2 to the rest of this section, see 2:1 on Τεκνία.

Ἐὰν εἴπωμεν. The writer uses this expression as a formulaic way of introducing a falsehood (cf. 1:8, 10).

Ἐὰν. Introduces the protasis (the "if . . ." statement) of a third class condition. Although many debate whether the following third class constructions introduce "present general" realities (likely) or "future more probable" realities, it is better to follow Porter (1989, 307), who argues that the subjunctive in such constructions simply expresses "projection without any statement of probability of its coming to pass." Or, put another way, the third class condition is more tentative than the first class condition and "simply projects some action or event for hypothetical consideration" (Porter 1994, 262). It is also important to go beyond common debates concerning whether the conditional clauses and some of the statements that follow reflect the views of the writer's opponents, and ask how each construction functions. As Longacre (1983, 7) points out, the conditional construction here, and frequently elsewhere, serves as a mitigated exhortation: "Do not claim to have fellowship with him and continue to walk in the darkness." Mitigation is a way of softening a command so as to make it more palatable to the listener/reader. It serves to urge a particular course of action gently rather than demand it (see also "Mitigated Exhortations" in the Introduction).

εἴπωμεν. Aor act subj 1st pl λέγω. Subjunctive with ἐάν. Porter (1994, 263) notes that 1:6-10 alternates between aorist and present tenses, "with the aorist tense used with the verb of saying and the present tense with the verb of doing. Emphasis rests on the verb of 'doing.'" The main clauses, i.e., the apodoses (the protases are structurally subordinate), are all present tense and carry the main hortatory line of the discourse forward.

ὅτι. Introduces the clausal complement (indirect discourse) of εἴπωμεν.

κοινωνίαν. Accusative direct object of ἔχομεν. On the meaning, see verse 3. The fronting (see 1:5 on σκοτία) of the object helps highlight the audacity of such a claim.

ἔχομεν. Pres act ind 1st pl ἔχω.

μετ' αὐτοῦ. Association. The antecedent is ὁ θεὸς (v. 5).

καὶ. The tendency is to take the conjunction as "adversative" (cf. Harris 2003, 61). Such an analysis, however, confuses issues of syntax with issues of translation. It is the semantic structure of the verse that points to a state of affairs that goes against the expectation raised by the first part of the protasis, *not* the conjunction καί, which is simply coordinate (cf. the discussion in Moule, 178).

ἐν τῷ σκότει περιπατῶμεν. An idiom (lit. "to walk in darkness") for living a lifestyle that is contrary to God's standards.

ἐν τῷ σκότει. Locative, in a metaphorical sense.

περιπατῶμεν. Pres act subj 1st pl περιπατέω. Subjunctive with ἐάν. The clause ἐν τῷ σκότει περιπατῶμεν is linked to εἴπωμεν by the καί. This verb focuses on lifestyle: "to live or behave in a customary manner" (LN 41.11). The present tense itself simply marks the verbal action as a process, with no emphasis on continuity (contra Brown, 197).

ψευδόμεθα καὶ οὐ ποιοῦμεν τὴν ἀλήθειαν. The conjunction introduces a clause that reiterates and thus emphasizes the negative nature of lying (cf. 2:4 on καί; Titrud, 247).

ψευδόμεθα. Pres mid ind 1st pl ψεύδομαι. Introduces the apodosis (the "then . . ." statement) of the conditional construction. The apodosis of each conditional statement in verses 6, 8, and 10 is framed with a verb or clause that makes the nature of the falsehood in the protasis crystal clear: ψευδόμεθα (1:6); πλανώμεν (1:8); ψεύστην ποιοῦμεν αὐτὸν (1:10). Miller (427) maintains that verbs that by their nature involve two parties, or a sense of reciprocity, tend to utilize the middle voice (e.g., δέχομαι, εἰσκαλέομαι). The verb ψεύδομαι falls under this category, more specifically coming under the category of "negative communication" (cf. Kemmer's category of "speech actions"). We might say that since ψεύδομαι fundamentally involves the interest of the liar, the middle form is required. For more on the voice, see "Deponency" in the Series Introduction.

οὐ ποιοῦμεν τὴν ἀλήθειαν. Litotes—a figure of speech in which a statement is made by negating the opposite idea. For example, "he is *not* a *bad* hockey player" means "he is a *good* hockey player." Here, "not doing the truth" is simply another way of saying "lying," with perhaps the added nuance of being a lifestyle.

ποιοῦμεν. Pres act ind 1st pl ποιέω.

τὴν ἀλήθειαν. Accusative direct object of ποιοῦμεν.

1:7 ἐὰν δὲ ἐν τῷ φωτὶ περιπατῶμεν ὡς αὐτός ἐστιν ἐν τῷ φωτί, κοινωνίαν ἔχομεν μετ᾽ ἀλλήλων καὶ τὸ αἷμα Ἰησοῦ τοῦ υἱοῦ αὐτοῦ καθαρίζει ἡμᾶς ἀπὸ πάσης ἁμαρτίας.

ἐὰν. Introduces the protasis of a third class condition (see 1:6 on Ἐὰν). The conditional construction functions as a mitigated exhortation: "You should walk in the light" (Longacre 1983, 7; cf. 1:6 on Ἐὰν).

δὲ. Introduces a contrast to the behavior outlined in the previous verse (but see 2:2 on ἀλλὰ).

ἐν τῷ φωτὶ περιπατῶμεν. An idiom (lit. "to walk in the light") for living a lifestyle that is in conformity with God's standards (see also 1:6 on ἐν τῷ σκότει περιπατῶμεν).

ἐν τῷ φωτὶ. Locative, in a metaphorical sense.

περιπατῶμεν. Pres act subj 1st pl περιπατέω. Subjunctive with ἐάν. On the semantics, see 1:6.

ὡς. Introduces the second half of a comparative construction.

αὐτός ἐστιν ἐν τῷ φωτὶ. This metaphorical construction is probably synonymous with the metaphor in 1:5, ὁ θεὸς φῶς ἐστιν, once again highlighting God's moral purity. The use of the prepositional phrase in this case, as opposed to an equative clause, simply provides structural balance with the first part of the comparison. The construction as a whole draws a correlation between God's character and believers' conduct.

ἐστιν. Pres act ind 3rd sg εἰμί. On the loss of accent, see 1:5 on ἐστιν.

κοινωνίαν. See 1:6. Here, the fronting (see 1:5 on σκοτία) of the term helps highlight the profundity of the claim..

ἔχομεν. Pres act ind 1st pl ἔχω. Introduces the apodosis of the conditional construction (cf. 1:6 on ψευδόμεθα), which in this case highlights a consequence of the protasis. On the present tense, see below on καθαρίζει.

μετ᾽ ἀλλήλων. Association.

τὸ αἷμα. Neuter nominative subject of καθαρίζει. Metonymy (see 2:2 on τοῦ κόσμου) for "death."

Ἰησοῦ. Possessive genitive.

τοῦ υἱοῦ. Genitive in apposition to Ἰησοῦ.

αὐτοῦ. Genitive of relationship.

καθαρίζει. Pres act ind 3rd sg καθαρίζω. Although it may be theologically appropriate to speak of Jesus' blood *continually* cleansing believers, the present tense simply portrays the event as a process or statement of fact, without reference to the continuity of the process. Right living leads to fellowship and cleansing.

ἡμᾶς. Accusative direct object of καθαρίζει.

ἀπὸ πάσης ἀμαρτίας. Separation. While πᾶς is often used hyperbolically (see, e.g., Acts 1:1, 18, 19; 2:12; 3:9, 18; 8:10; 24:5; 25:24; 26:20; Culy and Parsons, 16), here πάσης points to a profound literal truth (cf. 1:9).

1:8 ἐὰν εἴπωμεν ὅτι ἀμαρτίαν οὐκ ἔχομεν, ἑαυτοὺς πλανῶμεν καὶ ἡ ἀλήθεια οὐκ ἔστιν ἐν ἡμῖν.

ἐὰν εἴπωμεν. See 1:6.

ἐάν. Introduces the protasis of a third class condition (see 1:6 on Ἐάν). The conditional construction functions as a mitigated exhortation: "Do not claim to be without sin" (Longacre 1983, 7; cf. 1:6 on Ἐάν).

εἴπωμεν. Aor act subj 1st pl λέγω. Subjunctive with ἐάν.

ὅτι. Introduces the clausal complement (indirect discourse) of εἴπωμεν.

ἀμαρτίαν οὐκ ἔχομεν. Roughly equivalent to οὐχ ἡμαρτήκαμεν (1:10), though probably with more of a focus on culpability for sinful actions than on the actions themselves (cf. Brown, 205–6).

ἀμαρτίαν. Accusative direct object of ἔχομεν. The fronting (see 1:5 on σκοτία) of the object helps highlight the audacity of such a claim. The term serves as a literary hinge linking this verse to verse 7.

ἔχομεν. Pres act ind 1st pl ἔχω.

ἑαυτούς. Accusative direct object of πλανῶμεν.

πλανῶμεν. Pres act ind 1st pl πλανάω. On the significance of the present tense, see 1:7 on καθαρίζει. Introduces the apodosis of the conditional construction (cf. 1:6 on ψευδόμεθα).

ἡ ἀλήθεια οὐκ ἔστιν ἐν ἡμῖν. This idiomatic expression appears to serve as another label for those outside the community of believers (cf. ἐν τῇ σκοτίᾳ, 2:9). The sense of the idiom (see 1:6 on ἐν τῷ σκότει περιπατῶμεν) may be "we have rejected the truth" (cf. ὁ λόγος αὐτοῦ οὐκ ἔστιν ἐν ἡμῖν, 1:10).

ἔστιν. Pres act ind 3rd sg εἰμί. On the movement of the accent, see 1:5 on ἐστιν.

1:9 ἐὰν ὁμολογῶμεν τὰς ἁμαρτίας ἡμῶν, πιστός ἐστιν καὶ δίκαιος ἵνα ἀφῇ ἡμῖν τὰς ἁμαρτίας καὶ καθαρίσῃ ἡμᾶς ἀπὸ πάσης ἀδικίας.

ἐὰν. Introduces the protasis of a third class condition (see 1:6 on Ἐὰν). The conditional construction functions as a mitigated exhortation: "You should confess your sins" (Longacre 1983, 7; cf. 1:6 on Ἐὰν).

ὁμολογῶμεν. Pres act subj 1st pl ὁμολογέω. Subjunctive with ἐάν. Louw and Nida (33.275) define the verb in this context, "to acknowledge a fact publicly, often in reference to previous bad behavior." The public nature of this definition is consistent with the usage of this verb in Johannine literature (Westcott, 23). BDAG (708), on the other hand, distinguishes this usage (sense 3c: "to concede that something is factual or true . . . . w. focus on admission of wrongdoing") with the sense that ordinarily involves public acknowledgment of something (sense 4). Although *verbal* acknowledgment, rather than *public* acknowledgment, may be the focus, modern readers must beware of imposing their antipathy against public confession upon the text.

τὰς ἁμαρτίας. Accusative direct object of ὁμολογῶμεν. The plural form of the noun probably points to confession of specific sins rather than confession of sinfulness in general (cf. Smalley, 31).

ἡμῶν. Subjective genitive (see 1:1 on τῆς ζωῆς).

πιστός . . . καὶ δίκαιος. Predicate adjective. The fronting (see 1:5 on σκοτία) of part of the adjective phrase lends prominence to the statement (cf. Floor, 14; BDF §473).

ἐστιν. Pres act ind 3rd sg εἰμί. Introduces the apodosis of the conditional construction (cf. 1:6 on ψευδόμεθα). On the movement of the accent, see 1:5 on ἐστιν. The implied subject is God, who is the focus throughout this subsection, rather than Jesus.

δίκαιος. Given the contextual marker of confession of sins, the term probably carries its legal sense, which is captured by the English term "just" (cf. LN 66.5—"pertaining to being proper or right in the sense of being fully justified"). For God *not* to forgive in such circumstances would be *un*just, presumably because justice has already been fully satisfied through the cleansing effects of τὸ αἷμα Ἰησοῦ τοῦ υἱοῦ αὐτοῦ (v. 7) and the concomitant act of confession. Any negative inference from this statement (e.g., "If we do not confess our sins, he will not forgive our sins and wash us clean from all unrighteousness") is beyond the concerns of the letter.

ἵνα. Using traditional labels we would say that the ἵνα introduces a result clause or a clause that is epexegetical to πιστός . . . καὶ δίκαιος. It may be better, however, to argue that the verse is framed as a grounds-conclusion construction, with ἵνα introducing the conclusion (for more on semantic relationships between propositions, see, e.g., Beekman, Callow, and Kopesec). In other words, πιστός . . . καὶ δίκαιος substantiates the claim made by the ἵνα clause (Sherman and Tuggy, 34).

ἀφῇ. Aor act subj 3rd sg ἀφίημι. Subjunctive with ἵνα.

ἡμῖν. Dative of advantage (lit. "He forgives sins for us").

τὰς ἁμαρτίας. Accusative direct object of ἀφῇ.

καθαρίσῃ. Aor act subj 3rd sg καθαρίζω. Subjunctive with ἵνα.

ἡμᾶς. Accusative direct object of καθαρίσῃ.

ἀπὸ πάσης ἀδικίας. Separation. On πάσης, see 1:7. The term ἀδικίας should probably be viewed as synonymous with ἁμαρτία here (as in verse 7). Its choice likely reflects a stylistic effort to avoid repeating ἁμαρτία, which occurs just six words earlier.

1:10 ἐὰν εἴπωμεν ὅτι οὐχ ἡμαρτήκαμεν, ψεύστην ποιοῦμεν αὐτὸν καὶ ὁ λόγος αὐτοῦ οὐκ ἔστιν ἐν ἡμῖν.

This verse introduces the second half of an *inclusio* (see 1:6) and thus concludes the paragraph.

ἐὰν εἴπωμεν. See verse 6.

ἐὰν. Introduces the protasis of a third class condition (see 1:6 on Ἐάν). The conditional construction functions as a mitigated exhortation: "Do not claim that you have not sinned" (Longacre 1983, 7; cf. 1:6 on Ἐάν).

εἴπωμεν. Aor act subj 1st pl λέγω. Subjunctive with ἐάν.

ὅτι. Introduces the clausal complement (indirect discourse) of εἴπωμεν.

οὐχ ἡμαρτήκαμεν. It is unclear whether this expression is simply a stylistic variant of ἁμαρτίαν οὐκ ἔχομεν (1:8), with the stative aspect (perfect tense) being equivalent to the stative semantics of ἁμαρτίαν οὐκ ἔχομεν, or shifts the focus to actual acts of sin (so Brown, 211; see also 1:8 on ἁμαρτίαν οὐκ ἔχομεν).

ψεύστην. Accusative complement in an object-complement double accusative construction. In this construction, the second accusative (either a noun, adjective or participle) complements the direct object in that it predicates something about it (Wallace 1985, 93). Wallace's (1996, 181ff.) distinction between object-complement and person-thing double accusatives should probably be avoided, since in some cases the latter is appropriately labeled "object-complement," while in other instances the two accusatives represent a different syntactic phenomenon altogether (see comments on πολλάς κώμας in Acts 8:25 and ὑμᾶς in Acts 13:32 in Culy and Parsons, 160, 260). The complement usually follows the object. Its fronted position (see 1:5 on σκοτία) in this case probably highlights the seriousness of associating the term ψεύστην with God.

ποιοῦμεν. Pres act ind 1st pl ποιέω. Introduces the apodosis of the conditional construction (cf. 1:6 on ψευδόμεθα).

αὐτὸν. Accusative direct object of ποιοῦμεν. The referent is God, who is the focus throughout this subsection, rather than Jesus.

ὁ λόγος αὐτοῦ οὐκ ἔστιν ἐν ἡμῖν. Probably an idiom (see 1:6 on ἐν τῷ σκότει περιπατῶμεν) meaning, "We reject his message" or "We refuse to accept what he says" (cf. ἡ ἀλήθεια οὐκ ἔστιν ἐν ἡμῖν, 1:8).

ὁ λόγος. The modifier, αὐτοῦ, all but rules out taking this as the personified "Word" (contra GW).

αὐτοῦ. Subjective genitive (see 1:1 on τῆς ζωῆς) or genitive of source.

ἔστιν. Pres act ind 3rd sg εἰμί. On the movement of the accent, see 1:5 on ἐστιν.

2:1 Τεκνία μου, ταῦτα γράφω ὑμῖν ἵνα μὴ ἁμάρτητε. καὶ ἐάν · τις ἁμάρτῃ, παράκλητον ἔχομεν πρὸς τὸν πατέρα, Ἰησοῦν Χριστὸν δίκαιον·

Τεκνία. Vocative. The writer uses this familial term of endearment (the diminutive form of τέκνον) seven times in 1 John (2:12,

28; 3:7, 18; 4:4; 5:21). The diminutive form probably highlights both the level of endearment and the writer's position of superiority/authority within the relationship. Longacre (1983, 7) maintains that the use of the vocative, along with the reiteration of the verb γράφω, marks the beginning of a new paragraph. Others reject attributing such boundary marking power to the vocative (see "Genre and Structure" in the Introduction). The use of the vocative and return to a first person verb does mark a boundary of sorts, but it is better to view 2:1-2 as a sub-unit of 1:5–2:2 that serves as a "closure" of the larger unit (cf. Callow 1999). "The closure repeats and summarizes the main theme of the section and thereby marks the end of it" (Larsen 1991b, 52). Longacre's comment (1992, 273) on 2:1-6—"This is a hortatory paragraph, but the hortatory component is buried in the purpose clause of verse 1"—may therefore be applied to 1:5-2:2.

μου. Genitive of relationship.

ταῦτα. Accusative direct object of γράφω. In terms of syntax, the demonstrative pronoun should probably be taken as anaphoric, referring back to the preceding section, even though the letter as a whole accomplishes the following purpose as well (contra Westcott, 42; Brooke, 23).

γράφω. Pres act ind 1st sg γράφω. The writer continues to use present tense verbs of communication to carry the discourse forward (cf. 1:1 on ἀκηκόαμεν). Having established himself as a member of an elite group of eyewitnesses (see 1:1 on ἀκηκόαμεν), however, he now shifts from the first plural form (γράφομεν, 1:4) to first singular, since he is the one who is actually writing the letter.

ὑμῖν. Dative indirect object of γράφω.

ἵνα. Introduces a purpose clause that helps set the theme for the entire paragraph. It also serves, according to Longacre (1983, 9), as a mitigated exhortation ("Don't sin!"), which is followed by a series of reasons supporting the implied exhortation (cf. 1:6 on Ἐάν).

ἁμάρτητε. Aor act subj 2nd pl ἁμαρτάνω. The writer uses the aorist tense to portray the sin in view as a specific act rather than a process (present tense), effectively highlighting the absolute incompatibility of sinful behavior and a relationship with God.

καὶ. The use of the sentence-initial coordinate καὶ highlights thematic continuity (cf. 1:2 on καὶ), which is explicitly marked by the use of ἁμάρτῃ following ἁμάρτητε. The fact that a good English translation may require that the following proposition be introduced with a "but" or a "yet" does not mean that the καὶ is adversative, or contrastive (contra Brown, 215; Burdick, 130; Smalley, 35; Strecker, 35). Such an analysis confuses issues of syntax with issues of translation (cf. 2:20 on καὶ).

ἐάν. Introduces the protasis of a third class condition (see 1:6 on Ἐὰν).

τις. Nominative subject of ἁμάρτητε.

ἁμάρτῃ. Aor act subj 3rd sg ἁμαρτάνω. On the tense, see above on ἁμάρτητε. Subjunctive with ἐάν.

παράκλητον. This term is rare in other Greek literature and in the NT occurs only here and in the upper room discourse of the Fourth Gospel (14:16, 26; 15:26; 16:7), where the Holy Spirit, rather than Jesus, is the referent. Although Behm, along with most scholars (see, e.g., Brooke, 23; Strecker, 37) argues for a legal sense of the term (e.g., "advocate" or even "attorney"), Grayston (1981) presents evidence to the contrary and maintains that the term carries a more general sense of "supporter" or "sponsor," though it may be used in legal contexts at times. The role of the παράκλητος "is to give advice or to make a great person favourable to a suppliant" (Grayston 1981, 74). Thus, Grayston concludes (1981, 79–80) that the usage of the term in 1 John 2:1 "corresponds to the situation described by Philo where a person who had displeased the emperor needs a sponsor to propitiate him. In John's teaching, when a Christian has sinned the Father observes that the sinner is sponsored by Christ and is persuaded not to reject him and withdraw his truth." The focus, then, is not so much on the ability of the παράκλητος to defend someone, but rather on the *status* of the παράκλητος, which allows him to bring about a good outcome for the one being accused. The translation uses "advocate" in its non-legal sense.

ἔχομεν. Pres act ind 1st pl ἔχω. Introduces the apodosis of the conditional construction (cf. 1:6 on ψευδόμεθα).

πρὸς τὸν πατέρα. Used to link two personal referents, πρὸς typically carries a relational nuance (see 1:2). In this case, however, the contextual marker παράκλητον, which involves serving as an intermediary in the presence of someone else, points to a locative usage.

Ἰησοῦν Χριστόν. Accusative in apposition to παράκλητον.
δίκαιον. Accusative in apposition to Ἰησοῦν Χριστόν. The previous use of the term (1:9) occurred in the context of offering for-
giveness and, therefore, pointed to the "just" nature of God. Here,
the label serves to validate Jesus Christ as a qualified παράκλητος
and, thus, points to his righteous character.

**2:2 καὶ αὐτὸς ἱλασμός ἐστιν περὶ τῶν ἁμαρτιῶν ἡμῶν, οὐ περὶ
τῶν ἡμετέρων δὲ μόνον ἀλλὰ καὶ περὶ ὅλου τοῦ κόσμου.**

καὶ. The sentence-initial καὶ marks thematic continuity (see 1:2
on καὶ) and introduces a further comment on the theme of sin.
This syntactic link thus supports the view that "The advocacy that
the exalted Christ exercises for the community before the Father
is based on the atonement for sins accomplished in Jesus Christ's
redeeming sacrifice" (Strecker, 39).
αὐτὸς. Nominative subject (see 1:5 on αὕτη) of ἐστιν. The
explicit nominative subject pronoun keeps the focus on Jesus
Christ.
ἱλασμός. Predicate nominative (see 1:5 on αὕτη). Scholars
debate whether this term, and related terms, refers to propitiation
or expiation. Propitiation focuses on God's wrath being appeased,
while expiation focuses on the wiping away of sin. According to
Büchsel (317), Plutarch uses the term to focus on *both* "cultic propitiation of the gods and expiatory action in general." He goes on
to argue, however, that in 1 John "ἱλασμός does not imply propitiation of God." Instead, it focuses on "the setting aside of sin as
guilt against God. This is shown by the combination of ἱλασμός in
2:2 with παράκλητος in 2:1 and with the confession of sin in 1:8,
10." The use of ἱλασμός with περὶ τῶν ἁμαρτιῶν mirrors the use
of ἱλάσκομαι with περὶ τῶν ἁμαρτιῶν in the LXX (see, e.g., Exod
32:30). In the LXX, the focus appears to be more on expiation than
on propitiation, though certainty is elusive. Rather than deciding
between a focus on expiation or propitiation, it is probably better
simply to recognize that ἱλάσκομαι refers to dealing with the problem of sin, while ἱλασμός refers to the means by which sins are dealt
with, or "the means by which sins are forgiven" (LN 40.12).
ἐστιν. Pres act ind 3rd sg εἰμί. On the loss of accent, see 1:5 on
ἐστιν.

περὶ τῶν ἡμετέρων. Reference.

ἡμῶν. Subjective genitive (see 1:1 on τῆς ζωῆς).

οὐ . . . μόνον ἀλλὰ καὶ. "Not only . . . but also . . ."

ἀλλὰ. Most scholars treat contrast as an inherent nuance of δὲ (cf. Larsen, 1991a). Titrud (253), however, maintains that while "the inherent meaning of ἀλλὰ is contrast," δὲ depends on context to indicate a contrast. He goes on to concede, however, that "due to its function of marking what follows as something new and distinct, [δὲ] readily allows an adversative sense."

τῶν ἡμετέρων. See 1:3 on ἡ ἡμετέρα.

περὶ ὅλου τοῦ κόσμου. Elliptical form of περὶ τῶν ἁμαρτιῶν ὅλου τοῦ κόσμου.

τοῦ κόσμου. Subjective genitive (see 1:1 on τῆς ζωῆς). Metonymy for the "the people of the world." Metonymy is a figure of speech in which one term is used in place of another with which it is associated. In the expression, "he was reading the prophet Isaiah" (Acts 8:28), the writer ("the prophet Isaiah") is used as a metonymy for his writings ("the book that the prophet Isaiah wrote").

1 John 2:3-6

³This is how we know that we have come to know him, if we keep his commands. ⁴The one who claims, "I know him," and who does not keep his commands is a liar and the truth is not in him. ⁵Whoever keeps his word (shows that) the love of God has reached its goal in him. This is how we know that we have a relationship with him. ⁶The one who claims to continue to have a relationship with him ought to live in the same manner that he lived.

2:3 Καὶ ἐν τούτῳ γινώσκομεν ὅτι ἐγνώκαμεν αὐτόν, ἐὰν τὰς ἐντολὰς αὐτοῦ τηρῶμεν.

Καὶ. The use of the conjunction in the expression Καὶ ἐν τούτῳ γινώσκομεν (contrast 3:16; 4:2, 13; 5:2) may point the reader to look for thematic continuity between the following statement and what precedes (see 1:2 on καὶ), highlighting the fact that Jesus' role as universal ἱλασμός (2:2) does not preclude the absolute necessity of following his commands. Harris (2003, 74), on the other hand, implausibly argues that the conjunction carries long-range resumptive force: "The author, after discussing three claims

of the opponents in 1:6, 8, and 10 and putting forward three coun-
ter-claims of his own in 1:7, 1:9, and 2:1, is now returning to the
theme of God as light introduced in 1:5." Resumption of a topic
that far removed would require more than a simple conjunction
(cf. 1:3, where the writer chooses to reiterate part of the series of
relative clauses from 1:1 rather than using the typical resumptive
demonstrative pronoun).

ἐν τούτῳ. Instrumental. The demonstrative pronoun is cataphoric (see 1:5 on αὕτη), pointing forward to the ἐὰν clause. Here,
it helps make clear that the author is shifting to a new (though
related) topic. The use of this phrase with no noun antecedent for
the demonstrative pronoun is a favorite rhetorical device for the
author, appearing 12 times in 1 John, an additional five times in
the Gospel of John, and only 10 times elsewhere in the NT (Larsen
1990a, 27). The rhetorical function of ἐν τούτῳ is to place extra
emphasis on what the speaker is about to say or on what he has
just said (Larsen 1990a, 28). Indeed, "cataphora is almost always
a very marked feature" (Anderson and Anderson, 41). Larsen
(1990a, 33) points out that the author generally uses ἐν τούτῳ in
clauses in which "the main verb expresses the concept of knowledge or realization." Such clauses tend to be "at the very center
of John's theme. He wants to oppose certain false teachers who
did not accept that Christ had fully become a person like us at his
birth and that he remained a human person till his death" (Larsen
1990a, 33).

γινώσκομεν. Pres act ind 1st pl γινώσκω. The present tense carries along the main line of the argument (cf. 1:1 on ἀκηκόαμεν).
The verb introduces the apodosis of the third class condition (cf.
1:6 on ψευδόμεθα).

ὅτι. Introduces the clausal complement of γινώσκομεν. Such
complements may be thought of as introducing indirect discourse
with a verb of cognition.

ἐγνώκαμεν. Prf act ind 1st pl γινώσκω. The stative aspect (perfect tense) fits the writer's focus on the referents' current status.

αὐτόν. Accusative direct object of γινώσκομεν.

ἐὰν. Introduces the protasis of a third class condition (see 1:6
on Ἐὰν). The portrayal of what is expected of Christ's followers
in conditional or hypothetical terms produces a mitigated exhortation: "Keep his commands" (Longacre 1983, 9; cf. 1:6 on Ἐὰν).
The entire ἐὰν clause is epexegetical to τούτῳ (see 1:5 on ὅτι).

τὰς ἐντολὰς. Accusative direct object of τηρῶμεν. The fronting (see 1:5 on σκοτία) of the direct object makes it more prominent.

αὐτοῦ. Subjective genitive (see 1:1 on τῆς ζωῆς). Harris (2003, 76–77) argues that it is best to take the genitive modifiers of "commands" in 1 John as references to God the Father, since this is the clear sense in 3:23 and 4:21. Indeed, Harris has understated the case for clear references to God the Father in the other occurrences of ἡ ἐντολὴ with αὐτοῦ (see esp. 5:2, 3). Nevertheless, given the common Johannine focus on the unity between the Father and Son (see Culy 2010, 118–20) and 1 John's clear focus on knowing *both* the Father (2:14; 4:6, 7) and the Son (see 2:13, 14; 3:6), as well as the Holy Spirit (see 4:2), we may be going beyond the specificity of the text to attempt to choose a specific referent in every case (see also "Trinitarian Ambiguity" in the Introduction).

τηρῶμεν. Pres act subj 1st pl τηρέω. Subjunctive with ἐάν.

2:4 ὁ λέγων ὅτι Ἔγνωκα αὐτόν, καὶ τὰς ἐντολὰς αὐτοῦ μὴ τηρῶν, ψεύστης ἐστίν, καὶ ἐν τούτῳ ἡ ἀλήθεια οὐκ ἔστιν·

ὁ λέγων ὅτι Ἔγνωκα αὐτόν, καὶ τὰς ἐντολὰς αὐτοῦ μὴ τηρῶν. The whole participial construction, headed by the nominative ὁ λέγων . . . καὶ . . . μὴ τηρῶν, serves as the subject of ἔστιν.

ὁ λέγων. Pres act ptc masc nom sg λέγω (substantival). The use of the substantival participial construction here is roughly equivalent, in terms of semantics, to the protasis of a conditional construction. Harris (2003, 77–78) argues that the shift from third class conditional statements with first person plural verbs ("we say") to third person singular references with the substantival participles ("the one who . . .") "moves the second group of claims in 2:4-9 one step further away from the readers." While this analysis is true in referential terms, and certainly may point to a direct quotation of the writer's opponents (so Brown, 253), it does not address the question of the relative rhetorical force of the participial construction vis-à-vis the third class conditional statements. The participial constructions should probably also be viewed as mitigated exhortations ("Don't claim to know him when you don't keep his commands"; Longacre 1983, 9; cf. 1:6 on Ἐάν), with their

1 John 2:3-5   27

rhetorical force being more direct or accusatory (i.e., less mitigated) than the third class conditions (see also 2:23 on πᾶς).
ὅτι. Introduces the clausal complement (direct discourse) of
λέγων.
Ἔγνωκα. Prf act ind 1st sg γινώσκω. On the tense, see 2:3 on
ἐγνώκαμεν.
αὐτόν. Accusative direct object of Ἔγνωκα.
τὰς ἐντολὰς. Accusative direct object of τηρῶν. Again, the
fronted (see 1:5 on σκοτία) direct object is prominent.
αὐτοῦ. Subjective genitive (see 1:1 on τῆς ζωῆς).
ὁ . . . τηρῶν. Pres act ptc masc nom sg τηρέω (substantival). The
participle is linked to λέγω by the καὶ and governed by the same
article, making it part of a single substantival participial phrase.
ψεύστης. Predicate nominative (see 1:5 on ὁ θεὸς).
ἐστίν. Pres act ind 3rd sg εἰμί. On the retention of the accent,
see 1:5 on ἐστιν.
καὶ. The conjunction introduces a clause that reiterates what
it means to be a liar (cf. 1:6 on ψευδόμεθα καὶ οὐ ποιοῦμεν τὴν
ἀλήθειαν; Titrud, 248).
ἐν τούτῳ ἡ ἀλήθεια οὐκ ἔστιν. On this idiom (possibly meaning, "he has rejected the truth"), see 1:8 on ἡ ἀλήθεια οὐκ ἔστιν
ἐν ἡμῖν. The antecedent of the demonstrative pronoun is the participial construction ὁ λέγων ὅτι Ἔγνωκα αὐτόν, καὶ τὰς ἐντολὰς
αὐτοῦ μὴ τηρῶν.
ἡ ἀλήθεια. Nominative subject of the second ἔστιν.
ἔστιν. Pres act ind 3rd sg εἰμί. On the movement of the accent,
see 1:5 on ἐστιν.

**2:5 ὃς δ' ἂν τηρῇ αὐτοῦ τὸν λόγον, ἀληθῶς ἐν τούτῳ ἡ ἀγάπη
τοῦ θεοῦ τετελείωται. ἐν τούτῳ γινώσκομεν ὅτι ἐν αὐτῷ
ἐσμεν·**

ὃς δ' ἂν τηρῇ αὐτοῦ τὸν λόγον. The "headless" relative clause
(see 1:1 on Ὃ . . . ὃ) functions as the topic (see 1:1) of what follows, which will be picked up with the resumptive demonstrative
pronoun τούτῳ.
ὃς . . . ἂν. Nominative subject of τηρῇ. The relative pronoun
is used with the particle ἂν (or ἐάν) to form an indefinite relative

pronoun. Grammarians have often referred to ὅστις as an "indefinite relative pronoun." This is a misnomer since this relative pronoun is used with a definite antecedent approximately 90 percent of the time in the NT (see Culy 1989, 20, 30–31, n. 4). The indefinite relative pronoun (ὃς ἄν) introduces a contingency or condition (like a third class condition) and can appropriately be rendered, "whoever, whatever." Rhetorically, the use of this construction, rather than a third class condition, appears to carry a stronger invitation to be this type of person.

δʼ. The elided conjunction (δέ) introduces a contrast to the liar of 2:4 (but see 2:2 on ἀλλά).

τηρῇ. Pres act subj 3rd sg τηρέω. Subjunctive with ἄν.

αὐτοῦ τὸν λόγον. This expression is probably simply a stylistic variant of τὰς ἐντολὰς αὐτοῦ (2:4; so Harris 2003, 78; Strecker, 41).

αὐτοῦ. Subjective genitive (see 1:1 on τῆς ζωῆς). The label "possessive genitive" is best reserved for instances where the genitive noun modifies a concrete noun phrase.

τὸν λόγον. Accusative direct object of τηρῇ.

ἐν τούτῳ. The preposition could be viewed as denoting reference/respect or it could be locative. The antecedent of the demonstrative pronoun is the relative clause ὃς δʼ ἂν τηρῇ αὐτοῦ τὸν λόγον (see further above).

ἡ ἀγάπη. Nominative subject of τετελείωται.

τοῦ θεοῦ. Given the focus on "keeping" God's words/commands, and no indication that the focus shifts to God's actions, the genitive should probably be viewed as objective (see 1:1 on τῆς ζωῆς; so, e.g., Brooke, 32; Marshall, 125; Young, 30) rather than subjective (contra Bultmann, 25; Harris 2003, 79; Westcott, 49). Wendland (28), however, argues that this may well be an example of intentional ambiguity, or "semantic density," on the part of the author. Such ambiguity would be a literary rather than syntactic category, and should not be confused with the questionable label "plenary genitive" (see, e.g., Wallace, 119–21).

τετελείωται. Prf mid ind 3rd sg τελειόω. Although Louw and Nida themselves argue that the term in this context means either "to make perfect in the moral sense" (88.38) or "to cause to be truly and completely genuine" (73.7), this passage appears to be an example of τελειόω (as a middle voice form) being used to indicate, "to be completely successful in accomplishing some goal or attaining some state" (LN 68.31). The (hyperbolic) claim, then, is that such a person's ability to love God has reached a state of maturity (cf. Smalley, 49; Strecker, 41). Such a reading fits the semantics of the verse better than claiming that the verb points to a future event (contra Porter 1994, 41; Wallace, 581). The choice of perfect tense (stative aspect) is driven by the semantic focus on status.

ἐν τούτῳ. The preposition is instrumental. Some (Smalley, 50; Anderson and Anderson, 42) take the demonstrative pronoun as cataphoric (see 1:5 on αὕτη), referring to 2:6, while others (Burdick, 138; Harris 2003, 80) take it as anaphoric, referring to the first part of this verse ("keeping his word"). Clear cataphoric uses of the demonstrative pronoun in 1 John are usually followed either by an epexegetical ὅτι or ἵνα clause (1:5; 3:1, 8, 11, 16, 23; 4:9, 10, 13; 5:3, 14), an appositional noun phrase (2:25; 5:4, 6), a conditional construction (2:3), a construction introduced by the temporal marker ὅταν (5:2), or an instrumental construction (3:24). The same construction in 3:10 is ambiguous. Although the cataphoric pronoun may be followed by a finite clause (4:3), here the editors of the UBS⁴ are probably correct to place a comma before the prepositional phrase and a period at the end of this verse, indicating that the demonstrative is anaphoric.

γινώσκομεν. Pres act ind 1st pl γινώσκω. The present tense carries along the main line of the argument (cf. 1:1 on ἀκηκόαμεν).

ὅτι. Introduces the clausal complement of γινώσκομεν (see also 2:3 on ὅτι).

ἐν αὐτῷ. In this construction, where the referent is God, the function of the preposition should not be pressed. It is better to take such language of indwelling as an idiomatic means of highlighting the intimate nature of a relationship (see Culy 2010, 151).

ἐσμεν. Pres act ind 1st pl εἰμί. On the loss of accent, see 1:5 on ἐστιν.

2:6 ὁ λέγων ἐν αὐτῷ μένειν ὀφείλει καθὼς ἐκεῖνος περιεπάτησεν καὶ αὐτὸς [οὕτως] περιπατεῖν.

ὁ λέγων ἐν αὐτῷ μένειν. The whole participial construction, headed by the nominative ὁ λέγων, serves as the subject of ὀφείλει. On the rhetorical force of the construction, see 2:4 on ὁ λέγων.

ὁ λέγων. Pres act ptc masc nom sg λέγω (substantival).

ἐν αὐτῷ μένειν. This idiom (see 1:6 on ἐν τῷ σκότει περιπατῶμεν) points to continuity of relationship (cf. 2:5 on ἐν αὐτῷ).
Bultmann (26, n. 9) rightly argues that in contexts such as this,
where "abiding" has to do with personal affiliation (ἐν αὐτῷ), the
sense of μένειν is very close to the notion of "being faithful."

αὐτῷ. The referent is God the Father (see below on ἐκεῖνος).

μένειν. Pres act inf μένω ("indirect discourse"). So-called infinitives of indirect discourse are structurally infinitives that serve as
the direct object of a verb of communication.

ὀφείλει. Pres act ind 3rd sg ὀφείλω. The use of this verb, which
implies a degree of obligation, moves the level of urging closer to
a direct command (cf. the discussion of mitigation at 1:6 on Ἐάν).

καθώς. Introduces a comparison.

ἐκεῖνος. The explicit nominative subject pronoun is included to
introduce the second referent (the other is ὁ λέγων ἐν αὐτῷ μένειν)
in the comparative construction. The referent is Jesus Christ. Harris (2003, 80), following earlier scholars, maintains that "in 1
John there is a consistent switch in pronouns from αὐτός (autos)
to ἐκεῖνος (ekeinos) when a reference to Jesus Christ is clearly
introduced."

περιεπάτησεν. Aor act ind 3rd sg περιπατέω.

αὐτός. The use of the nominative pronoun, rather than the
accusative, makes it clear that the pronoun is not the subject of
the infinitive. Instead, it is resumptive and picks up the subject of
ὀφείλει (ὁ λέγων ἐν αὐτῷ μένειν) after the intervening parenthetical element (καθὼς ἐκεῖνος περιεπάτησεν).

[οὕτως]. The external evidence is relatively strong for both the
inclusion and exclusion of οὕτως. Strecker (43, n. 38) argues that
the reading without οὕτως would be the harder reading. It would
certainly be normal for a οὕτως clause to complete the thought of
a καθώς clause. In this particular construction, however, in which
οὕτως would be part of a complementary infinitival clause, it may
be more awkward with the adverb present in the text. Indeed, the
syntax is complicated by the discontinuity of ὀφείλει περιπατεῖν,
making it necessary to use καὶ and a resumptive pronoun (see
above on αὐτός). A "smoother" word order would be: ὁ λέγων
ἐν αὐτῷ μένειν ὀφείλει περιπατεῖν καθὼς ἐκεῖνος περιεπάτησεν.
Ultimately, the textual variation raises only questions of emphasis,

since the relationship between the καθώς clause and the rest of the verse is already made clear by the ὀφείλει plus infinitive construction. It seems most likely that the discontinuous syntax led the writer originally to include the explicit adverb, but that this was left out by many scribes because it is already implicit and/ or because it adds to the awkwardness caused by the resumptive construction.

περιπατεῖν. Pres act inf περιπατέω (complementary).

1 John 2:7-11

[7]Dear friends, I am not writing a new command to you, but rather an old command that you have had since the beginning. The old command is the message that you heard. [8]On the other hand, I *am* writing a new command to you—and this claim (that I am writing a new command) is true in and of itself and with respect to you—because the darkness is disappearing and the true light is now shining. [9]The one who claims to be in the light and yet hates his brother or sister is still in darkness. [10]The one who loves his brother and sister continues to be in the light and there is not something within him that will lead him to fall away. [11]But the one who hates his brother or sister is in the darkness, walks around in the darkness, and does not know where he is going, because the darkness has blinded his eyes.

2:7 Ἀγαπητοί, οὐκ ἐντολὴν καινὴν γράφω ὑμῖν, ἀλλ᾽ ἐντολὴν παλαιὰν ἣν εἴχετε ἀπ᾽ ἀρχῆς· ἡ ἐντολὴ ἡ παλαιά ἐστιν ὁ λόγος ὃν ἠκούσατε.

Ἀγαπητοί. Vocative (cf. 2:1 on Τεκνία). John uses this term of endearment six times between 2:7 and 4:11 (cf. 2 Pet 3:1-17, where the expression is used four times in 17 verses). The use of the vocative, along with the reiteration of the verb γράφω, once again helps mark the beginning of a new paragraph (cf. Longacre 1983, 10; Marshall, 128). Although a number of scholars (e.g., Marshall, 128; Westcott, 52) have suggested that the choice of ἀγαπητοί rather than τεκνία (2:1, 12, 28; 3:7, 18; 4:4; 5:21) may be driven by the theme of this section of the letter (i.e., love), the fact that τεκνία is later used in a context focusing on love (3:18), and ἀγαπητοί is repeatedly used in contexts not focusing on love

(3:2, 21; 4:1) suggests that the writer's motivation for his choice of vocatives cannot be so narrowly defined.

ἐντολὴν καινὴν. The accusative direct object of γράφω is naturally fronted (see 1:5 on σκοτία) as the constituent that will be contrasted with ἐντολὴν παλαιάν.

γράφω. Pres act ind 1st sg γράφω. The writer continues to use present tense verbs of communication to carry the discourse forward (cf. 1:1 on ἀκηκόαμεν).

ὑμῖν. Dative indirect object of γράφω.

ἀλλ'. See 2:2.

ἐντολὴν παλαιάν. Accusative direct object of an implicit γράφω.

ἣν. Accusative direct object of εἴχετε.

εἴχετε. Impf act ind 2nd pl ἔχω.

ἀπ' ἀρχῆς. Temporal. It is probably best to view this phrase as a general reference to what has been true for a long time (so Brooke, 35), rather than as a specific reference either to the beginning of their Christian experience (Burdick, 142; Marshall, 129; Westcott, 52) or the beginning of the Christian era (the teaching of Christ himself or the preaching of the gospel; Brown, 265).

ἡ ἐντολὴ ἡ παλαιά. Nominative subject of ἐστιν. Here, the status of this phrase as subject is made clear by the fact that it is the topic of what precedes (cf. 1:5 on ὁ θεός; see also Young, 65).

ἐστιν. Pres act ind 3rd sg εἰμί. On the loss of accent, see 1:5 on ἐστιν.

ὁ λόγος. Predicate nominative.

ὅν. Accusative direct object of ἠκούσατε.

ἠκούσατε. Aor act ind 2nd pl ἀκούω.

2:8 πάλιν ἐντολὴν καινὴν γράφω ὑμῖν, ὅ ἐστιν ἀληθὲς ἐν αὐτῷ καὶ ἐν ὑμῖν, ὅτι ἡ σκοτία παράγεται καὶ τὸ φῶς τὸ ἀληθινὸν ἤδη φαίνει.

πάλιν. Here, the term is used to indicate that the writer is going to restate an important point, in this case in contrasting terms ("on the other hand").

ἐντολὴν καινὴν. The accusative direct object of γράφω is naturally fronted (see 1:5 on σκοτία) as the topic of what follows.

γράφω. Pres act ind 1st sg γράφω. The present tense (particularly with the verb of communication) carries along the main line of the argument (cf. 1:1 on ἀκηκόαμεν).

ὑμῖν. Dative indirect object of γράφω.

ὅ ἐστιν ἀληθὲς ἐν αὐτῷ καὶ ἐν ὑμῖν. Efforts to unravel the meaning of this relative clause and its relationship to the rest of the verse have, for the most part, been unsuccessful. The neuter gender of the relative pronoun makes it clear that the antecedent cannot be ἐντολὴν καινὴν, which is feminine. The most likely antecedent is the whole preceding statement: ἐντολὴν καινὴν γράφω ὑμῖν (so Brooke, 36; Strecker, 50; cf. Moule, 130). The relative clause is introduced, then, to diffuse the contradiction between the claim in verse 7 and the claim being made here. If this analysis is correct, then αὐτῷ, which is typically viewed as a (masculine gender) reference to Christ (e.g., Burdick, 143; Brown, 266; Smalley, 57; Strecker, 50), should probably be viewed as neuter and coreferential with ὅ, its nearest possible antecedent.

In the early manuscripts, it is unclear whether αυτω is a personal pronoun (αὐτῷ) or a reflexive pronoun (αὑτῷ). When the reflexive pronoun is contracted, e.g., ἑαυτοῦ to αὑτοῦ, the shortened form is formally identical to αὐτοῦ in manuscripts that predate the introduction of breathing marks and accents, making it impossible to determine whether the author intended a personal pronoun or a reflexive pronoun. In John 2:24, for example, where manuscripts vary between ἑαυτόν and αυτον, Westcott-Hort read αυτον as αὑτόν, while the UBS[4] reads it as αὐτόν. Analogous textual variation is found in Luke 12:21 between ἑαυτῷ and αυτω. The latter should likely be read as αὑτῷ (see Robertson, 689), though some argue that the contracted reflexive had died out by the NT period (cf. Tiller, 44). The textual history of 1 John 5:10 provides a good example of scribes apparently interpreting the personal pronoun as having reflexive force. Many manuscripts read ἐν ἑαυτῷ, while others read εν αυτω, which could be accented either ἐν αὑτῷ or ἐν αὐτῷ. Ultimately, deciding which breathing mark is correct is irrelevant since the personal pronoun itself frequently carries reflexive force. As Robertson (680) notes, "In pre-Homeric times the pronominal stem was reflexive," and in the period during which the NT was composed, personal pronouns continued to be used reflexively (Robertson, 681), even though distinctive reflexive forms, like ἑαυτοῦ, were becoming more common. Since personal pronouns function reflexively when the antecedent of the pronoun is the subject of the clause in which it occurs (see Tiller), whether we read ἐν αὐτῷ or ἐν αὐτῷ, the present text should be rendered: "which is true in *itself.*"

In this proposed reading, both uses of the preposition ἐν should be labeled "reference." The relative clause then points out that the claim to be writing a new command (or new reminder of an old command) is both self-evidently true (the author had never written it before) and also true with respect to the readers (to whom the writer had previously never written). In the more traditional reading, in which αὐτῷ refers to Christ, the sense of the relative clause is that the love command found expression in both the life of Jesus and the life of the readers (cf 4:17).

ὅ. Nominative subject of ἐστιν. As Porter (1994, 249) notes, "In instances where the relative pronoun is referring to an extended phrase rather than to a particular word or a group of words . . . the neuter pronoun is often used" (see also above).

ἐστιν. Pres act ind 3rd sg εἰμί. On the loss of accent, see 1:5 on ἐστιν.

ἀληθὲς. Predicate adjective.

ὅτι. Causal. What proposition, though, does the ὅτι clause support? Virtually all scholars link it, in some way, to the preceding relative clause. Smalley (57), for example, maintains that it provides evidence for the relative clause: "this is realized in him and also in you *because* the darkness is fading" (cf. Strecker, 50). If the ὅτι clause modifies the relative clause, however, the semantics of the verse would make better sense if it related only to the second half of the relative clause (so Burdick, 143). Brown (268), on the other hand, maintains that the ὅτι clause provides both a "reason for the newness of the commandment" and a "reason for the way in which it is true in Christ and the Christian." If the above analysis of ὅ ἐστιν ἀληθὲς ἐν αὐτῷ καὶ ἐν ὑμῖν is correct, however, the relative clause should be viewed as a parenthetical comment, with the ὅτι clause providing a reason for πάλιν ἐντολὴν καινὴν γράφω ὑμῖν. In this reading, the writer uses the eschatological invasion of τὸ φῶς, which was brought about through the death and resurrection of Jesus Christ, as a support for his ethical exhortations. He is thus reminding the readers how they should be living, precisely because of the fact that the culmination of the ages has been set in motion. The precise nature of the metaphorical reference to ἡ σκοτία and τὸ φῶς is left open.

ἡ σκοτία. Nominative subject of παράγεται.

παράγεται. Pres mid ind 3rd sg παράγω.

τὸ φῶς τὸ ἀληθινὸν. Neuter nominative subject of φαίνει.

φαίνει. Pres act ind 3rd sg φαίνω.

2:9 ὁ λέγων ἐν τῷ φωτὶ εἶναι καὶ τὸν ἀδελφὸν αὐτοῦ μισῶν ἐν τῇ σκοτίᾳ ἐστὶν ἕως ἄρτι.

ὁ λέγων ἐν τῷ φωτὶ εἶναι καὶ τὸν ἀδελφὸν αὐτοῦ μισῶν. The whole participial construction, headed by the nominative ὁ λέγων ... καὶ ... μισῶν, serves as the subject of ἐστὶν. On the rhetorical force of the construction, see 2:4 on ὁ λέγων.

ὁ λέγων. Pres act ptc masc nom sg λέγω (substantival).

ἐν τῷ φωτὶ εἶναι. This idiom is roughly equivalent to ἐν τῷ φωτὶ περιπατεῖν (2:6), with the emphasis, however, being more on one's status (εἶναι) than on one's conduct (περιπατεῖν). As such, it is another Johannine label for those inside the broad community of believers (cf. 1:8).

εἶναι. Pres act inf εἰμί ("indirect discourse"; see 2:6 on μένειν).

καὶ. Although, given the semantics of the verse, we may translate the conjunction with a concessive or adversative expression in English, in terms of syntax, the conjunction is coordinate (contra, e.g., Harris 2003, 87).

τὸν ἀδελφὸν. Accusative direct object of μισῶν. The expression ἀδελφὸς serves as a technical term for "believers" (contra Bultmann, 28), with no gender distinction intended.

αὐτοῦ. Genitive of relationship.

ὁ ... μισῶν. Pres act ptc masc nom sg μισέω (substantival). The participle is linked to λέγων by the καὶ and governed by the same article. The verb is clearly an antonym for ἀγαπάω in 1 John, as is made clear in 4:20 (see also 3:14-15), where the use of the two verbs suggests that μισέω in 1 John (with a human direct object) focuses on "lack of love" (cf. Strecker, 52, n. 29) rather than strong antipathy or hostility (contra Brown, 269; Burdick, 145).

ἐν τῇ σκοτίᾳ ἐστίν. Another Johannine label for those outside the community of believers (cf. ἡ ἀλήθεια οὐκ ἔστιν ἐν ἡμῖν; 1:8). **ἐστὶν.** Pres act ind 3rd sg εἰμί. On the retention of the accent, see 1:5 on ἐστιν.

ἕως ἄρτι. The temporal qualifier makes it clear that "hating one's brother" and "being in the light" are mutually exclusive.

2:10 ὁ ἀγαπῶν τὸν ἀδελφὸν αὐτοῦ ἐν τῷ φωτὶ μένει, καὶ σκάνδαλον ἐν αὐτῷ οὐκ ἔστιν·

ὁ ἀγαπῶν τὸν ἀδελφὸν αὐτοῦ. The whole participial construction, headed by the nominative ὁ ἀγαπῶν, serves as the subject of μένει. On the rhetorical force of the construction, see 2:4 on ὁ λέγων.

ὁ ἀγαπῶν. Pres act ptc masc nom sg ἀγαπάω (substantival).

τὸν ἀδελφὸν. Accusative direct object of ἀγαπῶν. On the meaning, see 2:9.

αὐτοῦ. Genitive of relationship.

ἐν τῷ φωτὶ μένει. See 2:9 on ἐν τῷ φωτὶ εἶναι. The use of μένει rather than ἐστιν (2:9) highlights continuity of state and implies at least the theoretical possibility of deserting the light (contra Harris 2003, 81).

μένει. Pres act ind 3rd sg μένω.

σκάνδαλον ἐν αὐτῷ οὐκ ἔστιν. The antecedent of αὐτῷ is most likely the topic of the verse (ὁ ἀγαπῶν τὸν ἀδελφὸν αὐτοῦ) rather than τῷ φωτὶ (contra Smalley, 62). The idiom means something like, "there is no fault in him," or better, "there is not something within him that will lead him to fall away, i.e., fail to remain in the light" (cf. NJB; BDAG, 926; Stälin, 356–57). The writer appears to be concerned with "hatred" of one's brother being a potential σκάνδαλον, rather than claiming that those who love their brother are free from *anything* that could cause them to stumble.

σκάνδαλον. Neuter nominative subject of ἔστιν. On the meaning, see above.

ἔστιν. Pres act ind 3rd sg εἰμί. On the movement of the accent, see 1:5 on ἐστιν.

2:11 ὁ δὲ μισῶν τὸν ἀδελφὸν αὐτοῦ ἐν τῇ σκοτίᾳ ἐστὶν καὶ ἐν τῇ σκοτίᾳ περιπατεῖ, καὶ οὐκ οἶδεν ποῦ ὑπάγει, ὅτι ἡ σκοτία ἐτύφλωσεν τοὺς ὀφθαλμοὺς αὐτοῦ.

ὁ δὲ μισῶν τὸν ἀδελφὸν αὐτοῦ. The whole participial construction, headed by the nominative ὁ . . . μισῶν, serves as the subject of ἐστὶν. On the rhetorical force of the construction, see 2:4 on ὁ λέγων.

ὁ . . . μισῶν. Pres act ptc masc nom sg μισέω (substantival).

δὲ. The conjunction introduces a contrast to ὁ ἀγαπῶν τὸν ἀδελφὸν αὐτοῦ (2:10; but see 2:2 on ἀλλὰ).

τὸν ἀδελφὸν. Accusative direct object of μισῶν. On the meaning, see 2:9.

αὐτοῦ. Genitive of relationship.

ἐν τῇ σκοτίᾳ. See 2:9.

ἐστὶν. Pres act ind 3rd sg εἰμί. The use of the verb ἐστὶν rather than μένει (2:10) places the focus on present status rather than continuity of status, while περιπατεῖ places the focus on behavior. On the retention of the accent, see 1:5 on ἐστιν.

ἐν τῇ σκοτίᾳ περιπατεῖ. See 1:6 on ἐν τῷ σκότει περιπατῶμεν.

περιπατεῖ. Pres act ind 3rd sg περιπατέω. The verb here should be translated using its literal sense ("walk"), since it is part of a larger metaphor (walking around in the dark and not knowing where you are going).

οἶδεν. Prf act ind 3rd sg οἶδα.

ποῦ ὑπάγει. The interrogative clause serves as the syntactic direct object of οἶδεν.

ὑπάγει. Pres act ind 3rd sg ὑπάγω.

ὅτι. Causal.

ἡ σκοτία. Nominative subjective of ἐτύφλωσεν.

ἐτύφλωσεν. Aor act ind 3rd sg τυφλόω. The sense of the metaphor, ἡ σκοτία ἐτύφλωσεν τοὺς ὀφθαλμοὺς αὐτοῦ, appears to be that his status or metaphorical location ("in the dark") has led to the complete loss of spiritual perception.

τοὺς ὀφθαλμοὺς. Accusative direct object of ἐτύφλωσεν.

αὐτοῦ. Genitive of possession.

1 John 2:12-17

¹²I am writing to you, dear children, because your sins have been forgiven for the sake of his name. ¹³I am writing to you, fathers, because you have known the one who was from the beginning. I am writing to you, young men, because you have conquered the Evil One. ¹⁴I have written to you, children, because you have known the Father. I have written to you, fathers, because you have known him who was from the beginning. I have written to you, young men, because you are strong, and the word of God remains in you, and you have conquered the Evil One. ¹⁵Do not love the world or the things in the world. If anyone does love the world, the love of the Father is not in him. ¹⁶For everything that is in the world—the desire of the flesh, the desire of the eyes, and the pride concerning (one's) life—is not from the Father but from the world. ¹⁷Now, the world and its desires pass away, but the one who does the will of God remains forever.

2:12 Γράφω ὑμῖν, τεκνία, ὅτι ἀφέωνται ὑμῖν αἱ ἁμαρτίαι διὰ τὸ ὄνομα αὐτοῦ.

Γράφω. Pres act ind 1st sg γράφω. The writer continues to use present tense verbs of communication to carry the discourse forward (cf. 1:1 on ἀκηκόαμεν).

ὑμῖν. Dative indirect object of Γράφω.

τεκνία. Vocative. The use of the vocative, along with the reiteration of the verb γράφω, once again helps mark the beginning of a new paragraph (cf. 2:1 on Τεκνία). According to Longacre (1983, 11–14), this paragraph serves as the first peak (a point of particular prominence) in the discourse, marked by the use of the imperative mood (verse 15) for the first time (see also "Genre and Structure" in the Introduction). There is significant debate regarding how the various familial terms (τεκνία, πατέρες, νεανίσκοι, and παιδία) in verses 12-14 should be understood. Some scholars have taken τεκνία/παιδία, πατέρες, and νεανίσκοι as references to three distinct groups of people, who are distinguished by age or spiritual maturity. In light of the earlier use of τεκνία in 2:1 as a designation for the readers as a group (see

also the note at 2:1), the original readers would have likely read
πατέρες and νεανίσκοι in verse 13 as two sub-groups within the
larger group of τεκνία. Although the introduction of παιδία in
verse 14 may well have suggested to the readers that *three* groups
were in fact in view, the fact that παιδία is used in 2:18 to refer to
the readers as a whole suggests that it is synonymous with τεκνία
in 1 John (cf. the textual variation at 3:7). Louw and Nida (9.46)
define them both as "a person of any age for whom there is a
special relationship of endearment and association." Whether we
see literary references to two groups or three, ultimately we must
still determine whether *actual* groups are intended, or whether
the writer is using the divisions merely as a rhetorical device.
Against the former is the fact that the writer would expect Christians of all ages and levels of maturity to have had their sins
forgiven, to have known him who was from the beginning, and to
have overcome the Evil One. This suggests that the distinctions
are most likely a rhetorical device that is used to highlight key
characteristics of the readers' experience.

ὅτι. Causal (so Brooke, 44; Burdick, 172–73; Bultmann, 31;
Westcott, 58). Brown (300) notes that both Augustine and the Vul-
gate assumed the causal view. Harris (2003, 94; cf. Brown, 301),
on the other hand, argues that "If the uses of *hoti* are understood
as causal, it is difficult to see why the author immediately gives a
warning in the section which follows about loving the world. The
confidence he has expressed in his readers (if the *hoti*-clauses are
understood as causal) would appear to be ill-founded if he is so
concerned about their relationship to the world as 2:15-17 seems
to indicate." Such an analysis fails to recognize that statements of
confidence or commendation are often interspersed with strong
warnings in letters in order to soften the tone (see esp. Hebrews).

ἀφέωνται. Prf pass ind 3rd pl ἀφίημι.

ὑμῖν. Dative of advantage.

αἱ ἁμαρτίαι. Nominative subject of ἀφέωνται.

διὰ. Causal.

τὸ ὄνομα αὐτοῦ. Metonymy (see 2:2 on τοῦ κόσμου) for "him."

2:13 γράφω ὑμῖν, πατέρες, ὅτι ἐγνώκατε τὸν ἀπ' ἀρχῆς. γράφω ὑμῖν, νεανίσκοι, ὅτι νενικήκατε τὸν πονηρόν.

γράφω. Pres act ind 1st sg γράφω. On the tense, see 2:12.
ὑμῖν. Dative indirect object of γράφω.
πατέρες. Vocative. The writer uses this term here and in verse 14. While the designation by itself suggests respect and/or deference, as a member of the larger group of τεκνία/παιδία (see 2:12 on τεκνία) the πατέρες remain subordinate to the author of 1 John.
ὅτι. Causal (see 2:12).
ἐγνώκατε. Prf act ind 2nd pl γινώσκω. On the tense, see 2:3 on ἐγνώκαμεν.
τὸν ἀπ' ἀρχῆς. The article functions as a "nominalizer" (also known as a "substantivizer")—a word (or affix) that changes the following word, phrase, or clause into a substantive. The case of the nominalizer is determined by its syntactic role in the sentence. Here, τὸν ἀπ' ἀρχῆς is the accusative direct object of ἐγνώκατε. The expression is a clear reference back to 1:1 (see note), making Jesus Christ the referent (contra Stott, 97). As part of a title, it is likely that ἀπ' ἀρχῆς refers to Christ's preexistence (so Brooke, 45; Smalley, 73; Westcott, 60) rather than to the beginning of his ministry (contra Brown, 303; Harris 2003, 96).
γράφω. Pres act ind 1st sg γράφω.
ὑμῖν. Dative indirect object of γράφω.
νεανίσκοι. Vocative. Lit. "a young man beyond the age of puberty, but normally before marriage" (LN 9.32; see also 2:12 on τεκνία).
ὅτι. Causal (see 2:12).
νενικήκατε. Prf act ind 2nd pl νικάω. The verb νικάω is a key term in Johannine literature that occurs once in the Fourth Gospel, six times in 1 John, 17 times in Revelation, and just four times elsewhere in the NT.
τὸν πονηρόν. Accusative direct object of νενικήκατε. The use of the masculine form rather than the neuter (as in ℵ) points to a personal referent: Σατανᾶς (Smalley, 75).

2:14 ἔγραψα ὑμῖν, παιδία, ὅτι ἐγνώκατε τὸν πατέρα. ἔγραψα ὑμῖν, πατέρες, ὅτι ἐγνώκατε τὸν ἀπ' ἀρχῆς. ἔγραψα ὑμῖν, νεανίσκοι, ὅτι ἰσχυροί ἐστε καὶ ὁ λόγος τοῦ θεοῦ ἐν ὑμῖν μένει καὶ νενικήκατε τὸν πονηρόν.

ἔγραψα. Aor act ind 1st sg γράφω. The shift from the present tense in the previous verse to the aorist here is striking, and has been the subject of much debate. The variation in the textual history suggests that some scribes and translators were puzzled by the shift in tense and presumably changed the aorist tense to present (1175 *Byz* [K] *l* 147 *l* 422 *l* 590 *l* 592 *l* 603 *l* 883 *l* 1159 *l* 1141 it^ar, t, z vg^cl, ww Ambrose Augustine). Some scholars maintain that the shift to the aorist is driven by the fact that the writer is now referring to the preceding part of the letter (Brooke, 41–43; cf. Westcott, 60), an earlier letter (2 or 3 John; so Strecker, 55), or the Gospel of John (so Ross, 162–63). Many claim that the tense change is merely a stylistic device (Bultmann, 31; Brown, 297; Burdick, 175). Longacre (1983, 13) has noted, however, that all uses of γράφω preceding verse 14 are present tense (1:4; 2:1, 7, 8, 12, 13a, 13b), while all those from this point on are aorist (2:14a, 14b, 14c, 21, 26; 5:13), making the shift at this point a "watershed of the book." Such an observation is not inconsistent with the way that the tenses have been analyzed thus far. Given the limited correlations between verbal aspect and prominence outlined in the Introduction (see "Verbal Aspect and Prominence"), the use of the aorist tense here appears to effectively downgrade the prominence of the statement. As has been noted, the present tense verbs (particularly verbs of communication) carry the hortatory line of the discourse forward. The shift to the aorist tense here would then help mark this material as being of another nature, i.e., stopping or pausing the forward movement of the argument (cf. Porter 1994, 37). Such an analysis is certainly consistent with the semantics of verse 14. Indeed, subsequent uses of the aorist tense with γράφω (2:14b, 14c, 21, 26; 5:13) also occur in contexts where the writer is summarizing what has gone before rather than moving the discourse forward. All of this *suggests* that the shift should not simply be explained as stylistic variation, but rather was the natural choice for the writer given the nature of the information being presented: "Rather than using the more heavily marked Present to re-introduce his repeated assertions the author uses the less heavily marked Aorist in the second set so as not to detract emphasis from the message itself" (Porter 1989, 229).

ὑμῖν. Dative indirect object of ἔγραψα.

παιδία. Vocative. A near synonym of τεκνία (see LN 9.46; cf. 2:12 on τεκνία).

ὅτι. Causal (see 2:12).

ἐγνώκατε. Prf act ind 2nd pl γινώσκω. On the tense, see 2:3 on ἐγνώκαμεν.

τὸν πατέρα. Accusative direct object of ἐγνώκατε.

πατέρες. Vocative. See 2:13.

ὅτι. Causal (see 2:12).

ἐγνώκατε τὸν ἀπ' ἀρχῆς. See 2:13.

νεανίσκοι. Vocative. See 2:13.

ὅτι. Causal (see 2:12).

ἰσχυροί. Predicate adjective.

ἐστε. Pres act ind 2nd pl εἰμί. On the loss of accent, see 1:5 on εἰσιν.

ὁ λόγος τοῦ θεοῦ ἐν ὑμῖν μένει. The idiom (see 1:6 on ἐν τῷ σκότει περιπατῶμεν) probably indicates the continuing embracing of the truth (contrast ἡ ἀλήθεια οὐκ ἔστιν ἐν ἡμῖν; 1:8). The nuance of continuity comes from the semantics of the verb itself not its tense (cf. 2:6 on ἐν αὐτῷ μένειν and 2:10 on ἐν τῷ φωτὶ μένει).

τοῦ θεοῦ. If a label must be offered, subjective genitive (see 1:1 on τῆς ζωῆς) or source probably best captures the semantics of the construction.

μένει. Pres act ind 3rd sg μένω.

νενικήκατε τὸν πονηρόν. See 2:13.

2:15 Μὴ ἀγαπᾶτε τὸν κόσμον μηδὲ τὰ ἐν τῷ κόσμῳ. ἐάν τις ἀγαπᾷ τὸν κόσμον, οὐκ ἔστιν ἡ ἀγάπη τοῦ πατρὸς ἐν αὐτῷ·

ἀγαπᾶτε. Pres act impv 2nd pl ἀγαπάω (prohibition). The use of the imperative mood marks this verse and section as particularly prominent (five of the thirteen imperative verbs in 1 John occur in 2:15-29). The imperfective aspect (present tense) should not be pressed to imply that the readers were currently loving the world and needing to stop (contra Burdick, 176). Rather, it is the natural choice for prohibiting an action that is viewed as a process and follows the trend of using the present tense to mark mainline material (see also "Verbal Aspect and Prominence" in the

Introduction). As Porter notes (1994, 226), summarizing Boyer: "Boyer in his recent study of the imperative has estimated that the negated present imperative in the NT calls for the cessation of something already being done in only 74 of 174 instances. In other words, in 100 of the 174 instances the negated present imperative is not to be interpreted as calling for cessation of ongoing activity. This is a far cry from the percentages needed to support the traditional rule."

τὸν κόσμον. Accusative direct object of ἀγαπᾶτε.

τὰ ἐν τῷ κόσμῳ. This expression likely refers to the tangible things that ὁ κόσμος has to offer. The article functions as a nominalizer (see 2:13 on τὸν), changing the locative prepositional phrase into a substantive that is part of the compound accusative direct object of ἀγαπᾶτε.

ἐάν. Introduces the protasis of a third class condition (see 1:6 on Ἐάν). Longacre (1983, 13) once again argues that the conditional construction functions as a mitigated command: "Don't love the world" (cf. 1:6 on Ἐάν). This passage illustrates the importance of making a distinction between a mitigated "command" and a mitigated "exhortation." One would not expect a mitigated or softened command to follow a *direct* command. Additional exhortations of any sort, on the other hand, may be used to support a direct command (see also "Mitigated Exhortations" in the Introduction).

τις. Nominative subject of ἀγαπᾷ.

ἀγαπᾷ. Pres act subj 3rd sg ἀγαπάω. Subjunctive with ἐάν (the indicative form would be the same).

τὸν κόσμον. Accusative direct object of ἀγαπᾷ.

ἔστιν. Pres act ind 3rd sg εἰμί. Introduces the apodosis of the conditional construction (cf. 1:6 on ψευδόμεθα). On the movement of the accent, see 1:5 on ἐστιν.

ἡ ἀγάπη. Nominative subject of ἔστιν.

τοῦ πατρὸς. Objective genitive (see 1:1 on τῆς ζωῆς). Wendland (28) argues that this may well be an example of intentional ambiguity, or "semantic density," on the part of the author. Such ambiguity would be a literary rather than syntactic category, and should not be confused with the questionable label "plenary genitive" (see, e.g., Wallace, 119–21).

ἐν αὐτῷ. Locative, in a metaphorical sense.

2:16 ὅτι πᾶν τὸ ἐν τῷ κόσμῳ, ἡ ἐπιθυμία τῆς σαρκὸς καὶ ἡ ἐπιθυμία τῶν ὀφθαλμῶν καὶ ἡ ἀλαζονεία τοῦ βίου, οὐκ ἔστιν ἐκ τοῦ πατρὸς ἀλλ' ἐκ τοῦ κόσμου ἐστίν.

ὅτι. Causal.

πᾶν. Neuter nominative subject of ἔστιν.

τὸ ἐν τῷ κόσμῳ. The article τὸ functions as an adjectivizer—a word (or affix) that changes the following word, phrase, or clause into an adjectival modifier (cf. nominalizers; see 2:13 on τὸν ἀπ' ἀρχῆς). The whole expression, τὸ ἐν τῷ κόσμῳ, functions like an attributive adjective modifying the substantival πᾶν, and thus agrees with it in case, number, and gender.

ἐν τῷ κόσμῳ. Locative.

ἡ ἐπιθυμία τῆς σαρκὸς. Harris (2003, 99) argues that this expression "refers to everything that is the desire of human beings as human beings: all that meets their wants and needs." It is unlikely, given the context, however, that the term carries a (partially) neutral sense here (cf. Strecker, 59, n. 22).

ἡ ἐπιθυμία . . . καὶ ἡ ἐπιθυμία . . . καὶ ἡ ἀλαζονεία. Nominatives in apposition to πᾶν.

τῆς σαρκὸς. Genitive of source or subjective genitive (see 1:1 on τῆς ζωῆς; so Porter 1994, 95; Moule, 40).

ἡ ἐπιθυμία τῶν ὀφθαλμῶν. This expression focuses more on appetites that are activated through visual stimuli and lead to covetousness (Kruse, 95).

τῶν ὀφθαλμῶν. Subjective genitive (see 1:1 on τῆς ζωῆς) or perhaps genitive of source.

ἡ ἀλαζονεία. Louw and Nida (88.219) define this term as "a state of pride or arrogance, but with the implication of complete lack of basis for such an attitude."

τοῦ βίου. Here, βίος likely means, "the resources which one has as a means of living" (LN 57.18), and may also include one's status. The genitive could be taken as objective (cf. Strecker's [59] translation: "the pride in riches") or source (cf. Porter's [1994, 95] translation: "life-originating pride").

ἔστιν. Pres act ind 3rd sg εἰμί. On the movement of the accent, see 1:5 on ἐστιν.

ἐκ τοῦ πατρὸς . . . ἐκ τοῦ κόσμου. Source/Origin (but see 2:19 on ἦσαν ἐξ).

45

ἀλλ'. See 2:2.

ἐστίν. On the retention of the accent, see 1:5 on ἐστιν.

2:17 καὶ ὁ κόσμος παράγεται καὶ ἡ ἐπιθυμία αὐτοῦ, ὁ δὲ ποιῶν
τὸ θέλημα τοῦ θεοῦ μένει εἰς τὸν αἰῶνα.

καὶ. The sentence-initial καὶ marks thematic continuity (see 1:2
on καὶ) with what precedes.

ὁ κόσμος . . . καὶ ἡ ἐπιθυμία. Nominative subject of παράγεται.

παράγεται. Pres mid ind 3rd sg παράγω. Although the same
verb is used in 2:8 in the present tense to speak of a present reality,
such a time reference is made clear through its use with ἤδη. The
time reference here (if any) must be determined through reference
to the present context. The present tense portrays the action as a
process (imperfective aspect), but it is not clear that the claim is
that the world is currently passing away (cf. Schnackenburg, 123;
contra Burdick, 181; Harris 2003, 101)—though such a reading
would not be inconsistent with the writer's theology—or that
it *will* pass away. Since the following proposition, which uses
another present tense verb (μένει) with the temporal expression εἰς
τὸν αἰῶνα, points to a reality that extends to the indefinite future,
and the first proposition contrasts with the second (introduced by
δὲ), one could attempt to capture the contrast in English using
future tense verbs in both propositions: "The world *will* pass away
along with its desire(s), but the one who does the will of God *will*
remain forever." It may be better, however, given the fact that the
writer did not choose future tense verbs, to take the present tense
here as simply stating a claim about reality: the world is destined
for destruction, but those who do God's will are destined to live
forever (cf. the translation).

αὐτοῦ. It is unclear whether the genitive is subjective ("the
thing this world desires") or objective ("the desire for the things
of the world").

ὁ . . . ποιῶν τὸ θέλημα τοῦ θεοῦ. The whole participial construction, headed by the nominative ὁ . . . ποιῶν, serves as the
subject of μένει. On the rhetorical force of the construction, see
2:4 on ὁ λέγων.

ὁ . . . ποιῶν. Pres act ptc masc nom sg ποιέω (substantival).

δὲ. Introduces a contrast to the previous proposition (but see 2:2 on ἀλλὰ).

τὸ θέλημα. Neuter accusative direct object of ποιῶν.

τοῦ θεοῦ. Subjective genitive (see 1:1 on τῆς ζωῆς).

μένει. Pres act ind 3rd sg μένω. The use of μένει highlights continuity of state (cf. 2:10), with the following phrase making that continuity open-ended.

εἰς τὸν αἰῶνα. A temporal idiom (see 1:6 on ἐν τῷ σκότει περιπατῶμεν) denoting "unlimited duration of time, with particular focus upon the future" (LN 67.95).

1 John 2:18-29

[18]Children, it is the last hour, and just as you have heard that the antichrist is coming, even now many antichrists have already appeared. This is how we know that it is the last hour. [19]They went out from us but they did not belong to us. For if they had belonged to us, they would have remained with us. Instead, (they left) in order that they might reveal themselves, namely, that none of them belong to us. [20]Now, *you* have an anointing from the Holy One, and you all know (the truth).

[21]I have not written to you because you do not know the truth, but because you *do* know it and (you know) that no lie comes from the truth. [22]Who is the liar? The one who denies that Jesus is the Christ. This one is the antichrist, the one who (in effect) denies both the Father and the Son. [23]Everyone who denies the Son does not have the Father either. The one who confesses the Son (on the other hand) also has the Father. [24]As for you, let that which you have heard from the beginning remain in you. If that which you heard from the beginning remains in you, you also will remain in the Son and in the Father. [25]And this is the promise that he has promised to us, eternal life.

[26]I have written these things to you concerning those who would deceive you. [27]As for you, the anointing that you received from him remains in you, and you (thus) have no need for anyone to teach you. Instead, as his anointing teaches you about all things—and is true and not a lie—yes, just as it taught you, remain in him.

[28]And now, dear children, continue in your relationship with him, so that when he does appear we will have confidence and not be driven in shame from his presence at his coming. [29]If you really know that he is righteous, you will also know that everyone who practices righteousness has been born of him.

2:18 Παιδία, ἐσχάτη ὥρα ἐστίν, καὶ καθὼς ἠκούσατε ὅτι ἀντίχριστος ἔρχεται, καὶ νῦν ἀντίχριστοι πολλοὶ γεγόνασιν· ὅθεν γινώσκομεν ὅτι ἐσχάτη ὥρα ἐστίν.

Παιδία. See 2:14. The use of the vocative, with the shift to a new theme, helps mark the beginning of a new paragraph (cf. Strecker, 62; see also 2:1 on Τεκνία).

ἐσχάτη ὥρα. Nominative subject of ἐστίν. Attempts to argue that ἐσχάτη ὥρα refers to the entire period between Christ's ascension and Second Coming in this context distract attention from the rhetorical force of the expression. The original readers likely would have simply taken ἐσχάτη ὥρα as a reference to the imminent culmination of the ages. Such eschatological imminency is a frequent theme in the NT that serves rhetorically as a motivation both to perseverance and right living.

ἐστίν. Pres act ind 3rd sg εἰμί. On the retention of the accent, see 1:5 on ἐστιν.

καθὼς. Introduces a comparison.

ἠκούσατε. Aor act ind 2nd pl ἀκούω.

ὅτι. Introduces the clausal complement (indirect discourse) of ἠκούσατε.

ἀντίχριστος. Louw and Nida (53.83) attempt to diffuse the debate over whether the expression (used only here and in 2:22; 4:3; and 2 John 7 in the NT) focuses on opposition to Christ or attempting to take Christ's place by defining ἀντίχριστος as "one who is opposed to Christ, in the sense of usurping the role of Christ." Harris (2003, 106), on the other hand, connects the label ἀντίχριστος with deception: "the opponents, who are trying to deceive the believers of the community to which the author is writing, are deceivers, and *deceit* is linked to the coming of the Antichrist, so the opponents themselves may be labeled 'deceivers' and 'antichrists' since they foreshadow *the* Antichrist who is to come." The fact that it is highly improbable that the opponents had attempted to sway the readers of the letter by portraying themselves as "christs" suggests that general opposition to Christ or his purposes is in view, rather than active attempts to replace Christ or usurp his role. There has also been some debate regarding the significance of the anarthrous ἀντίχριστος. Smalley (91, n. a, 98; cf. Westcott, 70), for example, argues that the lack of article suggests that the term was being used as a proper name by the time the letter was written. Harris (2003, 106) counters by pointing out that the article is present in subsequent references to the ἀντίχριστος in 2:22; 4:3; and 2 John 7. The subsequent use of articular forms, however, does not rule out Smalley's argument. Indeed, in narrative, "When a participant is first mentioned, reference to him or her by name typically is *anarthrous*. However, once (s)he has been introduced, subsequent references to him or her by name within the same incident are *arthrous*" (Levinsohn 1992, 100). Such a practice may carry over into other genres. If so, the articular use of the term in 2 John 7 would suggest knowledge of a prior letter that is closely connected to 2 John.

ἔρχεται. Pres mid ind 3rd sg ἔρχομαι. Miller (428) suggests that the use of the middle form with this verb is conditioned by its reflexive semantics that involve "moving oneself in one direction or another," or "self-propulsion" (Kemmer). For more on the voice, see "Deponency" in the Series Introduction.

γεγόνασιν. Prf act ind 3rd pl γίνομαι.

ὅθεν. Here, the adverb is used as an inferential conjunction: "from which."

γινώσκομεν. Pres act ind 1st pl γινώσκω.

ὅτι. Introduces the clausal complement of γινώσκομεν (see also 2:3 on ὅτι).

ἐσχάτη ὥρα ἐστίν. See above.

2:19 ἐξ ἡμῶν ἐξῆλθαν, ἀλλ᾽ οὐκ ἦσαν ἐξ ἡμῶν· εἰ γὰρ ἐξ ἡμῶν ἦσαν, μεμενήκεισαν ἂν μεθ᾽ ἡμῶν· ἀλλ᾽ ἵνα φανερωθῶσιν ὅτι οὐκ εἰσὶν πάντες ἐξ ἡμῶν·

ἐξ ἡμῶν. Separation. The fronting (see 1:5 on σκοτία) of the prepositional phrase makes it more prominent. The use of the preposition ἐκ, along with the verb ἐξέρχομαι, makes it clear that the writer is referring to a group of individuals who, at one time, had been a part of the community to which he is addressing the letter. Rather than debating whether the first person plural pronoun identifies the writer as part of the congregation to which he writes (cf. Smalley, 101) or is a reference to the universal church (so Westcott, 71), it is better to focus on the rhetorical function of the pronoun, which is to draw a sharp distinction between the community of faith and those who have abandoned it.

ἐξῆλθαν. Aor act ind 3rd pl ἐξέρχομαι.

ἀλλ'. The adversative conjunction introduces a proposition that is "contraexpectation" (see also 2:2). The fact that someone departed "from us" would imply that they had belonged to "our" group. On the contrary, the writer tells the readers, they were never really "of us" at all.

ἦσαν ἐξ. The most appropriate label for the use of ἐκ with the verb εἰμί is probably "source/origin." Louw and Nida (89.3) describe this function as: "a marker of the source from which someone or something is physically or psychologically derived" (LN 89.3). Smalley (201) argues that εἶναι ἐκ serves as "a characteristically Johannine expression denoting the nature of something by referring to its origin." It may be appropriate, however, to add that the expression in John's writings appears to serve as yet another identity marker, introducing that to which someone belongs (see also 3:10 on ἔστιν ἐκ τοῦ θεοῦ).

ἦσαν. Impf ind 3rd pl εἰμί. The use of the imperfect in the second class condition should not be pressed to imply that the protasis speaks of a *present* state of affairs (as most grammarians claim; cf. Strecker, 64, n. 19). Porter (1994, 260; see also *idem*, 1989, 305) argues that the protasis in such conditions need not have "any temporal relation to the referential world."

εἰ. Introduces the protasis of a second class (contrary to fact) condition.

γάρ. The conjunction would typically be labeled "causal" here, since what follows introduces the grounds for the conclusion expressed in the statement, οὐκ ἦσαν ἐξ ἡμῶν. Larsen (1991a, 36), however, suggests that "γάρ is simply an explanatory particle that introduces some further information which the author/ speaker wishes to give his readers/hearers so that they can better understand some word or aspect of the previous sentence or clause. In some cases, there may be a causal relationship between the explanatory new information and the previous statement. But if that is so, it is not signaled by γάρ, but shown by the context."

ἐξ. See above on ἦσαν ἐξ.

μεμενήκεισαν. Plprf act ind 3rd pl μένω. The use of μένει highlights continuity of state (cf. 2:10).

ἄν. Introduces the apodosis of the second class condition (see also above on εἰ).

μεθ᾽ ἡμῶν. Association.

ἀλλ᾽. In this second use of the conjunction in this verse, it again introduces a contraexpectation (see also 2:2). Here, however, the contraexpectation clause is left implicit ("but *they went out from us* in order that . . ."; cf. John 1:8; 9:3; 11:52; 13:18).

ἵνα. Introduces a purpose clause that modifies an implicit ἐξῆλθαν.

φανερωθῶσιν ὅτι. Aor subj 3rd pl φανερόω. On the surface, it would appear that the third person *passive* form rules out taking the ὅτι clause as a clausal complement of φανερωθῶσιν ("in order that *they* might be shown/revealed *that* . . ."). If the verb is passive, the ὅτι clause would have to be taken as epexegetical: "in order that they might be revealed, namely . . ." It appears that some scribes (630 1505 2495 *pc* it^{h, z} syr^{p, hmg}) took the verb as passive and thus attempted to smooth out the awkward sense that resulted by changing the verb to third singular φανερωθῇ ("in order that *it* might be revealed that . . .). The verb form, however, may well be middle rather than passive (see "Deponency" in the Series Introduction on the -θη- morpheme) and therefore carry the sense here of "to reveal oneself" (cf. BDAG, 1048). In this reading, the ὅτι clause would remain epexegetical.

οὐκ. Given its position, the negativizer modifies the verb, rather than πάντες (contra Bultmann, 37), making it clear that the point is that "all (of them) were not of us" rather than "not all of them were of us."

εἰσὶν. Pres act ind 3rd pl εἰμί. On the retention of the accent, see 1:5 on ἐστιν.

πάντες. Nominative subject of εἰσὶν or perhaps predicate nominative.

ἐξ. See above on ἦσαν ἐξ.

2:20 καὶ ὑμεῖς χρῖσμα ἔχετε ἀπὸ τοῦ ἁγίου, καὶ οἴδατε πάντες.

καὶ. The conjunction here does not appear to explicitly build on a theme introduced in the previous verse (cf. 1:2 on καὶ). When we compare 2:19-20 with 2:26-27, however, it appears that having the

χρῖσμα is the referential opposite of not being ἐξ ἡμῶν (1:19) and
the opposite of being among τῶν πλανώντων (2:26). There is thus
thematic continuity but no lexical links between the current verse
and the preceding one. Although it may be appropriate to translate
this verse beginning with a "but," we should beware of using such
a translation to identify the conjunction καί as "adversative" (contra Dana and Mantey, 250). The contrast is made clear through
a combination of the explicit nominative subject pronoun (ὑμεῖς)
and the positive semantics of the verse, which contrast with οὐκ
ἦσαν ἐξ ἡμῶν and οὐκ εἰσὶν πάντες ἐξ ἡμῶν (2:19). Persson (21)
argues that the conjunction links the main proposition of this verse
with the main proposition of verse 18, with verse 19 serving as a
parenthetical comment on antichrists. This view, which depends
on viewing the coming of many antichrists and the anointing as
two grounds for a putative exhortation, is not consistent with the
syntax.

ὑμεῖς. The explicit nominative subject pronoun highlights the
contrast between the readers and those who "went out from us."

χρῖσμα. Neuter accusative direct object of ἔχετε. The term
occurs only here and in 2:27 (twice) in the NT. Grouping χρῖσμα
with the cognate verb χρίω, Louw and Nida (37.107) define it,
"to assign a person to a task, with the implication of supernatu-
ral sanctions, blessing, and endowment." Scholars tend to debate
whether the expression refers to the Holy Spirit (so most scholars),
the teachings of the Gospel/the Word of God (Grayston 1984, 87;
Houlden, 79), or both (Marshall, 155). Elsewhere, the Holy Spirit
is portrayed as the "instrument" with which someone is anointed
(see LXX Isa 61:1; Acts 10:38; cf. 2 Cor 1:21-22). Perhaps more
important are the parallels between Jesus' discourse on the Holy
Spirit in John 14 and 1 John 2. "In 1 John 2:27 believers are told
that they 'received' the χρῖσμα (*chrisma*), while in John 14:17
Jesus contrasts his disciples with the 'world' who cannot 'receive'
the Paraclete. In 1 John 2:27 the χρῖσμα (*chrisma*) is said to
'remain in' believers, while in John 14:17 Jesus tells the disciples
that the Paraclete 'remains with you and will be in you.' 1 John
2:27 says that the χρῖσμα (*chrisma*) 'teaches you [believers] about
all things,' while in John 14:26 Jesus says, 'the Paraclete will teach
you everything.' Finally, in 1 John 2:20 knowledge ('and [*sic.*] all
of you know') is the result of having the χρῖσμα (*chrisma*), while
in John 14:17 knowledge is given by the Paraclete" (Harris 2003,

111). Such parallels suggest that the Holy Spirit is in view here, in which case, χρῖσμα should be taken as an example of personification (see 1:2 on ἡ ζωὴ; see also 2:27).

ἔχετε. Pres act ind 2nd pl ἔχω.

ἀπὸ τοῦ ἁγίου. Source. The use of the substantival form of ἅγιος as a messianic designation elsewhere in the NT (cf. Mark 1:24; Luke 4:34; John 6:69; Acts 3:14; Rev 3:7) makes a reference to Jesus here more likely (so most scholars) than a reference to God (contra BDAG, 11; Burdick, 198). As Harris (2003, 113) notes, Jesus is also repeatedly described as the one who conveys the Holy Spirit to his followers (John 15:26; 16:7; Acts 2:33).

καὶ. In the syntax, the conjunction simply introduces a coordinate clause. In terms of semantics, however, the conjoined clause, οἴδατε πάντες, introduces the result of the previous event, or conclusion drawn from the previous statement. Titrud (250) suggests that in cases such as this, "By syntactically elevating what is logically subordinate, the author is placing more prominence (emphasis) on the clause than it would have had if introduced by a subordinating conjunction" (see also 2:27; 3:9).

οἴδατε. Prf act ind 2nd pl οἶδα.

πάντες. Nominative subject of οἴδατε. The direct object of οἴδατε is left unstated. The awkwardness of the text without a direct object appears to have led to variation in the textual history of this verse. The UBS⁴ reading is supported by א B P Y 398 1838 1852 copˢᵃ arm Jerome Hesychiusˡᵃᵗ, while there is widespread manuscript evidence for the accusative πάντα (A C 33 81 322 323 436 614 945 1067 1175 1243 1292 1409 1505 1611 1735 1739 1852 2138 2298 2344 2464 *Byz* [K] *Lect* itᵃʳ, ʰ, ᶻ vg syrᵖ, ʰ copᵇᵒ eth geo slav Cyril-Jerusalemᵈᵘᵇˡᵉᵐ Didymusᵈᵘᵇ). The context, which contrasts the readers with those who have deserted the community of faith, coupled with the fact that the nominative is the harder reading and also has early support, favors the nominative reading, though an early scribal error cannot definitively be ruled out.

2:21 οὐκ ἔγραψα ὑμῖν ὅτι οὐκ οἴδατε τὴν ἀλήθειαν, ἀλλ᾽ ὅτι οἴδατε αὐτήν, καὶ ὅτι πᾶν ψεῦδος ἐκ τῆς ἀληθείας οὐκ ἔστιν.

ἔγραψα. Aor act ind 1st sg γράφω. On the tense, see 2:14 on ἔγραψα.

ὑμῖν. Dative indirect object of ἔγραψα.

ὅτι ... ὅτι ... ὅτι. The function of the three ὅτι clauses in this verse is difficult to determine. (1) All three could be viewed as causal ("I did not write because . . ."; so NASB, NIV, NEB; Brooke, 57; Strecker, 67, n. 36). (2) All three could be taken as introducing clausal complements of ἔγραψα ("I did not write *that* . . . but *that* . . . and *that* . . ."). Despite the strong scholarly support for this view (Bultmann, 38, n. 13; Brown, 350; Harris 2003, 115; Haas, de Jonge, and Swellengrebel, 66–67; Schnackenburg, 144), it makes little sense in the context of the letter for the author to say that he has written to them about their knowledge of the truth, assuring them of something they already know (cf. Strecker, 67, n. 36). (3) The first two could be taken as causal and the third as introducing a clausal complement of either (a) ἔγραψα ("I did not write *because* . . . but *because* . . . and *that* . . ."; so KJV, RSV), or (b) the preceding οἴδατε ("I did not write *because* . . . but *because* you know it and (you know) *that* . . ."; so CEV, GW, NCV, NRSV, REB, RSV; Dodd, 55; Smalley, 109–10). Option (3a) should be rejected as untenable due to the use of καὶ preceding the third ὅτι, which somehow links the following ὅτι clause with the preceding one. Harris (2003, 115) argues that taking any of the ὅτι clauses as causal "is grammatically awkward because there is no direct object expressed for the verb ἔγραψα. . . . If the *hoti*-clauses were causal we should have expected a direct object such as ταῦτα." While a ὅτι clause is frequently used as a clausal complement of γράφω in the NT (introducing the content of what is or was written), this phenomenon generally occurs as part of a formula (with the perfect tense) for introducing a Scripture quotation (e.g., γέγραπται ὅτι). Even Mark 12:19, which appears to have an analogous construction, is a reference to Scripture. Furthermore, γράφω is frequently used without an explicit direct object. Indeed, the NET Bible, which follows Harris (its general editor) here, takes the ὅτι clause that follows γράφω in Revelation 21:5, where no explicit direct object is present, as causal (cf. 1 Cor 9:10, where the ὅτι is taken as causal with the passive ἐγράφη). Thus, given the fact that John is not introducing a Scripture quotation, and direct objects need not be supplied with γράφω, the causal reading for the first two occurrences appears to be more natural. This narrows the options to (1) and (3b). Although either reading is plausible, the semantics and the use of the conjunction preceding the third ὅτι clause points toward option (3b). In terms of semantics, it is

54   1 John 2:18-29

difficult to determine how "every lie is not from the truth" could
serve as a reason for writing. Harris (2003, 115) argues against
(3b) on the basis that the καί that introduces the third ὅτι clause is
coordinate rather than epexegetical. He is correct in viewing the
conjunction as coordinate but incorrect in arguing that this rules
out (3b). The καί, in fact, links the third ὅτι clause to αὐτὴν, making it part of a compound direct object of the preceding οἴδατε.
The writer thus begins by stating that the readers should not think
that he is writing "because" (first ὅτι clause) they lack knowledge
of the truth. Quite the contrary, he is writing precisely "because"
(second ὅτι clause) they *do* know the truth *and* (καί) they know
"that" (third ὅτι clause) the lies of his opponents have a different
source. This analysis is consistent with the author's practice of
reminding readers of what they already know rather than convey-
ing new information (Persson, 20–21).

οἴδατε. Prf act ind 2nd pl οἶδα.
τὴν ἀλήθειαν. Accusative direct object of οἴδατε.
ἀλλ'. See 2:2.
αὐτήν. Accusative direct object of οἴδατε
πᾶν ψεῦδος. Neuter nominative subject of ἔστιν.
ἐκ τῆς ἀληθείας. Source/Origin (but see 2:19 on ἦσαν ἐξ).
ἔστιν. Pres act ind 3rd sg εἰμί. On the movement of the accent, see
1:5 on ἐστιν.

**2:22 Τίς ἐστιν ὁ ψεύστης εἰ μὴ ὁ ἀρνούμενος ὅτι Ἰησοῦς οὐκ
ἔστιν ὁ Χριστός; οὗτός ἐστιν ὁ ἀντίχριστος, ὁ ἀρνούμενος
τὸν πατέρα καὶ τὸν υἱόν.**

Τίς. Predicate nominative (see 1:5 on αὕτη). The rhetorical
question, introduced by Τίς, functions as a "focus-forcing" device,
i.e., it draws attention to the piece of new information that is
provided in the writer's response to the question (Anderson and
Anderson, 45).
ἐστιν. Pres act ind 3rd sg εἰμί. On the loss of accent, see 1:5 on
ἐστιν.
ὁ ψεύστης. Nominative subject (see 1:5 on αὕτη) of ἐστιν.
εἰ μή. Louw and Nida (89.131) describe this expression as "a
marker of contrast by designating an exception—'except that, but,
however, instead, but only.'"

ὁ ἀρνούμενος ὅτι Ἰησοῦς οὐκ ἔστιν ὁ Χριστός. Constructions introduced by εἰ μὴ should probably be viewed as elliptical. In this case, the whole participial construction, headed by the
nominative ὁ ἀρνούμενος, serves as the subject of an implied verb
and predicate (ἐστιν ὁ ψεύστης).

ὁ ἀρνούμενος. Pres mid ptc masc nom sg ἀρνέομαι (substantival). Miller (427) accounts for the use of the middle form with
this verb by listing it as a verb that involves reciprocity, or more
specifically, a situation "where two parties are involved and where
the removal of one party would render the verb meaningless and no
action possible." For more on the voice, see "Deponency" in the
Series Introduction.

ὅτι. Introduces the clausal complement of ἀρνούμενος, which
should probably be taken as direct discourse (so Burdick, 200;
Smalley, 111), given the presence of the negative οὐκ: "the one
who denies (Jesus, by saying) 'Jesus is not the Christ.'"

Ἰησοῦς οὐκ ἔστιν ὁ Χριστός. The use of the negativizer οὐκ
in a clause that gives the content of the verb ἀρνέομαι is analogous
to a double negative and intensifies the semantics (cf. 1:5 on οὐκ
... οὐδεμία).

Ἰησοῦς. Although in equative clauses the articular noun is normally the subject (see 1:5 on ὁ θεὸς), where one of the nominative
constituents is a proper noun, it will generally be the subject of the
sentence regardless of whether or not it is articular (see Wallace,
44, 45, n. 25; contra Carson 1987, 642–44).

ἔστιν. Pres act ind 3rd sg εἰμί. On the movement of the accent,
see 1:5 on ἐστιν.

ὁ Χριστός. Predicate nominative (see above on Ἰησοῦς).

οὗτός. Nominative subject (see 1:5 on αὕτη) of ἐστιν. The second accent comes from the enclitic ἐστιν (see 1:5 on ἐστιν).

ἐστιν. Pres act ind 3rd sg εἰμί.

ὁ ἀντίχριστος. Predicate nominative (see 1:5 on αὕτη). On the
meaning, see 2:18.

ὁ ἀρνούμενος. Pres mid ptc masc nom sg ἀρνέομαι. The participle could be taken as either attributive (modifying ὁ ἀντίχριστος)
or substantival (and thus nominative in apposition to ὁ ἀντίχριστος),
as the editors of the UBS[4] imply through the insertion of a comma
between the two constituents. On the voice, see above.

τὸν πατέρα καὶ τὸν υἱόν. Accusative direct object of ἀρνούμενος.

2:23 πᾶς ὁ ἀρνούμενος τὸν υἱὸν οὐδὲ τὸν πατέρα ἔχει· ὁ ὁμολογῶν τὸν υἱὸν καὶ τὸν πατέρα ἔχει.

πᾶς ὁ ἀρνούμενος τὸν υἱόν. The whole participial construction, headed by the nominative πᾶς ὁ ἀρνούμενος, functions as the subject of ἔχει. In constructions where πᾶς is followed by an articular participle one could take either πᾶς or the participle as substantival. If πᾶς is viewed as substantival, the participle will be attributive. Since the nominative singular πᾶς does not require an article to make it substantival, and indeed is never articular, either analysis is acceptable (cf. BDF §413[2]; Robertson, 772–73). Rhetorically, the use of πᾶς with an articular participle is more forceful than the simple substantival construction (e.g., ὁ ἀρνούμενος; cf. Paul's quotation of LXX Isa 28:16 in Rom 10:11, where he adds πᾶς to the simple substantival participle to strengthen the universal focus).

ὁ ἀρνούμενος. Pres mid ptc masc nom sg ἀρνέομαι (substantival or attributive; see above). On the voice, see 2:22.

τὸν υἱόν. Accusative direct object of ἀρνούμενος.

τὸν πατέρα ἔχει. This expression, which probably highlights relationship, is another way of identifying those who are part of the community of faith. The writer picks up this same language in 5:12 to highlight the defining characteristic of those who possess life: ὁ ἔχων τὸν υἱὸν ἔχει τὴν ζωήν· ὁ μὴ ἔχων τὸν υἱὸν τοῦ θεοῦ τὴν ζωὴν οὐκ ἔχει.

τὸν πατέρα. Accusative direct object of ἔχει.

ἔχει. Pres act ind 3rd sg ἔχω.

ὁ ὁμολογῶν τὸν υἱόν. The whole participial construction, headed by the nominative ὁ ὁμολογῶν, serves as the subject of ἔχει. On the rhetorical force of the construction, see 2:4 on ὁ λέγων.

ὁ ὁμολογῶν. Pres act ptc masc nom sg ὁμολογέω (substantival). Here, the verb means, "to express openly one's allegiance to a proposition or person" (LN 33.274; cf. 1:9 on ὁμολογῶμεν).

τὸν υἱόν. Accusative direct object of ὁμολογῶμεν.

τὸν πατέρα. Accusative direct object of ἔχει.

2:24 ὑμεῖς ὃ ἠκούσατε ἀπ' ἀρχῆς ἐν ὑμῖν μενέτω· ἐὰν ἐν ὑμῖν μείνῃ ὃ ἀπ' ἀρχῆς ἠκούσατε, καὶ ὑμεῖς ἐν τῷ υἱῷ καὶ ἐν τῷ πατρὶ μενεῖτε.

ὑμεῖς. The pendent, or "hanging," nominative serves as the topic (see 1:1) of what follows.

ὃ ἠκούσατε ἀπ᾽ ἀρχῆς. The headless relative clause (see 1:1 on Ὃ . . . ὃ), which is fronted (see 1:5 on σκοτία) for emphasis (cf. 2:27), serves as the subject of μενέτω. Some manuscripts (𝔐 syrʰ Augustine) add οὖν after the pronoun to make the logical connection between this verse and what precedes more explicit.

ὃ. Accusative direct object of ἠκούσατε.

ἠκούσατε. Aor act ind 2nd pl ἀκούω.

ἀπ᾽ ἀρχῆς. Temporal (see 2:7).

ἐν ὑμῖν μενέτω. The use of μένω highlights continuity of state (cf. 2:10). In this case, the idiom refers to continued adherence to the subject of the imperative verb.

μενέτω. Pres act impv 3rd sg μένω. The imperative clause marks the beginning of the "hortatory heart of the paragraph," which reaches its climax with the imperative statement in verse 27 (Longacre 1992, 273). For more on the significance of the tense and mood, see 2:15 on ἀγαπᾶτε and "Verbal Aspect and Prominence" in the Introduction.

ἐὰν. Introduces the protasis of a third class condition (see 1:6 on Ἐὰν) that serves to urge the readers to respond appropriately to the preceding imperative by portraying the "remaining" as a reality that is open to question.

μείνῃ. Aor act subj 3rd sg μένω. Subjunctive with ἐὰν. On the semantics, see above on ἐν ὑμῖν μενέτω.

ὃ ἀπ᾽ ἀρχῆς ἠκούσατε. The headless relative clause (see 1:1 on Ὃ . . . ὃ) functions as the subject of μείνῃ. On its internal syntax, see above.

ἐν τῷ υἱῷ καὶ ἐν τῷ πατρὶ μενεῖτε. When μένειν ἐν is used with a personal object of the preposition, as here, the idiom points to a continued relationship (see 2:6 on ἐν αὐτῷ μένειν).

μενεῖτε. Fut act ind 2nd pl μένω.

2:25 καὶ αὕτη ἐστὶν ἡ ἐπαγγελία ἣν αὐτὸς ἐπηγγείλατο ἡμῖν, τὴν ζωὴν τὴν αἰώνιον.

καὶ. The use of καὶ here, highlighting thematic continuity (see 1:2 on καὶ), may indicate that ἡ ἐπαγγελία and ὃ ἠκούσατε ἀπ᾽ ἀρχῆς (2:24) are coreferential.

αὕτη. Predicate nominative (see 1:5 on αὕτη). The demonstrative is cataphoric (cf. 1:5 on αὕτη), pointing forward to τὴν ζωὴν τὴν αἰώνιον (contra Brown, 357, who argues that it primarily points back to verse 24).

ἐστὶν. Pres act ind 3rd sg εἰμί. On the retention of the accent, see 1:5 on ἐστιν.

ἡ ἐπαγγελία. Nominative subject (see 1:5 on αὕτη) of ἐστὶν.

ἥν. Accusative direct object of ἐπηγγείλατο.

αὐτὸς. Nominative subject of ἐπηγγείλατο (intensive). The referent is Jesus Christ.

ἐπηγγείλατο. Aor mid ind 3rd sg ἐπαγγέλλομαι. The writer adds extra rhetorical force through the use of a verb that is cognate with the preceding noun (cf. 5:4; Anderson and Anderson, 44). Miller (427) maintains that verbs that by their nature involve two parties, or a sense of reciprocity, tend to utilize the middle voice. Although she does not list this verb in her charts, it fits well in the category of "positive communication" with verbs like ἀποφτέγγομαι and μαρτύρομαι. For more on the voice, see "Deponency" in the Series Introduction.

ἡμῖν. Dative indirect object of ἐπηγγείλατο. A few scribes (B 1241 1292* 1881 *l* 1441 vg^mss) inadvertently changed the pronoun to ὑμῖν.

τὴν ζωὴν τὴν αἰώνιον. We would expect this noun phrase to be nominative in apposition to αὕτη (though some may identify ἡ ἐπαγγελία as the appositional element). At first glance, it may appear that the case of τὴν ζωὴν τὴν αἰώνιον has been attracted to the relative pronoun. Attraction occurs when a relative pronoun takes the case of its antecedent rather than the case it would bear as a constituent of the relative clause (see also 3:24 on οὗ). Occasionally, "inverse" attraction occurs, resulting in the antecedent taking on the case of the relative pronoun (for more on inverse attraction see Culy and Parsons, 210). Here, however, the relative clause modifies ἡ ἐπαγγελία and is syntactically unrelated to τὴν ζωὴν τὴν αἰώνιον. The accusative case is likely due to ellipsis, with τὴν ζωὴν τὴν αἰώνιον serving as the accusative direct object of an implied (αὐτὸς) ἐπηγγείλατο (ἡμῖν).

2:26 Ταῦτα ἔγραψα ὑμῖν περὶ τῶν πλανώντων ὑμᾶς.

Ταῦτα. Neuter accusative direct object of ἔγραψα. The antecedent is most naturally taken as the immediately preceding context
of 2:18-25 (so Burdick, 204; Bultmann, 40; Brooke, 61; Westcott,
78), but a reference to the entire letter cannot be ruled out (cf. Smalley, 122).

ἔγραψα. Aor act ind 1st sg γράφω. On the tense, see 2:14 on
ἔγραψα.

ὑμῖν. Dative indirect object of ἔγραψα.

περὶ. Reference.

τῶν πλανώντων. Pres act ptc masc gen pl πλανάω (substantival). Genitive object of the preposition περὶ. While "those *trying*
to deceive you" may be an appropriate translation, it provides no
basis for labeling the *tense* "conative present." The tense merely
portrays the event as a process. The "conative" nature of the event
is derived from the context not the syntax of the verb (contra
Strecker, 76).

ὑμᾶς. Accusative direct object of πλανώντων.

**2:27 καὶ ὑμεῖς τὸ χρῖσμα ὃ ἐλάβετε ἀπ' αὐτοῦ μένει ἐν ὑμῖν,
καὶ οὐ χρείαν ἔχετε ἵνα τις διδάσκῃ ὑμᾶς· ἀλλ' ὡς τὸ αὐτοῦ
χρῖσμα διδάσκει ὑμᾶς περὶ πάντων, καὶ ἀληθές ἐστιν καὶ οὐκ
ἔστιν ψεῦδος, καὶ καθὼς ἐδίδαξεν ὑμᾶς, μένετε ἐν αὐτῷ.**

καὶ. See 2:20 on καὶ.

ὑμεῖς. The pendent, or "hanging," nominative serves as the
topic (see 1:1) of what follows (cf. 2:24).

τὸ χρῖσμα. Neuter nominative subject of μένει. On the meaning, see 2:20. The subject along with its modifying relative clause,
ὃ ἐλάβετε ἀπ' αὐτοῦ, is fronted (see 1:5 on σκοτία) to highlight
(along with the topic construction) the contrast between the readers and τῶν πλανώντων (v. 26; cf. 2:20).

ὃ. Accusative direct object of ἐλάβετε.

ἐλάβετε. Aor act ind 2nd pl λαμβάνω.

ἀπ' αὐτοῦ. Source. The referent is Jesus Christ (τοῦ ἁγίου;
2:20).

μένει ἐν ὑμῖν. The use of μένει highlights continuity of state
(cf. 2:10). Depending on whether one takes τὸ χρῖσμα personally

or impersonally, the verb may point to continuity of relationship or continued adherence to the subject of the verb (cf. 2:24 on ἐν ὑμῖν μείνῃ).

μένει. Pres act ind 3rd sg μένω.

καὶ. In the syntax, the conjunction simply introduces a coordinate clause. In terms of semantics, however, the conjoined clause, οὐ χρείαν ἔχετε ἵνα τις διδάσκῃ ὑμᾶς, introduces the result that follows from the previous statement. Titrud (250) suggests that in cases such as this, "By syntactically elevating what is logically subordinate, the author is placing more prominence (emphasis) on the clause than it would have had if introduced by a subordinating conjunction" (see also 2:20; 3:9).

χρείαν. Accusative direct object of ἔχετε.

ἔχετε. Pres act ind 2nd pl ἔχω.

ἵνα. Introduces a clause that is epexegetical to χρείαν (contra Wallace, 473, who lists it as a result clause, probably due to the fact that the entire clause, καὶ οὐ χρείαν ἔχετε ἵνα τις διδάσκῃ ὑμᾶς, introduces a result of what precedes).

τις. Nominative subject of διδάσκῃ.

διδάσκῃ. Pres act subj 3rd sg διδάσκω. Subjunctive with ἵνα.

ὑμᾶς. Accusative direct object of διδάσκῃ.

ἀλλ'. See 2:2.

ὡς. The particle could be viewed as "a marker of cause or reason, implying the special nature of the circumstances" (LN 89.37). As such it would introduce the grounds for the conclusion or exhortation that is introduced by μένετε. It is more likely, however, that the particle functions here as a "relatively weak . . . [marker] of a relationship between events or states" (LN 64.12).

αὐτοῦ. Subjective genitive (see 1:1 on τῆς ζωῆς), with Jesus being the agent of the anointing.

τὸ . . . χρῖσμα. Neuter nominative subject of διδάσκει. This should probably be viewed as an example of personification (see 1:2 on ἡ ζωή), with the referent being the Holy Spirit (see 2:20).

διδάσκει. Pres act ind 3rd sg διδάσκω.

ψεῦδος. Accusative direct object of διδάσκει.

περὶ πάντων. Reference. A tantalizingly vague and strikingly broad (hyperbolic) designation of the content of the teaching (cf. John 14:26).

καὶ. The coordinate conjunction links the following clause to the clause introduced by ὡς.

ἀληθές. Predicate adjective.

ἐστιν. Pres act ind 3rd sg εἰμί. On the loss of accent, see 1:5 on ἐστιν. The implied subject is χρῖσμα.

καί. The conjunction introduces a clause that reiterates ἀληθές ἐστιν (cf. 1:6 on ψευδόμεθα καὶ οὐ ποιοῦμεν τὴν ἀλήθειαν; Titrud, 248).

ἔστιν. Pres act ind 3rd sg εἰμί. On the movement of the accent, see 1:5 on ἐστιν.

ψεῦδος. Predicate adjective.

καὶ καθώς. The conjunction is used with καθώς (a marker "of similarity in events and states, with the possible implication of something being in accordance with something else"; LN 64.14) to resume and strengthen the comparison introduced earlier by ὡς.

ἐδίδαξεν. Aor act ind 3rd sg διδάσκω. The implied subject could either be χρῖσμα (so Bultmann, 41; Westcott, 79), which is the implied subject of the preceding conjoined clause (ἀληθές ἐστιν καὶ οὐκ ἔστιν ψεῦδος) and the explicit subject of the clause before it (τὸ αὐτοῦ χρῖσμα διδάσκει ὑμᾶς περὶ πάντων), or (less likely) Christ, the referent of the syntactically more distant pronoun αὐτοῦ at the beginning of this verse (so Burdick, 205; Houlden, 75; Smalley, 127).

ὑμᾶς. Accusative direct object of ἐδίδαξεν.

μένετε ἐν αὐτῷ. On the semantics, see above on μένει ἐν ὑμῖν.

μένετε. Pres act ind/impv 2nd pl μένω. The textual variant μενεῖτε (049 𝔐) indicates that certain scribes read this as an indicative, but they also changed the tense to future. Elsewhere in the NT, ἀλλὰ ὡς always introduces a comparison that follows a negative proposition (Matt 22:30; 26:39; John 7:10; 21:8; Rom 9:32; 1 Cor 3:1; 4:14; 2 Cor 2:17a, b; 7:14; 11:17; Gal 4:14; Eph 5:15; 6:6; 1 Pet 2:16) except here and in Ephesians 5:24. In Ephesians 5:24, ἀλλὰ ὡς introduces the grounds for an implicit command that is introduced by οὕτως καί. Although οὕτως καί is absent here and the semantics of the two propositions are not parallel as in Ephesians 5:24, an imperative reading still makes better sense of the whole verse (so Burdick, 207; Bultmann, 41; Schnackenburg, 149; Smalley, 127; contra Brooke, 63–64; Westcott, 81). The fact that the following verse uses the imperative form (μένετε) does not rule out an imperative here, since there is a paragraph break between 2:27 and 2:28. On the significance of the imperative form here, see also 2:24 on μενέτω, 2:15 on ἀγαπᾶτε, and "Verbal Aspect and Prominence" in the Introduction.

2:28 Καὶ νῦν, τεκνία, μένετε ἐν αὐτῷ, ἵνα ἐὰν φανερωθῇ σχῶμεν παρρησίαν καὶ μὴ αἰσχυνθῶμεν ἀπ' αὐτοῦ ἐν τῇ παρουσίᾳ αὐτοῦ.

Καὶ νῦν, τεκνία. Vocatives (cf. 2:1 on Τεκνία) are frequently used at the beginning of a new paragraph in 1 John, and Longacre (1992, 274) argues that this paragraph concludes the introduction of the letter. Given the use of the vocative with the transitional Καὶ νῦν and an imperative verb, it is indeed appropriate to see a boundary here. Verses 28-29, however, are better viewed as a sub-unit of 2:3-29 that serves as a "closure" of the section (see 2:1 on Τεκνία) and anticipates what follows (cf. Larsen 1991b, 52–53). The conjunction and adverb together may be used to highlight a key point in a hortatory discourse, either oral (cf. Culy and Parsons, 78, on Acts 4:29) or written (see 2 John 5). Here, the statement serves to summarize and reinforce the preceding ethical peak (2:12-17), which focuses on not loving the world, and dogmatic peak (2:18-27), which focuses on proper Christology (see also "Genre and Structure" in the Introduction).

μένετε ἐν αὐτῷ. On the meaning, see 2:6 on ἐν αὐτῷ μένειν.

αὐτῷ. Given the fact that the following verb and final αὐτοῦ (used with τῇ παρουσίᾳ) almost certainly refer to Jesus Christ and his Parousia, he is the likely referent of the pronoun here as well, though the writer may have been intentionally ambiguous (see "Trinitarian Ambiguity" in the Introduction).

μένετε. Pres act impv 2nd pl μένω. Given its use with Καὶ νῦν and the vocative τεκνία, the form μένετε should be taken as imperative rather than indicative. On the significance of the imperative mood, see 2:15 on ἀγαπᾶτε and "Verbal Aspect and Prominence" in the Introduction.

ἵνα. Purpose.

ἐὰν. Louw and Nida (67.32) maintain that this conjunction may be used to refer to "a point of time which is somewhat conditional and simultaneous with another point of time" (LN 67.32). Citing this passage as an example, BDAG (268) claims that at times the meaning of ἐάν "approaches closely that of ὅταν." Similarly, Young (184) notes, "Ἐάν can be used as a temporal conjunction to convey a future event that is contemporaneous with another future event." It is quite possible, however, that these definitions have been influenced more by English usage than by Greek syntax. The author of this letter is fond of clothing propositions that are readily accepted as true in hypothetical language, i.e., third class conditions (see 2:29; 5:15). Rhetorically, such constructions appear to force the reader to the conclusion that the apodosis of the conditional construction should also be readily accepted as true. In the present case, the writer is arguing that if the readers heed his warning to "remain in him," they will most certainly have confidence "if" he appears. Since English does not use conditional language with readily accepted truths, however, most translators have used "when" rather than "if." In an attempt to capture some of the conditional nuance of the syntax, while still working within the framework of English grammar, I have rendered the clause "when he *does* appear."

φανερωθῇ. Aor subj 3rd sg φανερόω. The verb could be viewed as either middle or passive voice (see 3:8; "Deponency" in the Series Introduction; cf. BDAG , 1048). Subjunctive with ἐάν.

σχῶμεν. Aor act subj 1st pl ἔχω. Subjunctive with ἵνα. The shift from second person plural (μένετε) to first person plural links the readers' need to "remain," and so have confidence, with the author's need to do likewise. Rhetorically, then, it supports the exhortation by reminding the readers that "We're all in this together."

παρρησίαν. Accusative direct object of σχῶμεν. Louw and Nida (25.158) define παρρησία as "a state of boldness and confidence, sometimes implying intimidating circumstances." The sense of παρρησία is certainly constrained by the phrase μὴ αἰσχυνθῶμεν, to which its clause is conjoined. The idea of "confidence" is, therefore, probably in view in this context. Given the fact, however, that in the Greco-Roman world, παρρησία was "the voice of friendship" (Plutarch, *Adul. amic.* [*Mor.*] 51C), and the context points to maintaining a relationship with the Son (μένετε ἐν αὐτῷ), παρρησία probably goes beyond simple confidence to highlight relational intimacy (for more, see Culy 2010, 53–56).

καὶ. The conjunction introduces a clause that amplifies the significance of σχῶμεν παρρησίαν (cf. 1:6 on ψευδόμεθα καὶ οὐ ποιοῦμεν τὴν ἀλήθειαν; Titrud, 248).

αἰσχυνθῶμεν. Aor pass subj 1st pl αἰσχύνω. Although some parse this form as passive deponent and others treat it as middle (as is clearly the case in Mark 8:38; see also "Deponency" in the Series Introduction on the nature of the -θη- morpheme) and thus render the whole expression something like "may not draw back in shame from him" (Brown, 381; cf. Brooke, 66), it may be preferable to view the form as a true passive with God or Jesus Christ being the unexpressed agent (cf. Smalley, 131), given its use with ἀπό (see below). "Shame" language is often used in an eschatological sense, as here (cf. Mark 8:38; Brown, 381).

ἀπ' αὐτοῦ. Separation. The entire expression, αἰσχυνθῶμεν ἀπ' αὐτοῦ, appears to point to a negative judgment that involves removal from the Son's presence. Some, however, have argued that the preposition introduces the agent of the passive verb (cf. Haas, de Jonge, and Swellengrebel, 74; Marshall, 166, n. 9).

ἐν τῇ παρουσίᾳ. Temporal. Although παρουσίᾳ can be used of someone "coming" or "arriving" in general (see 1 Cor 16:17), in the NT it is frequently used as a technical term for the eschatological coming of Christ, as here.

αὐτοῦ. Subjective genitive (see 1:1 on τῆς ζωῆς).

2:29 ἐὰν εἰδῆτε ὅτι δίκαιός ἐστιν, γινώσκετε ὅτι καὶ πᾶς ὁ ποιῶν τὴν δικαιοσύνην ἐξ αὐτοῦ γεγέννηται.

ἐάν. Introduces a third class condition (see 1:6 on Ἐάν). The use of a third class condition probably serves as a mild rebuke by calling into question a belief that the readers unquestionably embraced. The construction also highlights the fact that the proposition in the apodosis is an equally obvious truth (cf. 2:28 on ἐάν).

εἰδῆτε. Prf act subj 2nd pl οἶδα. Subjunctive with ἐάν. The shift between the perfect tense εἰδῆτε and the present tense γινώσκετε is probably governed by stylistic concerns, i.e., rules of collocation (γινώσκω is never used with ἐὰν in the NT), rather than indicating a difference in meaning (οἶδα does not occur in the present tense).

ὅτι. Introduces the clausal complement of εἰδῆτε (see also 2:3 on ὅτι).

δίκαιός. Predicate adjective. The second accent comes from the enclitic ἐστιν (see 1:5 on ἐστιν).

ἐστιν. Pres act ind 3rd sg εἰμί. On the loss of accent, see 1:5 on ἐστιν. The subject of the verb could be either Christ or God. In favor of the latter is the fact that the pronoun αὐτοῦ later in the verse almost certainly refers to the Father and has as its syntactic antecedent the unexpressed subject of ἐστιν. Harris (2003, 127–28) notes that ἐξ αὐτοῦ γεγέννηται "in the Johannine literature customarily refers to God and *never* refers unambiguously to Jesus." In favor of a reference to Christ is the fact that Jesus was described as "the righteous one" (δίκαιον) in 2:1, and was the topic of the previous verse, where at least the final two uses of the pronoun αὐτός referred to him. This appears to be another case where the striking unity between the Father and Son has led to referential ambiguity (see "Trinitarian Ambiguity" in the Introduction).

γινώσκετε. Pres act ind 2nd pl γινώσκω. Particularly given the use of the third class condition (see above on ἐὰν), the apodosis serves as a fairly strong (though mitigated) exhortation to righteous living (cf. 1:6 on Ἐὰν). As part of a third class condition, the verb should almost certainly be taken as indicative rather than imperative (contra Westcott, 82).

ὅτι. Introduces the clausal complement of γινώσκετε (see also 2:3 on ὅτι).

καὶ. The awkward position of the adverbial καί apparently led some scribes (B Ψ 𝔐 and some versions) to omit it (on the distinction between the conjunctive and adverbial roles of καί, see Titrud, 242–45).

πᾶς ὁ ποιῶν τὴν δικαιοσύνην. The whole participial construction, headed by the nominative πᾶς ὁ ποιῶν, functions as the subject of γεγέννηται. On the rhetorical force of πᾶς with an articular participle, see 2:23 on πᾶς ὁ ἀρνούμενος.

ὁ ποιῶν. Pres act ptc masc nom sg ποιέω (substantival or attributive; see 2:23 on πᾶς ὁ ἀρνούμενος).

τὴν δικαιοσύνην. Accusative direct object of ποιῶν.

ἐξ αὐτοῦ γεγέννηται. This expression, which also occurs in 3:9a, 9b; 4:7; 5:1a, 1b, 4, 18a, 18b, points to God (ἐξ αὐτοῦ) initiating spiritual life in his followers. Within the context of the conditional construction, the metaphor appears to focus on the transference of character traits from the Father to those who have been "born of him" (see also the discussion on σπέρμα αὐτοῦ ἐν αὐτῷ μένει at 3:9).

γεγέννηται. Prf pass ind 3rd sg γεννάω.

1 John 3:1-6

¹Just look at the kind of love the Father has given to us: we are called children of God. And that is what we are! For this reason the world does not know us, because it did not know him. ²Dear friends, we are presently God's children, and it has not yet been revealed exactly what we will be. We know (however) that when he does appear, we will be like him, since we will see him as he is. ³And everyone who has this hope in him purifies himself, just as he is pure. ⁴Everyone who practices sin, also practices lawlessness. Indeed, sin is lawlessness. ⁵Now, you know that he was revealed (in the first place) so that he might get rid of sin, and there is no sin in him (at all). ⁶Everyone who continues in relationship with him does not sin. Everyone who sins has neither seen him nor known him.

3:1 ἴδετε ποταπὴν ἀγάπην δέδωκεν ἡμῖν ὁ πατὴρ ἵνα τέκνα θεοῦ κληθῶμεν· καὶ ἐσμέν. διὰ τοῦτο ὁ κόσμος οὐ γινώσκει ἡμᾶς ὅτι οὐκ ἔγνω αὐτόν.

ἴδετε. Aor act impv 2nd pl ὁράω/εἶδον. The imperative form of ὁράω/εἶδον serves to draw the attention of the readers to an important point. In this case, the imperative marks the beginning of a new paragraph and the vocative, which typically occurs at the beginning of paragraphs in 1 John (cf. 2:1 on Τεκνία), is not introduced until verse 2 (Longacre 1992, 274). For more on the significance of the tense and mood, see 2:15 on ἀγαπᾶτε and "Verbal Aspect and Prominence" in the Introduction.

ποταπὴν. The interrogative ποταπός (equivalent to ποῖος; Strecker, 86, n. 2; LN 58.30) simply raises an indirect question regarding the nature of the thing it modifies. Used with the expression ἴδετε (or ἴδε; Mark 13:1), however, it calls attention to the wondrous nature of the thing being described.

ἀγάπην. Accusative direct object of δέδωκεν.

δέδωκεν. Prf act ind 3rd sg δίδωμι. The use of the perfect tense, along with the interjection ἴδετε and interrogative ποταπὴν, marks the proposition as particularly prominent.

ἡμῖν. Dative indirect object of δέδωκεν.

ὁ πατήρ. Nominative subject of δέδωκεν.

ἵνα. Introduces a clause that is epexegetical to ἀγάπην (contra Strecker, 87, who attributes a telic/final nuance to it).

τέκνα. Nominative complement in a subject-complement double nominative construction (contra, e.g., Young, 13, who calls it a "nominative of appellation"). When a double accusative construction is passivized, the result is a double nominative construction. Passivization involves making the accusative direct object of an active verb the nominative subject of the passive verb. Since complements will always bear the same case as the constituent that they "complement," passivized double accusative constructions will contain two nominative constituents, a nominative subject and a nominative complement.

θεοῦ. Genitive of relationship.

κληθῶμεν. Aor pass subj 1st pl καλέω. Subjunctive with ἵνα.

καὶ ἐσμέν. This conjoined clause is omitted by 1175 *Byz* [K L] *Lect* vgᵐˢ. Its strong external attestation (𝔓⁷⁴ᵛⁱᵈ ℵ A B C P Ψ 33 81 et al.) suggests its originality (see also Metzger, 642). As the text stands, the conjunction introduces a clause that reiterates and thus emphasizes the previous proposition (cf. 1:6 on ψευδόμεθα καὶ οὐ ποιοῦμεν τὴν ἀλήθειαν; Titrud, 248).

ἐσμέν. Pres act ind 1st pl εἰμί. On the retention of the accent, see 1:5 on ἐστιν.

διὰ τοῦτο. This expression refers to a reason that supports the proposition it introduces. Technically, the demonstrative pronoun could be either anaphoric or (more likely) cataphoric (see 1:5 on αὕτη). Harris (2003, 130) notes that when διὰ τοῦτο is used to refer to what follows in the Gospel of John (six times: 5:16, 18; 8:47; 10:17; 12:18, 39), there is always an epexegetical ὅτι clause accompanying it, while when it refers to what precedes (nine times: 1:31; 6:65; 7:21-22; 9:23; 12:27; 13:11; 15:19; 16:15; 19:11), it is never followed by a ὅτι clause. He goes on to maintain that the same pattern holds true in the three uses of the expression in the Johannine Letters (see also 4:5; 3 John 10). Haas, de Jonge, and Swellengrebel (77), on the other hand, prefer to take the demonstrative pronoun as anaphoric and view the subsequent ὅτι as providing an additional explanation (cf. Strecker, 87).

ὁ κόσμος. Nominative subject of γινώσκει. Metonymy (see 2:2 on τοῦ κόσμου) for "the people of the world."

γινώσκει. Pres act ind 3rd sg γινώσκω.

ἡμᾶς. Accusative direct object of γινώσκει.

ὅτι. Introduces a clause that is epexegetical to τοῦτο (or perhaps causal; see above on διὰ τοῦτο).

ἔγνω. Aor act ind 3rd sg γινώσκω.

αὐτόν. Accusative direct object of ἔγνω. The pronoun could once again refer to either Jesus Christ or God the Father. Given the fact that αὐτόν is the one that the world did not know (ἔγνω), a likely reference to the incarnation (cf. John 1:10—ἐν τῷ κόσμῳ ἦν, καὶ ὁ κόσμος δι' αὐτοῦ ἐγένετο, καὶ ὁ κόσμος αὐτὸν οὐκ ἔγνω), the former seems more likely (notice also the intertextual link between τέκνα θεοῦ κληθῶμεν and ἔδωκεν αὐτοῖς ἐξουσίαν τέκνα θεοῦ γενέσθαι in John 1:12). The fact that similar statements are made with clear reference to the Father (John 17:25—πάτερ δίκαιε, καὶ ὁ κόσμος σε οὐκ ἔγνω, ἐγὼ δέ σε ἔγνων), however, coupled with the writer's propensity for not drawing sharp distinctions between the Father and the Son (see "Trinitarian Ambiguity" in the Introduction), suggests that we should be cautious in making strong claims here.

3:2 Ἀγαπητοί, νῦν τέκνα θεοῦ ἐσμεν, καὶ οὔπω ἐφανερώθη τί ἐσόμεθα. οἴδαμεν ὅτι ἐὰν φανερωθῇ ὅμοιοι αὐτῷ ἐσόμεθα, ὅτι ὀψόμεθα αὐτὸν καθώς ἐστιν.

Ἀγαπητοί. Vocative (cf. 2:1 on Τεκνία and 3:1 on ἴδετε).

νῦν. The adverb sets up the temporal contrast that will be introduced with the future ἐσόμεθα.

τέκνα. Predicate nominative.

θεοῦ. Genitive of relationship.

ἐσμεν. Pres act ind 1st pl εἰμί. On the loss of accent, see 1:5 on ἔστιν.

καὶ. Although a good English rendering may use "but," the conjunction itself is coordinate not adversative (contra Burdick, 232). The semantic contrast is set up by νῦν and οὔπω. Once again, we must be careful not to confuse issues of syntax with translation issues.

ἐφανερώθη. Aor pass ind 3rd sg φανερόω.

τί ἐσόμεθα. The interrogative clause functions as a clausal subject of ἐφανερώθη.

τί. Predicate nominative (of ἐσόμεθα).

ἐσόμεθα. Fut ind 1st pl εἰμί.

οἴδαμεν. Prf act ind 1st pl οἶδα. Some manuscripts (𝔐 syr cop^(sa, bo)) add δὲ after the verb in order to make the contrast between

this proposition and preceding one explicit (but see 2:2 on ἀλλά).
Greenlee (48), however, rejects the view that any contrast should
be seen here.

ὅτι. Introduces the clausal complement of οἴδαμεν (see also 2:3
on ὅτι).

ἐάν. Introduces a third class condition (see 1:6 on Ἐάν). On its
use in this context, see 2:28.

φανερωθῇ. Aor subj 3rd sg φανερόω. The verb could be
viewed as either middle or passive voice (see 3:8; "Deponency"
in the Series Introduction; cf. BDAG, 1048). Subjunctive with
ἐάν. The implied subject of the verb could be either (a) the same
as the subject of ἐφανερώθη ("We know that when *what we will
be* is revealed . . ."; so Harris 2003, 131–32; and Brown, 393–94,
who renders the clause: "But we know that at this revelation"), or
(b) Jesus Christ (so most scholars). Three factors point to the latter option as preferable. First, if the subject of φανερωθῇ is Jesus
Christ, then the following pronouns (αὐτῷ and αὐτόν) have a clear
antecedent. Second, and more important, the verb φανερωθῇ is
conceptually linked to and further explained by the verb ὀψόμεθα,
which follows. The fact that the object of this verb is almost certainly Christ (contra Brown, 395) makes it likely that Christ is also
the subject of the passive verb φανερωθῇ. Finally, if the analysis of
καὶ presented in 1:2 is correct, then the lack of thematic continuity
(i.e., no καὶ) between this clause and the previous one supports a
different subject for φανερωθῇ than for ἐφανερώθη.

ὅμοιοι. Predicate adjective.

αὐτῷ. Dative complement of ὅμοιοι. The antecedent is most
likely Jesus Christ (so most scholars; contra Brown, 394–95;
Haas, de Jonge, and Swellengrebel, 78–79).

ὅτι. Causal. Given its location, the ὅτι clause must provide the
reason for the narrower claim, ὅμοιοι αὐτῷ ἐσόμεθα, rather than
the broader claim οἴδαμεν ὅτι ἐὰν φανερωθῇ ὅμοιοι αὐτῷ ἐσόμεθα.

ὀψόμεθα. Fut mid ind 1st pl ὁράω. Cooper (594; cited by Conrad, 8, n. 18) maintains that the volitional nature of the future tense
frequently led to the use of middle voice morphology (see also
"Deponency" in the Series Introduction).

αὐτόν. Accusative direct object of ὀψόμεθα. The antecedent is
most likely Jesus Christ (so most scholars; contra Brown, 394–95;
Haas, de Jonge, and Swellengrebel, 78–79).

καθώς. Introduces a comparison.

ἐστιν. Pres act ind 3rd sg εἰμί. On the loss of accent, see 1:5 on
ἐστιν.

**3:3 καὶ πᾶς ὁ ἔχων τὴν ἐλπίδα ταύτην ἐπ' αὐτῷ ἁγνίζει ἑαυτὸν
καθὼς ἐκεῖνος ἁγνός ἐστιν.**

καὶ. See 1:2 on καὶ.

πᾶς ὁ ἔχων τὴν ἐλπίδα ταύτην ἐπ' αὐτῷ. The whole participial construction, headed by the nominative πᾶς ὁ ἔχων, functions as the subject of ἁγνίζει. On the rhetorical force of πᾶς with
an articular participle, see 2:23 on πᾶς ὁ ἀρνούμενος (cf. 2:4 on
ὁ λέγων). Here, the semantics of the verse as a whole, though the
main verb is indicative, point to a mitigated command (see "Mitigated Exhortations" in the Introduction) that urges the readers to
purify themselves (cf. Strecker, 91). As Longacre (1992, 274)
notes, verses 3-6 form the "hortatory body of the paragraph."

ὁ ἔχων. Pres act ptc masc nom sg ἔχω (substantival or attributive; see 2:23 on πᾶς ὁ ἀρνούμενος).

τὴν ἐλπίδα. Accusative direct object of ἔχων.

ταύτην. The antecedent is the content of 3:2b.

ἐπ' αὐτῷ. The preposition is used to introduce the object of the
implicit verbal idea in τὴν ἐλπίδα (cf. the use of ἐλπίζω with ἐπί
in 1 Tim 4:10; 5:5; 6:17; 1 Pet 1:13). The referent of the demonstrative pronoun is most likely Jesus Christ, but could be God the
Father (see 3:1 on αὐτόν).

ἁγνίζει. Pres act ind 3rd sg ἁγνίζω. This verb, which occurs 7
times in the NT (John 11:55; Acts 21:24, 26; 24:18; Jas 4:8; 1 Pet
1:22), is a near synonym for καθαρίζω. The two verbs appear to
be used interchangeably in James 4:8. Indeed, while it could be
argued that καθαρίζω is used of outward cleansing (χεῖρας) and
ἁγνίζει of inward cleansing (καρδίας) in James 4:8, καθαρίζω is
used with τὰς καρδίας as its object in Acts 15:9. Here, the choice
of ἁγνίζει is dictated by the following use of ἁγνός. The verb
should be understood in an ethical ("avoid sinning") rather than
a cultic sense ("undergo purification rites"; cf. Strecker, 91–92;
Smalley, 149).

ἑαυτὸν. Accusative direct object of ἁγνίζει.

καθώς. Introduces a comparison.

ἐκεῖνος. Nominative subject of ἐστιν (cf. 1:5 on αὕτη). The referent is Jesus Christ (see also 2:6).

ἁγνός. Predicate adjective (see 1:5 on αὕτη).

ἐστιν. Pres act ind 3rd sg εἰμί. On the loss of accent, see 1:5 on ἐστιν.

3:4 Πᾶς ὁ ποιῶν τὴν ἁμαρτίαν καὶ τὴν ἀνομίαν ποιεῖ, καὶ ἡ ἁμαρτία ἐστὶν ἡ ἀνομία.

Πᾶς ὁ ποιῶν τὴν ἁμαρτίαν. The whole participial construction, headed by the nominative Πᾶς ὁ ποιῶν, functions as the subject of ποιεῖ. On the rhetorical force of πᾶς with an articular participle, see 2:23 on πᾶς ὁ ἀρνούμενος.

ὁ ποιῶν τὴν ἁμαρτίαν. The expression should probably be viewed as synonymous with ὁ ἁμαρτάνων (contra Smalley, 154, who takes the construction as "emphatic"). The choice of the periphrastic expression is dictated by its connection with τὴν ἀνομίαν ποιεῖ here (the verb ἀνομέω is not used in the NT) and its contrast with ὁ ποιῶν τὴν δικαιοσύνην in 2:29 (cf. Brown, 398; see also 3:8).

ὁ ποιῶν. Pres act ptc masc nom sg ποιέω (substantival or attributive; see 2:23 on πᾶς ὁ ἀρνούμενος).

τὴν ἁμαρτίαν. Accusative direct object of ποιῶν. The term ἀνομία differs from ἁμαρτία in that it carries the nuance of rebellion or willful rejection of an established standard ("to behave with complete disregard for the laws or regulations of a society"; LN 88.139). Strecker (94) notes that this term is frequently used in both Jewish and Christian apocalyptic literature "to describe the activity of Satan against God immediately before the end" (cf. the eschatological language in 1 John, e.g., ἐσχάτη ὥρα ἐστίν, 2:18).

ποιεῖ. Pres act ind 3rd sg ποιέω.

καὶ. The conjunction should not be taken to contain a causal element (contra Strecker, 94, n. 5). Here it introduces a clause that reiterates the preceding statement (cf. 1:6 on ψευδόμεθα καὶ οὐ ποιοῦμεν τὴν ἀλήθειαν; Titrud, 248).

ἡ ἁμαρτία. Nominative subject of ἐστίν. Where two articular nominative nouns are used in an equative construction (X = Y), as here, the one that is the topic of what precedes will be the subject.

72   1 John 3:1-6

ἐστὶν. Pres act ind 3rd sg εἰμί. On the retention of the accent, see 1:5 on ἐστιν.

ἡ ἀνομία. Predicate nominative.

3:5 καὶ οἴδατε ὅτι ἐκεῖνος ἐφανερώθη ἵνα τὰς ἁμαρτίας ἄρῃ, καὶ ἁμαρτία ἐν αὐτῷ οὐκ ἔστιν.

καὶ. The sentence-initial καὶ marks thematic continuity (see 1:2 on καὶ) and introduces a further comment on the inappropriateness of sin in the life of the Christian.

οἴδατε. Prf act ind 2nd pl οἶδα.

ὅτι. Introduces the clausal complement of οἴδατε (see also 2:3 on ὅτι).

ἐκεῖνος. Nominative subject of ἐφανερώθη. The referent is Jesus Christ (see also 2:6).

ἐφανερώθη. Aor ind 3rd sg φανερόω. The verb could be viewed as either middle or passive voice (see 3:8; "Deponency" in the Series Introduction; cf. BDAG, 1048).

ἵνα. Introduces a purpose clause.

τὰς ἁμαρτίας ἄρῃ. The language suggests an echo of John 1:29—Ἴδε ὁ ἀμνὸς τοῦ θεοῦ ὁ αἴρων τὴν ἁμαρτίαν τοῦ κόσμου (Smalley, 156).

τὰς ἁμαρτίας. Accusative direct object of ἄρῃ. It is impossible to determine whether the author wrote τὰς ἁμαρτίας or τὰς ἁμαρτίας ἡμῶν. Both readings have strong external support and the pronoun is implicit in the UBS[4] reading.

ἄρῃ. Aor act subj 3rd sg αἴρω. Subjunctive with ἵνα.

καὶ ἁμαρτία ἐν αὐτῷ οὐκ ἔστιν. Smalley (157) notes the parallel expression in John 7:18—καὶ ἀδικία ἐν αὐτῷ οὐκ ἔστιν.

καὶ. The καὶ marks thematic continuity (see 1:2 on καὶ) with the preceding clause.

ἁμαρτία. Nominative subject of ἔστιν.

ἐν αὐτῷ. Locative, in a metaphorical sense. The antecedent of αὐτῷ is ἐκεῖνος. There is no syntactic or contextual basis for maintaining that the pronoun could possibly refer to the Christian (contra Smalley, 157–58).

ἔστιν. Pres act ind 3rd sg εἰμί. On the movement of the accent, see 1:5 on ἐστιν. The present tense should not be pressed to imply "the *eternally* sinless character of Jesus" (contra Smalley, 157), however theologically accurate such a claim may be.

3:6 πᾶς ὁ ἐν αὐτῷ μένων οὐχ ἁμαρτάνει· πᾶς ὁ ἁμαρτάνων οὐχ ἑώρακεν αὐτὸν οὐδὲ ἔγνωκεν αὐτόν.

πᾶς ὁ ἐν αὐτῷ μένων. The whole participial construction, headed by the nominative πᾶς ὁ . . . μένων, functions as the subject of ἁμαρτάνει (see also 3:3 on πᾶς). On the rhetorical force of πᾶς with an articular participle, see 2:23 on πᾶς ὁ ἀρνούμενος.

ἐν αὐτῷ μένων. On the meaning, see 2:6 on ἐν αὐτῷ μένειν.

ὁ . . . μένων. Pres act ptc masc nom sg μένω (substantival or attributive; see 2:23 on πᾶς ὁ ἀρνούμενος).

ἁμαρτάνει. Pres act ind 3rd sg ἁμαρτάνω. The author's statement here with the present tense verb has led to widespread debate regarding the meaning of the passage. Given the writer's penchant for absolute statements, the rhetorical force of this statement must be kept in mind. His concern is not with projected eschatological realities (contra Wallace, 524–25). Rather, his bold statement serves "in the parenthetical context . . . [as] a warning to the community to draw the necessary conclusions from the liberating indicative of the Christ-event" (Strecker, 96; cf. Bultmann, 51). Or, as Smalley (159) puts it, the writer's statement makes it clear that "an intimate and ongoing relationship with Christ . . . precludes the practice of sin." Read within the context of the rest of the letter, it is clear that the writer does not necessarily expect a sinless life for those who "remain in him." He had made it clear in 2:1 that sin *may* occur in the believer's life. His ethical standards, both here and elsewhere in the letter, however, are incredibly high. It is important, then, not to water down his statement by pressing the present tense to imply a focus on continual or habitual sin (contra e.g., Burdick, 239; Young, 108), as though the writer were claiming that true Christians may sin as long as it is not continual or habitual. The tense simply portrays the sin as a process without regard to the event's frequency of recurrence—a process that should have no place in the life of one who "remains in him."

πᾶς ὁ ἁμαρτάνων. Nominative subject of ἑώρακεν. On the rhetorical force of πᾶς with an articular participle, see 2:23 on πᾶς ὁ ἀρνούμενος.

ὁ ἁμαρτάνων. Pres act ptc masc nom sg ἁμαρτάνω (substantival or attributive; see 2:23 on πᾶς ὁ ἀρνούμενος). On the tense, see above on ἁμαρτάνει. **ἑώρακεν.** Prf act ind 3rd sg ὁράω. On the tense, see 2:3 on ἐγνώκαμεν. While most would agree that the literal sense of ὁράω is not in view, it is not clear whether the sense here is "to take special notice of something, with the implication of concerning oneself" (LN 30.45), "to come to understand as the result of perception" (LN 32.11), "to experience an event or state, normally in negative expressions indicating what one will not experience" (LN 90.79), "to be mentally or spiritually perceptive . . . w. focus on cognitive aspect" (BDAG, 720), or something else. It is likely that ἑώρακεν and ἔγνωκεν are close in meaning in this context, with the former focusing more on general experience of Christ and the latter focusing on actual relationship. The earlier uses of ὁράω, particularly the parallel perfect uses of the verb in chapter 1, suggest that the writer may be contrasting his eyewitness experience of Christ, which led to a changed lifestyle, with his opponents' lack of eyewitness experience, which led them to take a less serious view of sin.

αὐτόν. Accusative direct object of ἑώρακεν. The referent is Jesus Christ, since he is the only possible antecedent in verses 5-6.

ἔγνωκεν. Prf act ind 3rd sg γινώσκω. On the tense, see 2:3 on ἔγνωκεν.

αὐτόν. Accusative direct object of ἔγνωκεν. The referent is Jesus Christ (see above).

1 John 3:7-12

⁷Dear children, let no one deceive you. The one who practices righteousness is righteous, even as (Jesus) is righteous. ⁸The one who practices sin (on the other hand) belongs to the devil, because the devil has been sinning since the beginning. For this reason, the Son of God was revealed, that he might destroy the works of the devil. ⁹Everyone who has been born of God does not practice sin, since God's seed remains in him and he is not able to sin, because he has been born of God.

¹⁰This is how the children of God and the children of the devil may be distinguished: anyone who does not practice righteousness does not belong to God, and (the same is true of) the one who does not love

his brother or sister. [11]For this is the message that you have heard from the beginning: we should love one another—[12]not as Cain did; he was from the Evil One and murdered his brother. And why did he murder him? Because his deeds were evil, but his brother's were righteous.

3:7 Τεκνία, μηδεὶς πλανάτω ὑμᾶς· ὁ ποιῶν τὴν δικαιοσύνην δίκαιός ἐστιν, καθὼς ἐκεῖνος δίκαιός ἐστιν·

Τεκνία. The use of the vocative (cf. 2:1 on Τεκνία), along with the imperative verb, helps mark a paragraph break. Some scribes (A P 33 et al.) replaced τεκνία with its synonym παιδία.
μηδεὶς. Substantival nominative subject of πλανάτω.
πλανάτω. Pres act impv 3rd sg πλανάω. On the significance of the tense and mood, see 2:15 on ἀγαπάτε and "Verbal Aspect and Prominence" in the Introduction.
ὑμᾶς. Accusative direct object of πλανάτω.
ὁ ποιῶν. Pres act ptc masc nom sg ποιέω (substantival). The participial construction, ὁ ποιῶν τὴν δικαιοσύνην, functions as the subject of ἐστιν.
τὴν δικαιοσύνην. Accusative direct object of ποιῶν.
δίκαιός. Predicate adjective. The second accent comes from the enclitic ἐστιν (see 1:5 on ἐστιν).
ἐστιν. Pres act ind 3rd sg ἐστιν. On the loss of accent, see 1:5 on ἐστιν.
καθὼς. Introduces a comparison.
ἐκεῖνος. Nominative subject (see 1:5 on αὕτη) of ἐστιν. The referent is Jesus Christ (see also 2:6).
δίκαιός ἐστιν. See above.

3:8 ὁ ποιῶν τὴν ἁμαρτίαν ἐκ τοῦ διαβόλου ἐστίν, ὅτι ἀπ' ἀρχῆς ὁ διάβολος ἁμαρτάνει. εἰς τοῦτο ἐφανερώθη ὁ υἱὸς τοῦ θεοῦ, ἵνα λύσῃ τὰ ἔργα τοῦ διαβόλου.

ὁ ποιῶν τὴν ἁμαρτίαν. The choice of this near synonym for ὁ ἁμαρτάνων (3:6) is probably dictated by the contrast being drawn with ὁ ποιῶν τὴν δικαιοσύνην (3:7; see also 3:4 on ὁ ποιῶν τὴν ἁμαρτίαν).
ὁ ποιῶν. Pres act ptc masc nom sg ποιέω (substantival). The participial construction, ὁ ποιῶν τὴν ἁμαρτίαν, functions as the

subject of ἐστίν. On the rhetorical force of the construction, see 2:4 on ὁ λέγων.

ἐκ τοῦ διαβόλου. Source/Origin (but see 2:19 on ἦσαν ἐξ).

ἐστίν. Pres act ind 3rd sg εἰμί. On the retention of the accent, see 1:5 on ἐστιν.

ὅτι. Causal.

ἀπ' ἀρχῆς. Temporal. The specific temporal reference (perhaps to the Garden of Eden) is left unstated.

ὁ διάβολος. Nominative subject of ἁμαρτάνει. Louw and Nida (12.34) describe this term as "a title for the Devil, literally 'slanderer.'" The title likely carried more semantic freight than the English term "devil." Foerster (73) suggests that the closest English equivalent is "adversary," with the work of the διάβολος always implying "an attempt . . . to separate God and man."

ἁμαρτάνει. Pres act ind 3rd sg ἁμαρτάνω. The present tense of this verb simply portrays the action as a process, while the temporal marker ἀπ' ἀρχῆς sets the boundaries of the process as extending from the distant past to the present. Interpreters should beware of imposing both nuances on the tense itself and viewing it as a "habitual present" (contra Smalley, 169), one of many highly questionable tense labels (see "Using the *Baylor Handbook on the Greek New Testament*" in the Series Introduction). To capture the sense of ἀπ' ἀρχῆς . . . ἁμαρτάνει in English requires the use of a perfect progressive construction ("has been sinning . . .").

εἰς. Purpose.

τοῦτο. Cataphoric (see 1:5 on αὕτη).

ἐφανερώθη. Aor pass ind 3rd sg φανερόω. It would be possible, following Strecker (101, n. 52; cf. Brown, 406), to view this and other cases of ἐφανερώθη in 1 John, where Jesus is the subject, as middle forms: "the Son of the God has revealed himself" (see "Deponency" in the Series Introduction on the nature of the -θη- morpheme).

ὁ υἱὸς τοῦ θεοῦ. It is unclear whether this expression should be taken primarily as an ontological claim or a messianic title. Given the focus on Jesus' role in 1 John, the latter option is most likely (cf. Matt 26:63, where the high priest clearly uses the expression as a messianic title: ὁ Χριστὸς ὁ υἱὸς τοῦ θεοῦ).

ὁ υἱὸς. Nominative subject of ἐφανερώθη.

τοῦ θεοῦ. Genitive of relationship.

ἵνα. The ἵνα clause should probably be taken as epexegetical to the demonstrative pronoun, which (with εἰς) introduces purpose.
λύσῃ. Aor act subj 3rd sg λύω. Subjunctive with ἵνα.
τὰ ἔργα. Accusative direct object of λύσῃ.
τοῦ διαβόλου. Subjective genitive (see 1:1 on τῆς ζωῆς).

3:9 Πᾶς ὁ γεγεννημένος ἐκ τοῦ θεοῦ ἁμαρτίαν οὐ ποιεῖ, ὅτι σπέρμα αὐτοῦ ἐν αὐτῷ μένει· καὶ οὐ δύναται ἁμαρτάνειν, ὅτι ἐκ τοῦ θεοῦ γεγέννηται.

Πᾶς ὁ γεγεννημένος ἐκ τοῦ θεοῦ. The whole participial construction, headed by the nominative Πᾶς ὁ γεγεννημένος, functions as the subject of ποιεῖ. On the rhetorical force of πᾶς with an articular participle, see 2:23 on πᾶς ὁ ἀρνούμενος. Strecker's (101) claim that the use of the πᾶς indicates that "the community is being addressed as a whole" reflects an overly literal reading of the adjective that ignores its rhetorical function.
ὁ γεγεννημένος. Prf pass ptc masc nom sg γεννάω (substantival or attributive; see 2:23 on πᾶς ὁ ἀρνούμενος).
ἐκ τοῦ θεοῦ. The most appropriate label is probably "source." Used with γεννάω, however, the preposition ἐκ specifically introduces the one who produces the "offspring" (cf. 2:29 on ἐξ αὐτοῦ γεγέννηται).
ἁμαρτίαν. Accusative direct object of ποιεῖ.
ποιεῖ. Pres act ind 3rd sg ποιέω. On the tense, see 3:6 on ἁμαρτάνει.
ὅτι. Causal.
σπέρμα αὐτοῦ ἐν αὐτῷ μένει. Attempts to take σπέρμα as a reference to the Word of God/Gospel (so Dodd, 77–78) or the Holy Spirit (Brown, 411; Schnackenburg, 175) fail to situate the interpretation of the term in its metaphorical context (ὁ γεγεννημένος ἐκ τοῦ θεοῦ). In this context, the expression as a whole probably highlights the transference of character traits—spiritual DNA, as it were—through spiritual descent from the Father (cf. Smalley, 172). As Strecker (103) puts it: "anyone who is born of God and therefore is of one nature with God lives in irreconcilable opposition to every kind of sinful action."
σπέρμα. Neuter nominative subject of μένει.

αὐτοῦ. Possessive genitive. The antecedent is τοῦ θεοῦ.
ἐν αὐτῷ μένει. The use of μένει highlights continuity of state (cf. 2:10).
μένει. Pres act ind 3rd sg μένω.
καὶ. In the syntax, the conjunction simply introduces a coordinate clause. In terms of semantics, however, the conjoined clause, οὐ δύναται ἁμαρτάνειν, introduces the result of the preceding clause. Titrud (250) suggests that in cases such as this, "By syntactically elevating what is logically subordinate, the author is placing more prominence (emphasis) on the clause than it would have had if introduced by a subordinating conjunction" (see also 2:20, 27).
δύναται. Pres mid ind 3rd sg δύναμαι. The middle voice is likely conditioned by the fact that "the subject is the center of gravity" (Miller, 429; for more, see "Deponency" in the Series Introduction).
ἁμαρτάνειν. Pres act inf ἁμαρτάνω (complementary).
ὅτι. Causal.
ἐκ τοῦ θεοῦ. See above. The fronting (see 1:5 on σκοτία) of the prepositional phrase (in contrast to ὁ γεγεννημένος ἐκ τοῦ θεοῦ) makes it more prominent.
γεγέννηται. Prf pass ind 3rd sg γεννάω. On the tense, see 2:3 on ἐγνώκαμεν.

3:10 ἐν τούτῳ φανερά ἐστιν τὰ τέκνα τοῦ θεοῦ καὶ τὰ τέκνα τοῦ διαβόλου· πᾶς ὁ μὴ ποιῶν δικαιοσύνην οὐκ ἔστιν ἐκ τοῦ θεοῦ, καὶ ὁ μὴ ἀγαπῶν τὸν ἀδελφὸν αὐτοῦ.

ἐν τούτῳ. Instrumental. The demonstrative pronoun should probably be taken as cataphoric (so Brooke, 90; Bultmann, 53; Harris 2003, 151; Strecker, 104; see also 1:5 on αὕτη), pointing forward to the πᾶς clause, rather than anaphoric (contra Brown, 416; but see below on πᾶς ὁ μὴ ποιῶν δικαιοσύνην), though some scholars simply claim that it refers to both (Schnackenburg, 176, n. 181; Smalley, 179). On the rhetorical function of this expression, see 2:3.
φανερά. Neuter plural predicate adjective.
ἐστιν. Pres act ind 3rd sg εἰμί. Neuter plural subjects

1 John 3:9-10   79

characteristically take singular verbs (see Wallace, 399–400). On the loss of accent, see 1:5 on ἐστιν.

τὰ τέκνα . . . καὶ τὰ τέκνα. Neuter nominative subject of ἐστιν.

τὰ τέκνα τοῦ διαβόλου. Similar language is found in John 8:44—ὑμεῖς ἐκ τοῦ πατρὸς τοῦ διαβόλου ἐστὲ.

τοῦ θεοῦ, τοῦ διαβόλου. Genitive of relationship.

πᾶς ὁ μὴ ποιῶν δικαιοσύνην. The whole participial construction, headed by the nominative πᾶς ὁ . . . ποιῶν, functions as the subject of ἐστιν. On the rhetorical force of πᾶς with an articular participle, see 2:23 on πᾶς ὁ ἀρνούμενος.

ὁ . . . ποιῶν. Pres act ptc masc nom sg ποιέω (substantival or attributive; see 2:23 on πᾶς ὁ ἀρνούμενος).

δικαιοσύνην. Accusative direct object of ποιῶν.

ἔστιν ἐκ τοῦ θεοῦ. The most appropriate label for the use of ἐκ with the verb εἰμί is probably "source/origin." It is not clear, however, whether this expression is synonymous with "born of God" (ὁ γεγεννημένος ἐκ τοῦ θεοῦ; v. 9) and/or focuses more on identity and character (see 2:19 on ἦσαν ἐξ). The contrasting designation, ἐκ τοῦ πονηροῦ, occurs in 3:12. It is likely that the birth language (γεννάω; 2:29; 3:9a, 9b; 4:7; 5:1a, 4, 18a, 18b) and familial language (τὰ τέκνα τοῦ θεοῦ; cf. John 8:44—ὑμεῖς ἐκ τοῦ πατρὸς τοῦ διαβόλου ἐστὲ) both point to relational links that are evident in one's behavior and character (cf. John 8:44—καὶ τὰς ἐπιθυμίας τοῦ πατρὸς ὑμῶν θέλετε ποιεῖν).

ἔστιν. Pres act ind 3rd sg εἰμί. On the movement of the accent, see 1:5 on ἐστιν.

καὶ. Although some take the conjunction as epexegetical ("that is, anyone who does not love his brother"; so Bultmann, 54; Smalley, 181; Strecker, 105), it is preferable to take the conjunction as introducing a clause that is coordinate with the preceding one and in which οὐκ ἔστιν ἐκ τοῦ θεοῦ is implied.

ὁ μὴ ἀγαπῶν τὸν ἀδελφὸν αὐτοῦ. The whole participial construction, headed by the nominative ὁ . . . ἀγαπῶν, serves as the subject of an implicit οὐκ ἔστιν ἐκ τοῦ θεοῦ. On the rhetorical force of the construction, see 2:4 on ὁ λέγων.

ὁ . . . ἀγαπῶν. Pres act ptc masc nom sg ἀγαπάω (substantival).

τὸν ἀδελφὸν. Accusative direct object of ἀγαπῶν. On the meaning, see 2:9.

αὐτοῦ. Genitive of relationship.

3:11 Ὅτι αὕτη ἐστὶν ἡ ἀγγελία ἣν ἠκούσατε ἀπ' ἀρχῆς, ἵνα ἀγαπῶμεν ἀλλήλους·

Ὅτι. Causal. Many have noted the structural parallel to 1:5 (Καὶ ἔστιν αὕτη ἡ ἀγγελία), with some arguing that 3:11 marks the beginning of the second major section of the letter, which extends to 5:12 (see, e.g., Brown, 126, who argues that 1:5 and 3:11 each set the theme for the half of the letter that follows). Although such an analysis may make good sense of the themes of the letter, it ignores the surface structure. The ὅτι makes it clear that syntactically 3:11 is subordinate to 3:10. Typical corroborating markers of a new paragraph or section do not appear until 3:13.
αὕτη. Predicate nominative (see 1:5 on αὕτη). The demonstrative is cataphoric (see 1:5 on αὕτη).
ἐστὶν. Pres act ind 3rd sg εἰμί. On the retention of the accent, see 1:5 on ἐστιν.
ἡ ἀγγελία. Nominative subject (see 1:5 on αὕτη) of ἐστὶν. On the meaning of this term, see 1:5. Some scribes (א C P Ψ et al.) substituted the more common ἐπαγγελία, which occurs 52 times in the NT (ἀγγελία occurs only here and in 1:5 in the NT).
ἣν. Accusative direct object of ἠκούσατε.
ἀπ' ἀρχῆς. Temporal (see 2:7).
ἵνα. Introduces a clause that is epexegetical to αὕτη (see 1:5 on ὅτι).
ἀγαπῶμεν. Pres act subj 1st pl ἀγαπάω. Subjunctive with ἵνα.
ἀλλήλους. Accusative direct object of ἀγαπῶμεν.

3:12 οὐ καθὼς Κάϊν ἐκ τοῦ πονηροῦ ἦν καὶ ἔσφαξεν τὸν ἀδελφὸν αὐτοῦ· καὶ χάριν τίνος ἔσφαξεν αὐτόν; ὅτι τὰ ἔργα αὐτοῦ πονηρὰ ἦν, τὰ δὲ τοῦ ἀδελφοῦ αὐτοῦ δίκαια.

καθὼς. Introduces a comparison.
Κάϊν. Most translations render what follows Κάϊν using a relative clause (e.g., NRSV: "We must not be like Cain who was from the evil one and murdered his brother"). Although such translations may be natural, syntactically Κάϊν is the subject of an

implied verb and predicate (ἠγάπησεν τὸν ἀδελφὸν αὐτοῦ; "not as Cain '*loved*' his brother"), while ἐκ τοῦ πονηροῦ ἦν is a new independent clause. The diaeresis over the *iota* indicates that the vowel is not part of a diphthong, but rather is syllabic (Κά-ιν).

ἐκ τοῦ πονηροῦ. On the meaning of this expression, see 3:10 on ἔστιν ἐκ τοῦ θεοῦ and 2:19 on ἦσαν ἐξ.

τοῦ πονηροῦ. The use of this title, which refers to ὁ διάβολος (3:8), makes the connection between Cain, whose works were "evil" (τὰ ἔργα αὐτοῦ πονηρὰ ἦν), and his "father" more explicit.

ἦν. Impf ind 3rd sg εἰμί.

ἔσφαξεν. Aor act ind 3rd sg σφάζω. The use of the aorist tense helps mark this material as background or supplemental material that does not serve to carry the argument forward. The choice of this term ("to slaughter, either animals or persons; in contexts referring to persons, the implication is of violence and mercilessness"; LN 20.72), which occurs only here and in Revelation in the NT, highlights the heinous nature of Cain's crime.

τὸν ἀδελφὸν. Accusative direct object of ἔσφαξεν.

αὐτοῦ. Genitive of relationship.

χάριν. This preposition, which takes a genitive modifier and serves as "a marker of a reason, often with the implication of an underlying purpose" (LN 89.29), occurs just nine times in the NT (also Luke 7:47; Gal 3:19; Eph 3:1, 14; 1 Tim 5:14; Titus 1:5, 11; Jude 16). It actually serves as a "postposition" generally, i.e., it generally follows its genitive modifier. It should not be mistaken for the noun χάρις, which is identical in form in the accusative singular and from which it is derived (Robertson, 486–88). The expression, χάριν τίνος, is unique to the NT (Strecker, 109, n. 12).

τίνος. Genitive object of the preposition χάριν. On the force of the rhetorical question that follows, see 2:22 on Τίς.

ἔσφαξεν. See above.

αὐτόν. Accusative direct object of ἔσφαξεν.

ὅτι. Causal.

τὰ ἔργα. Neuter nominative subject of ἦν.

αὐτοῦ. Subjective genitive (see 1:1 on τῆς ζωῆς).

πονηρὰ. Predicate adjective.

ἦν. Impf ind 3rd sg εἰμί. Neuter plural subjects characteristically take singular verbs (see Wallace, 399–400).

τὰ. The noun ἔργα is left implicit.

τοῦ ἀδελφοῦ. Subjective genitive (see 1:1 on τῆς ζωῆς). On the meaning, see 2:9.

δίκαια. Predicate adjective.

1 John 3:13-18

¹³Do not be surprised, brothers and sisters, if the world hates you. ¹⁴We know that we have moved from death to life because we love (our) brothers and sisters. The one who does not love (his brothers and sisters) remains in death. ¹⁵Everyone who hates his brother or sister is a murderer; and you know that no murderer has eternal life remaining in him. ¹⁶This is how we know (what) love (is): he laid down his life for us. So, we ought to lay down our lives for our brothers and sisters. ¹⁷But whoever has material possessions and notices a brother or sister in need and (still) refuses to have compassion on him, how can the love of God remain in him? ¹⁸Dear children, do not love (others merely) with (your) speech or by what you say, but truly (love them) by what you do.

3:13 [καὶ] μὴ θαυμάζετε, ἀδελφοί, εἰ μισεῖ ὑμᾶς ὁ κόσμος.

[καὶ]. The editors of the UBS⁴ were not able to determine with any degree of certainty whether the original text had the conjunction or not. The conjunction is found in ℵ Cᵛⁱᵈ P Ψ 1739 itʳ, ⁶⁵ syrᵖ arm eth, while it is absent in A B K L 33 81 614 *Byz Lect* itʰ vg syrʰ copˢᵃ, ᵇᵒ, ᶠᵃʸ et al. The conjunction could have been added, either intentionally or intuitively, to make explicit the thematic continuity (see 1:2 on καὶ) with what precedes. The fact that the link is relatively weak (the world's treatment of Christians is being set against Cain's treatment of his brother), however, may have led some scribes to omit it intuitively. The preceding word (δίκαια) could also have led to an accidental omission (cf. Metzger, 643) or insertion of the καί.

θαυμάζετε. Pres act impv 2nd pl θαυμάζω. On the significance of the tense and mood, see 2:15 on ἀγαπάτε and "Verbal Aspect and Prominence" in the Introduction.

ἀδελφοί. On the meaning, see 2:9. The use of the vocative,

along with an imperative verb provides evidence for a paragraph break (cf. 2:1 on Τεκνία).

εἰ. The conjunction should probably be taken as introducing a first class condition. The choice of the first class rather than third class condition (which is predominant in 1 John), moves the reader away from hypothetical situations (see 1:6 on Ἐὰν) to more likely situations, though the first class condition itself simply presents an assertion for the sake of argument (see, e.g., Wallace, 690–94), without reference to whether or not it is true in reality. BAGD (219), however, treats εἰ as a complementizer equivalent to ὅτι here, noting that such a usage is attested elsewhere after verbs of emotion. Similarly, Young (185) argues that "Εἰ functions as a complementizer to transform an embedded sentence into a complement noun clause. This function is common after verbs of emotion or wonder, but occurs with other verbs as well." The fact that θαυμάζω is frequently followed by a complement clause introduced by ὅτι (see, e.g., Luke 11:38; John 3:7; 4:27; Gal 1:6), however, raises the question of why the writer would switch to εἰ here, and suggests that we are simply dealing with a first class condition. An examination of the usage of verbs like θαυμάζω may have been what led BDAG (277–78) to change the entry for εἰ so that it no longer links the current usage to a verb of emotion (though the new entry—"marker of an indirect question as content, *that*"—leaves questions about the function of εἰ).

μισεῖ ὑμᾶς ὁ κόσμος. Although Smalley (187) views all three constituents here as "emphatic," the only constituent that may possibly be viewed as a marked word order is ὑμᾶς, since objects follow the subject in unmarked constructions (see 1:5 on σκοτία).

μισεῖ. Pres act ind 3rd sg μισέω.

ὑμᾶς. Accusative direct object of μισεῖ.

ὁ κόσμος. Nominative subject of μισεῖ. Metonymy (see 2:2 on τοῦ κόσμου) for "the people of the world."

3:14 ἡμεῖς οἴδαμεν ὅτι μεταβεβήκαμεν ἐκ τοῦ θανάτου εἰς τὴν ζωήν, ὅτι ἀγαπῶμεν τοὺς ἀδελφούς· ὁ μὴ ἀγαπῶν μένει ἐν τῷ θανάτῳ.

ἡμεῖς. The explicit nominative subject pronoun helps emphasize the contrast between the characteristic actions of the world and Cain (hatred and murder) and the characteristics of those who have crossed over from death to life.

οἴδαμεν. Prf act ind 1st pl οἶδα.

ὅτι. Introduces the clausal complement of οἴδαμεν (see also 2:3 on ὅτι).

μεταβεβήκαμεν ἐκ τοῦ θανάτου εἰς τὴν ζωήν. Similar language is found in John 5:24—μεταβέβηκεν ἐκ τοῦ θανάτου εἰς τὴν ζωήν.

μεταβεβήκαμεν. Prf act ind 1st pl μεταβαίνω. The perfect tense is required by the semantics of the verb and the ἐκ . . . εἰς construction that follows, both of which highlight the change from one state or place to another (cf. LN 13.51; BDAG, 638). As Smalley (188) notes, the verb "provides a graphic description of the believer's transition from the world of hatred and death to the realm of love and life."

ἐκ τοῦ θανάτου. Separation.

εἰς τὴν ζωήν. Locative, in a metaphorical sense.

ὅτι. Causal. More specifically, this ὅτι clause provides the grounds for the conclusion expressed in the statement οἴδαμεν ὅτι μεταβεβήκαμεν ἐκ τοῦ θανάτου εἰς τὴν ζωήν (so also Young, 260).

ἀγαπῶμεν. Pres act ind 1st pl ἀγαπάω. The present tense, which simply portrays the action as a process, should not be pressed to imply "that the need for brotherly love . . . is constant" (contra Smalley, 189).

τοὺς ἀδελφούς. Accusative direct object of ἀγαπῶμεν. On the meaning, see 2:9.

ὁ . . . ἀγαπῶν. Pres act ptc masc nom sg ἀγαπάω (substantival). Nominative subject of μένει. The text of the UBS⁴ is supported by ℵ A B 33 1739 it^(h, r, 65) vg cop^(bo, fay) arm, while a number of manuscripts (C K L Ψ 81 *Byz Lect* et al.) read ἀγαπῶν τὸν ἀδελφὸν and others (P 056 614 syr^(p, h) et al.) read ἀγαπῶν τὸν ἀδελφὸν αὐτοῦ. All three variants reflect the same content, since ἀγαπῶν τὸν ἀδελφὸν αὐτοῦ is implicit in the shortest reading. Since the UBS⁴ reading has strong external support and it appears that copyists were more likely to intuitively/accidentally include implicit information rather than omit it (consistent with the shorter reading principle), most scholars prefer the shorter reading.

μένει ἐν τῷ θανάτῳ. The use of μένει highlights continuity of state (cf. 2:10), in this case continuity in the state of death (lacking spiritual life).

μένει. Pres act ind 3rd sg μένω.

1 John 3:14-15   85

3:15 πᾶς ὁ μισῶν τὸν ἀδελφὸν αὐτοῦ ἀνθρωποκτόνος ἐστίν,
καὶ οἴδατε ὅτι πᾶς ἀνθρωποκτόνος οὐκ ἔχει ζωὴν αἰώνιον ἐν
αὐτῷ μένουσαν.

πᾶς ὁ μισῶν τὸν ἀδελφὸν αὐτοῦ. The whole participial construction, headed by the nominative πᾶς ὁ μισῶν, functions as the
subject of ἐστίν. In an equative clause (cf. 1:5 on ὁ θεὸς) such as this,
the heavier noun phrase (πᾶς ὁ μισῶν τὸν ἀδελφὸν αὐτοῦ) will tend
to be the subject and the shorter noun phrase (ἀνθρωποκτόνος) the
predicate. On the rhetorical force of πᾶς with an articular participle,
see 2:23 on πᾶς ὁ ἀρνούμενος.
ὁ μισῶν. Pres act ptc masc nom sg μισέω (substantival or attributive; see 2:23 on πᾶς ὁ ἀρνούμενος).
τὸν ἀδελφὸν. Accusative direct object of μισῶν. On the meaning,
see 2:9.
αὐτοῦ. Genitive of relationship.
ἀνθρωποκτόνος. Predicate nominative (see above). The whole
clause should probably be viewed as hyperbole (so Brown, 447; contra most scholars), on par with Jesus' statement in Matthew 5:21-22.
This term is used only here and in John 8:44 (to describe ὁ διάβολος)
in the NT.
ἐστίν. Pres act ind 3rd sg εἰμί. On the retention of the accent, see
1:5 on ἐστιν.
καὶ. The text should likely have a period or semi-colon preceding the conjunction rather than a comma. The clause-initial καὶ marks
thematic continuity (see 1:2 on καὶ) and introduces a further comment
on ἀνθρωποκτόνος.
οἴδατε. Prf act ind 2nd pl οἶδα.
ὅτι. Introduces the clausal complement of οἴδατε (see also 2:3 on
ὅτι).
πᾶς ἀνθρωποκτόνος. Nominative subject of ἔχει.
οὐκ ἔχει ζωὴν αἰώνιον ἐν αὐτῷ μένουσαν. The language
(μένω points to continuity in a particular state; cf. 2:10) suggests on
the surface that failure to love one's fellow believer, or perhaps active
"hatred" of one's fellow believer, leads to exclusion from both present
and eschatological privilege. This is consistent with the writer's earlier
argument that identifies loving one's fellow believers as a validation

of having passed from death to life (3:14; cf. 2:10; 3:10). Rhetorically, then, the indicative statement serves as a powerful reminder (cf. 1:6 on Ἐὰν) to believers not to allow themselves to slip into "hating" another believer.

ἔχει. Pres act ind 3rd sg ἔχω. Rather than claiming that the present tense of the verb "includes a durative force . . . and this is intensified by the phrase which follows" (Smalley, 191), it is better to recognize that the present tense simply portrays the event as a process, while it is the participle μένουσαν that provides the durative nuance.

ζωὴν αἰώνιον. Accusative direct object of ἔχει.

ἐν αὐτῷ. Locative.

μένουσαν. Pres act ptc fem acc sg μένω. The participle could be viewed as attributive (cf. Rogers and Rogers, 596) or as an accusative complement in an object-complement double accusative construction (see 1:10 on ψεύστην).

3:16 ἐν τούτῳ ἐγνώκαμεν τὴν ἀγάπην, ὅτι ἐκεῖνος ὑπὲρ ἡμῶν τὴν ψυχὴν αὐτοῦ ἔθηκεν· καὶ ἡμεῖς ὀφείλομεν ὑπὲρ τῶν ἀδελφῶν τὰς ψυχὰς θεῖναι.

ἐν τούτῳ. Instrumental. The demonstrative pronoun is cataphoric (see 1:5 on αὕτη), pointing forward to the ὅτι clause. On the rhetorical function of this expression, see 2:3.

ἐγνώκαμεν. Prf act ind 1st pl γινώσκω. The semantics of the verse drive the writer to use the perfect tense, i.e., he is going to appeal to a past event ("he gave his life for us") as the basis for a present reality ("we know what true love is"; see also 2:3).

τὴν ἀγάπην. Accusative direct object of ἐγνώκαμεν.

ὅτι. Introduces a clause that is epexegetical to τούτῳ (see 1:5 on ὅτι).

ἐκεῖνος. Nominative subject of ἔθηκεν. The referent is Jesus Christ (see also 2:6).

ὑπὲρ ἡμῶν. In this context, the preposition functions as "a marker of a participant who is benefited by an event or on whose behalf an event takes place" (LN 90.36). Louw and Nida's label "benefaction" (1:802) is preferable to the traditional label "substitution" or "representation." Although (1) the preposition (with the genitive) can denote "substitution," (2) it is theologically true that

Jesus died in place of his followers, and (3) at times the notions of substitution and benefaction cannot be distinguished with this term (cf. Harris 1975–78, 1197), the parallel use of the term below with reference to believers strongly suggests that benefaction, as defined above, is in focus here.

τὴν ψυχὴν . . . ἔθηκεν. An idiom meaning, "to die, with the implication of voluntary or willing action" (LN 23.113; cf. Strecker, 115; and Smalley, 193, who renders the verb "surrender").

τὴν ψυχὴν. Accusative direct object of ἔθηκεν.

αὐτοῦ. Possessive genitive.

ἔθηκεν. Aor act ind 3rd sg τίθημι.

καὶ. The clause-initial καὶ marks thematic continuity (see 1:2 on καὶ) and introduces a further comment on τὴν ψυχὴν . . . ἔθηκεν. Given the semantics of the verb ὀφείλομεν and the context, the conjunction cannot introduce a second clause governed by ὅτι ("By this we know what love is . . . we ought to lay down our lives . . ."; contra Smalley, 194).

ἡμεῖς. The explicit nominative subject pronoun (coupled with the conjunction; see above on καὶ) highlights the logical response of Christians to what Jesus Christ did for them, which will be introduced by ὀφείλομεν.

ὀφείλομεν. Pres act ind 1st pl ὀφείλω. On the semantics and rhetorical significance of this verb, see 2:6 on ὀφείλει. Smalley's contention (194) that "the present tense of the verb contains a durative force" is untenable. The present tense simply portrays the event as a process. Moreover, this verb *only* occurs in the imperfective aspect in the NT (30 times in the present tense, and 5 times in the imperfect).

ὑπὲρ τῶν ἀδελφῶν. Benefaction (see above on ὑπὲρ ἡμῶν). On the meaning of ἀδελφῶν, see 2:9.

τὰς ψυχὰς θεῖναι. On the idiom, see above. The use of the idiom here should probably be understood as a synecdoche (see 1:1 on αἱ χεῖρες ἡμῶν) of sorts. If the readers ought to be willing to give their lives for their fellow believers (one way of serving), then surely they should be quick to embrace all lesser forms of serving them.

τὰς ψυχὰς. Accusative direct object of θεῖναι.

θεῖναι. Aor act inf τίθημι (complementary).

3:17 ὃς δ' ἂν ἔχῃ τὸν βίον τοῦ κόσμου καὶ θεωρῇ τὸν ἀδελφὸν αὐτοῦ χρείαν ἔχοντα καὶ κλείσῃ τὰ σπλάγχνα αὐτοῦ ἀπ' αὐτοῦ, πῶς ἡ ἀγάπη τοῦ θεοῦ μένει ἐν αὐτῷ;

ὃς ... αὐτοῦ. The entire relative clause functions as the topic (see 1:1) of what follows, which will be picked up with the resumptive pronoun αὐτῷ.

ὃς ... ἄν. The indefinite relative pronoun (see 2:5 on ὅς ... ἄν) serves as the nominative subject of ἔχῃ. There is no syntactic basis for claiming that this construction "expresses a situation which occurs generally" (contra Smalley, 196; Strecker, 116).

δ'. Used in this context (see 2:2 on ἀλλὰ), the elided conjunction (δέ) introduces a contrast (but see 2:2 on ἀλλὰ) to the statement in the previous verse: ἡμεῖς ὀφείλομεν ὑπὲρ τῶν ἀδελφῶν τὰς ψυχὰς θεῖναι.

ἔχῃ. Pres act subj 3rd sg ἔχω. Subjunctive with ἄν. The present tense simply portrays the event as a process. It does not imply a situation that occurs "repeatedly" (contra Smalley, 196).

τὸν βίον. Accusative direct object of ἔχῃ. Used with τοῦ κόσμου, the sense here is "the resources which one has as a means of living" (LN 57.18). It is worth noting that the writer has chosen to use this expression rather than τὸν πλοῦτον ("riches, wealth"), making it clear that ὃς ἄν will include just about everyone, not just the rich, since all have resources.

τοῦ κόσμου. Attributive genitive.

θεωρῇ. Pres act subj 3rd sg θεωρέω. Subjunctive with ἄν. The choice of verb may imply a clear awareness of the plight of τὸν ἀδελφὸν. BDAG (454) defines the present usage as "to observe someth. with sustained attention" (cf. LN 24.14; Smalley, 196).

τὸν ἀδελφὸν. Accusative direct object of θεωρῇ. Given the use of this expression through 1 John, the focus appears to be on fellow believers (see 2:9).

αὐτοῦ. Genitive of relationship.

χρείαν. Accusative direct object of ἔχοντα.

ἔχοντα. Pres act ptc masc acc sg ἔχω. Accusative complement in an object-complement double accusative construction (see 1:10 on ψεύστην).

κλείσῃ τὰ σπλάγχνα αὐτοῦ. An idiom (lit. "he closes his intestines") meaning, "to refuse to show compassion" (LN 25.55).

κλείσῃ. Aor act subj 3rd sg κλείω. Subjunctive with ἄν.

τὰ σπλάγχνα. Accusative direct object of κλείσῃ.

αὐτοῦ. Genitive of possession.

ἀπ' αὐτοῦ. Separation.

πῶς. Bauer (82–83) maintains that πῶς introduces the rhetorical question as a means of denying that such a state of affairs is possible.

ἡ ἀγάπη. Nominative subject of μένει.

τοῦ θεοῦ. Probably objective genitive (see 1:1 on τῆς ζωῆς; cf. 2:5). When the writer asks, πῶς ἡ ἀγάπη τοῦ θεοῦ μένει ἐν αὐτῷ, his point is not that God's lack of love for someone results in that person's failure to love his brother (subjective genitive; contra Haas, de Jonge, and Swellengrebel, 92; Strecker, 117). Instead, the question points to the dissonance between claiming to love God and not demonstrating that love in action toward others in need. Wendland (28), however, argues that this may well be an example of intentional ambiguity, or "semantic density," on the part of the author. Such ambiguity would be a literary rather than syntactic category, and should not be confused with the questionable label "plenary genitive" (see, e.g., Wallace, 119–21).

μένει ἐν αὐτῷ. The use of μένει highlights continuity of state (cf. 2:10).

μένει. Pres act ind 3rd sg μένω. BDF §366(4) argues that the verb should be accented as a future (μενεῖ) rather than a present form.

3:18 Τεκνία, μὴ ἀγαπῶμεν λόγῳ μηδὲ τῇ γλώσσῃ ἀλλὰ ἐν ἔργῳ καὶ ἀληθείᾳ.

Τεκνία. Although vocatives frequently occur at the beginning of new paragraphs in 1 John (cf. 2:1 on Τεκνία), and some scholars see 3:18 as marking a new sub-section (see, e.g., Harris 2003, 152), it is probably better to follow Strecker (118), who argues that the "renewed address to the readers does not mean that a new section begins at this point, but rather that the whole of what has been said up to now will be summarized in this verse" (cf. Haas, de Jonge, and Swellengrebel, 92; Marshall, 196).

ἀγαπῶμεν. Pres act subj 1st pl ἀγαπάω (hortatory subjunctive). The use of the subjunctive with μή is typically labeled "prohibitive subjunctive" when the verb is second person. First person subjunctives of this nature are typically labeled "hortatory subjunctive" (so Wallace, 465, for this passage), since the subject is not "commanding" himself or herself to refrain from a particular action. With the hortatory subjunctive, the writer is exhorting the readers to join him or her in some action (McKay, 79). Since the hortatory subjunctive functions, however, as a "thinly veiled substitute for a second person imperative" (McKay, 79), the semantic distinction between a negative hortatory subjunctive and a prohibitive subjunctive should not be pressed. For more on the similarities, compare Gal 6:9 (τὸ δὲ καλὸν ποιοῦντες μὴ ἐγκακῶμεν), which McKay (78) treats as a hortatory subjunctive, with the semantically analogous 2 Thess 3:13 (μὴ ἐγκακήσητε καλοποιοῦντες), which McKay (80) labels a prohibitive subjunctive.

λόγῳ μηδὲ τῇ γλώσσῃ. Dative of instrument. Although Smalley (198) argues that this expression functions as a hendiadys (see further below), the lack of symmetry (one noun is anarthrous and one is articular) argues against this.

ἀλλά. The conjunction highlights the sharp contrast that is being drawn between loving speech and loving action (see also 2:2).

ἐν ἔργῳ καὶ ἀληθείᾳ. Instrumental. We should not see any semantic distinction between the prepositional phrase with ἐν and the earlier simple dative λόγῳ μηδὲ τῇ γλώσσῃ (contra Westcott, 115). The conjoined noun phrase ἔργῳ καὶ ἀληθείᾳ could be viewed as a hendiadys and thus rendered "genuine works" (so Bultmann, 56; cf. Haas, de Jonge, and Swellengrebel, 93). Strecker argues against this view, presumably because the two terms are not near synonyms. It is helpful, in this case, to draw a distinction between a "hendiadys" and a "doublet," though the two terms are often used interchangeably. A doublet refers to the use of two near synonyms, joined by a conjunction, to refer to a single idea. Doublets in Greek, such as τέρατα καὶ σημεῖα, serve to intensify the semantics of the conjoined terms. The traditional definition of hendiadys, on the other hand, refers to a construction that conjoins two nouns (from different semantic domains), with one noun functioning like an attributive modifier of the other. For example, in Gen 3:16, Eve is told by God, "I will greatly multiply your pains and pregnancies" meaning "I will greatly multiply your pains of pregnancy" (so Wenham, 81) or "I will greatly multiply your labor pains." Thus, while Strecker's (118) argument against

hendiadys here ("the relationship between action and truth cannot
be readily summarized in a single concept") would be valid with
respect to a doublet, a traditional hendiadys does not require conjoined near synonyms (for more on hendiadys, see esp. Avishur,
100–11).

ἀληθείᾳ. One should not try to read a deeper significance
("sharing in the revelation of God in Christ") into the use of this
term (contra Smalley, 199). The context and its use with the preposition ἐν points to the sense "pertaining to being a real or actual
event or state" (LN 70.4).

1 John 3:19-24

[19][So] That is how we will know that we belong to the truth and
will (be able to) convince our heart before him—[20]if our heart condemns (us)—that God is greater than our heart; indeed, he knows all
things. [21]Dear friends, if our heart does *not* condemn us, then we have
confidence before God [22]and we receive whatever we ask from him,
because we keep his commands and do what is pleasing before him.
[23]Now, this is his command, that we believe in the name of his Son
Jesus Christ and that we love one another, just as he commanded us to
do. [24]So then, it is the one who keeps his commands that continues to
have a relationship with him, and he with that person. This is how we
know that he continues to have a relationship with us, by his Spirit,
whom he has given to us.

3:19 [Καὶ] ἐν τούτῳ γνωσόμεθα ὅτι ἐκ τῆς ἀληθείας ἐσμέν, καὶ
ἔμπροσθεν αὐτοῦ πείσομεν τὴν καρδίαν ἡμῶν

[Καὶ]. Most manuscripts read καὶ ἐν τούτῳ (א C Ψ 81 322 323
945 1175 1241 1243 1739 1881 2298 *Byz Lect* itq syrp copsa, boms
arm eth slav Augustine). Others, however, omit the conjunction (A
B 436 1067 1409 1735 2344 2464 itar, h, t, z vg copbo, fay geo Clem-
ent), and still others read καὶ ἐκ τούτου (1292 1505 1611 1844
1852 2138 [syrh]). External evidence tends to favor the first reading, which the UBS[4] upgraded to a "C" rating. The conjunction,
if original, marked thematic continuity with what precedes. The
fact that the thematic link is relatively weak (it focuses on "truth,"
which is not a primary topic in what precedes) may have led some
scribes to omit it intuitively (cf. 3:13).

ἐν τούτῳ. Instrumental. The antecedent of τούτῳ is probably the statements in verse 18. On the rhetorical function of this expression, see 2:3.

γνωσόμεθα. Fut mid ind 1st pl γινώσκω. It is going beyond the syntax to claim that the future tense points to "a moment of crisis (for which reassurance may be needed)" (contra Smalley, 201). Instead, since the antecedent of τούτῳ is verse 18, the point is that if the readers love in the manner described, then they *will* know that they "are of the truth." Given the fact that "knowing" has a high degree of intellectual self-involvement (see Miller, 428), it is not surprising to find the middle voice being used. Cooper (594; cited by Conrad, 8, n. 18) points out that the volitional nature of the future tense is what has led to the use of middle morphology with many verbs (see also "Deponency" in the Series Introduction).

ὅτι. Introduces the clausal complement of γνωσόμεθα (see also 2:3 on ὅτι).

ἐκ τῆς ἀληθείας ἐσμέν. The use of a prepositional phrase, headed by ἐκ, once again highlights identity. Although this is then another way of saying that the readers belong to God, the term ἀληθείας does not itself refer to God (contra Westcott, 116).

ἐσμέν. Pres act ind 1st pl εἰμί. On the retention of the accent, see 1:5 on ἐστιν.

καί. The conjunction could either introduce a second clause that is linked to ἐν τούτῳ ("By this we will know that we belong to the truth and (by this) we will convince our heart before him") or introduce a new sentence ("And we will convince our heart before him, [20]because . . .") that is conjoined to [Καὶ] ἐν τούτῳ γνωσόμεθα ὅτι ἐκ τῆς ἀληθείας ἐσμέν. In the latter case, the ὅτι that begins verse 20 would probably be taken as causal (see below on verse 20). The use of two future verbs, however, suggests that they should be viewed as parallel/coordinate, thus favoring the former option.

ἔμπροσθεν αὐτοῦ. If the clause is read eschatologically, then ἔμπροσθεν αὐτοῦ πείσομεν τὴν καρδίαν ἡμῶν would be roughly synonymous with σχῶμεν παρρησίαν . . . ἐν τῇ παρουσίᾳ αὐτοῦ (2:28). Although the future tense of the verb πείσομεν may suggest an eschatological sense ("at the Judgment"), the use of a future verb (γνωσόμεθα) apparently to point to a (potentially) present reality in the previous clause (056 and 0142 read γινώσκομεν), and the similar expression apparently referring to prayer in 3:21 (see πρὸς τὸν θεόν), both suggest that a strictly eschatological sense should not be pressed in the present context.

πείσομεν τὴν καρδίαν ἡμῶν. Louw and Nida (25.166) argue that πείθω τὴν καρδίαν is an idiom meaning, "to exhibit confidence and assurance in a situation which might otherwise cause dismay or fear." Smalley (201) renders the verb "reassure" and points to 2 Maccabees 4:45 and Matthew 28:14 in support of this rendering (cf. BDAG, 791: "conciliate, pacify, set at ease/rest"). The verb, however, seems always to carry the sense "to convince someone to believe something and to act on the basis of what is recommended" (LN 33.301). Since this makes good sense of 2 Maccabees 4:45 and Matthew 28:14, we should not posit a new meaning for the verb, though the whole expression may in fact be an idiom.

πείσομεν. Fut act ind 1st pl πείθω. On the meaning, see above.

τὴν καρδίαν. Accusative direct object of πείσομεν.

ἡμῶν. Possessive genitive.

3:20 ὅτι ἐὰν καταγινώσκῃ ἡμῶν ἡ καρδία, ὅτι μείζων ἐστὶν ὁ θεὸς τῆς καρδίας ἡμῶν καὶ γινώσκει πάντα.

The contiguous ὅτι clauses in this verse make the syntax difficult to sort out. To begin, it is important to recognize that neither of the ὅτι clauses can introduce a clausal complement (object clause) of πείσομεν, since that verb already has a direct object (τὴν καρδίαν). (1) Some take the first ὅτι as causal and the second as introducing a clausal complement of an implicit verb (e.g., γινώσκομεν): "*because* if our heart condemns (us), (we know) *that* God is greater than our heart" (cf. Burdick 274–75, Bultmann, 57). (2) A second reading maintains that ὅτι should actually be read as ὅ τι, with ὅ τι ἐὰν being a rather emphatic way of stating that "*whatever/whenever* our heart condemns us," we continue to have confidence in God (Smalley, 200, 202; Westcott, 117; cf. the syntax in Mark 6:23; 1 Cor 16:2; Col 3:17). In this reading, the second ὅτι could be either causal ("we convince our heart before him, [20]whenever our heart condemns (us), because God is greater than our heart") or epexegetical ("we convince our heart before him, [20]whenever our heart condemns (us), that God is greater than our heart"). If this is the appropriate way to understand the first ὅτι/ὅ τι, it may be appropriate to render the first clause in verse 20, "regardless of how our heart condemns us." (3) A third reading takes both ὅτι clauses as epexegetical to the final clause of verse 19: "we convince our heart before him ²⁰that if our heart condemns (us), that God is greater than our heart." In this reading, the second ὅτι is used resumptively following the protasis (the second ὅτι is, in fact, omitted by A 33 *pc* it vg cop^(bo, sa^(mss))). Unfortunately, none of these analyses can be ruled out and certainty regarding the syntax of the passage remains elusive.

ὅτι. See above.

ἐὰν. Introduces the protasis of a third class condition (see 1:6 on Ἐὰν).

καταγινώσκῃ. Pres act subj 3rd sg καταγινώσκω. Subjunctive with ἐὰν.

ἡμῶν. Possessive genitive.

ἡ καρδία. Nominative subject of καταγινώσκῃ. Although the force of the protasis may best be captured by translating ἡ καρδία, "conscience," it may be appropriate either to take ἡμῶν ἡ καρδία as an example of synecdoche (see 1:1 on αἱ χεῖρες ἡμῶν), meaning "we," or to take the whole expression καταγινώσκῃ ἡμῶν ἡ καρδία as an idiomatic way of referring to "condemning oneself."

ὅτι. See above.

μείζων. Predicate adjective.

ἐστὶν. Pres act ind 3rd sg εἰμί. On the retention of the accent, see 1:5 on ἐστιν.

ὁ θεὸς. Nominative subject of ἐστὶν.

τῆς καρδίας. Genitive of comparison (with μείζων).

ἡμῶν. Possessive genitive.

καὶ. Epexegetical.

γινώσκει. Pres act ind 3rd sg γινώσκω.

πάντα. Neuter accusative direct object of γινώσκει.

3:21 Ἀγαπητοί, ἐὰν ἡ καρδία [ἡμῶν] μὴ καταγινώσκῃ, παρρησίαν ἔχομεν πρὸς τὸν θεόν,

Ἀγαπητοί. Vocative (see 2:7).

ἐὰν. Introduces the protasis of a third class condition (see 1:6 on Ἐὰν). Smalley (204) argues that the negative conditional statement, ἐάν . . . μὴ καταγινώσκῃ points to "a resolution of the tensions outlined in vv 19-20" and should thus be rendered "if our heart *no longer* condemns us." It is not clear from the syntax, however, that the semantics of the conditional clause should be so closely linked to verses 19-20.

ἡ καρδία [ἡμῶν] μὴ καταγινώσκῃ. It is unclear (1) whether or not the original text included the bracketed pronoun, and (2) whether or not the verb was followed by the pronoun ἡμῶν (genitive object of καταγινώσκῃ). Some manuscripts have a single pronoun following καρδία (e.g., codex C), others have a single pronoun following καταγινώσκῃ (e.g., codex A), others have pronouns in both positions (e.g., *Byz*), and still others have no pronouns at all (e.g., codex B). Ultimately, each variant only raises the question of whether the information conveyed by the pronouns is implicit or explicit.

ἡ καρδία. Nominative subject of καταγινώσκῃ.

[ἡμῶν]. Possessive genitive. On the textual issue, see above.

καταγινώσκῃ. Pres act subj 3rd sg καταγινώσκω. Subjunctive with ἐάν.

παρρησίαν. Accusative direct object of ἔχομεν. On the meaning, see 2:28.

ἔχομεν. Pres act ind 1st pl ἔχω.

πρὸς τὸν θεόν. Locative, in a metaphorical sense. The use of this expression with παρρησίαν may suggest an eschatological context (cf. 2:28), rather than a present confidence in prayer. The reference to prayer in the following verse (cf. also 5:14), however, suggests that present confidence is primarily in view, particularly if the analysis of the conjunction καί (v. 22) is correct.

3:22 καὶ ὃ ἐὰν αἰτῶμεν λαμβάνομεν ἀπ' αὐτοῦ, ὅτι τὰς ἐντολὰς αὐτοῦ τηροῦμεν καὶ τὰ ἀρεστὰ ἐνώπιον αὐτοῦ ποιοῦμεν.

καὶ. The conjunction should probably be taken as epexegetical (so Strecker, 124, n. 29).

ὃ ἐὰν αἰτῶμεν λαμβάνομεν. The language here is similar to language found at a number of points in the Fourth Gospel (see, e.g., 14:13-14; 15:7; 16:23-24). It is also worth noting that both

this language and the notion of παρρησία (3:21) are indicative of
the language of ideal friendship (see Culy 2010, 51–56, 152–55).
ὃ ἐὰν αἰτῶμεν. The relative clause functions as the direct object
of λαμβάνομεν.
ὃ ἐὰν. The indefinite relative pronoun (see 2:5 on ὅς . . . ἄν)
serves as the accusative direct object of αἰτῶμεν.
αἰτῶμεν. Pres act subj 1st pl αἰτέω. Subjunctive with ἐάν.
λαμβάνομεν. Pres act ind 1st pl λαμβάνω.
ἀπ' αὐτοῦ. Source.
ὅτι. Causal.
τὰς ἐντολὰς. Accusative direct object of τηροῦμεν.
αὐτοῦ. Subjective genitive (see 1:1 on τῆς ζωῆς).
τηροῦμεν. Pres act ind 1st pl τηρέω.
τὰ ἀρεστὰ. Accusative direct object of ποιοῦμεν.
ἐνώπιον αὐτοῦ. Locative, in a metaphorical sense. Smalley (206; following Westcott, 119) suggests that ἐνώπιον αὐτοῦ
points to God's "sight" or "regard," while ἔμπροσθεν αὐτοῦ (v.
19) focuses on God's "presence." Such a fine difference in meaning should probably be rejected (see, e.g., Harris 2003, 163; LN
83.33).
ποιοῦμεν. Pres act ind 1st pl ποιέω.

**3:23 καὶ αὕτη ἐστὶν ἡ ἐντολὴ αὐτοῦ, ἵνα πιστεύσωμεν τῷ
ὀνόματι τοῦ υἱοῦ αὐτοῦ Ἰησοῦ Χριστοῦ καὶ ἀγαπῶμεν
ἀλλήλους, καθὼς ἔδωκεν ἐντολὴν ἡμῖν.**

καὶ αὕτη ἐστὶν. See 1:5 on Καὶ ἔστιν αὕτη.
καὶ. The sentence-initial καὶ marks thematic continuity (see 1:2
on καὶ) and introduces a further comment on τὰς ἐντολὰς αὐτοῦ
(3:22).
αὕτη. Predicate nominative (see 1:5 on αὕτη). The demonstrative pronoun is cataphoric (see 1:5 on αὕτη), pointing forward to
the ἵνα clause.
ἐστὶν. Pres act ind 3rd sg εἰμί. On the retention of the accent,
see 1:5 on ἐστιν.
ἡ ἐντολὴ. Nominative subject (see 1:5 on αὕτη) of ἐστὶν.
αὐτοῦ. Subjective genitive (see 1:1 on τῆς ζωῆς). Given the content of the command, the referent must be God.

ἵνα. Introduces a clause that is epexegetical to αὕτη (see 1:5 on ὅτι). Any imperatival sense comes from the semantics of ἐντολὴ, rather than from the ἵνα (contra Strecker, 126).

πιστεύσωμεν. Aor act subj 1st pl πιστεύω. Subjunctive with ἵνα. The aorist tense, which may or may not be original (it appears in B 𝔐), portrays the act of belief as an event (completive aspect) and may downgrade the prominence of this proposition, presenting it as something that is an assumed foundation (or "background") for the hortatory discourse (see "Verbal Aspect and Prominence" in the Introduction). If this analysis of the tense is correct, then the variant present tense reading πιστεύωμεν (found in ℵ A C Ψ 33 et al.) would make believing in Jesus Christ part of the exhortation, rather than information that is already assumed to be true. Strecker (127) argues that the verb πιστεύσωμεν here "is not used in the intellectual sense of merely 'holding something to be true,' but has the meaning of 'acknowledging.'"

τῷ ὀνόματι. The dative complement is used with πιστεύω to introduce the object of belief. Commenting on 1 John 2:12, Brown (302) suggests that "We are dealing here with a Semitic outlook where 'name' stands for the very identity of the person . . ." Similarly, Brooke (104) maintains that the whole expression here "denotes the conviction that Christ really is that which His name implies Him to be."

τοῦ υἱοῦ. Probably possessive genitive (but see 2:5 on αὐτοῦ).

αὐτοῦ. Genitive of relationship.

Ἰησοῦ Χριστοῦ. Genitive in apposition to τοῦ υἱοῦ.

ἀγαπῶμεν. Pres act subj 1st pl ἀγαπάω. Subjunctive with ἵνα. The present tense both portrays the love directed at fellow believers as a process and may help mark this proposition as part of the main hortatory line of the discourse.

ἀλλήλους. Accusative direct object of ἀγαπῶμεν.

καθώς. Introduces a comparative clause that probably further explains ἀγαπῶμεν ἀλλήλους alone, rather than πιστεύσωμεν τῷ ὀνόματι τοῦ υἱοῦ αὐτοῦ Ἰησοῦ Χριστοῦ καὶ ἀγαπῶμεν ἀλλήλους.

ἔδωκεν. Aor act ind 3rd sg δίδωμι. The most natural syntactic subject would be God (see above on αὐτοῦ), but the readers would have remembered Jesus as the one who had given the love command (on the blurring of reference between the Father and the Son, see "Trinitarian Ambiguity" in the Introduction).

ἐντολὴν. Accusative direct object of ἔδωκεν.

ἡμῖν. Dative indirect object of ἔδωκεν.

3:24 καὶ ὁ τηρῶν τὰς ἐντολὰς αὐτοῦ ἐν αὐτῷ μένει καὶ αὐτὸς ἐν αὐτῷ· καὶ ἐν τούτῳ γινώσκομεν ὅτι μένει ἐν ἡμῖν, ἐκ τοῦ πνεύματος οὗ ἡμῖν ἔδωκεν.

καὶ. The sentence-initial καὶ marks thematic continuity (see 1:2 on καὶ) and introduces a further comment on ἐντολὴν (v. 23). As a whole, this verse provides a summary of this section and anticipates the next one (Larsen 1991b, 53; so also Titrud, 247).

ὁ τηρῶν τὰς ἐντολὰς αὐτοῦ. The whole participial construction, headed by the nominative ὁ τηρῶν, serves as the subject of μένει. On the rhetorical force of the construction, see 2:4 on ὁ λέγων.

ὁ τηρῶν. Pres act ptc masc nom sg τηρέω (substantival).

τὰς ἐντολὰς. Accusative direct object of τηρῶν.

αὐτοῦ. Subjective genitive (see 1:1 on τῆς ζωῆς). In terms of syntax, the most likely referent continues to be God the Father (but see 3:23 on ἔδωκεν).

ἐν αὐτῷ μένει. See 2:6. It is impossible to determine whether the referent of αὐτῷ is God or Jesus Christ (see "Trinitarian Ambiguity" in the Introduction).

μένει. Pres act ind 3rd sg μένω.

καὶ. Introduces a clause that is coordinate with the previous clause and in which the verb of the previous clause is implied.

αὐτὸς. Nominative subject of an implicit μένει. On the antecedent, see above on ἐν αὐτῷ μένει.

αὐτῷ. The antecedent of the second αὐτῷ is ὁ τηρῶν τὰς ἐντολὰς αὐτοῦ.

καὶ. The clause-initial καὶ marks thematic continuity (see 1:2 on καὶ) and introduces a further comment on "remaining."

ἐν τούτῳ. Instrumental. The demonstrative pronoun is cataphoric (see 1:5 on αὕτη), pointing forward to ἐκ τοῦ πνεύματος οὗ ἡμῖν ἔδωκεν. On the rhetorical function of this expression, see 2:3.

γινώσκομεν. Pres act ind 1st pl γινώσκω.

ὅτι. Introduces the clausal complement of γινώσκομεν (see also 2:3 on ὅτι).

μένει ἐν ἡμῖν. This idiom, built on the verb μένω, once again

points to continuity of relationship (see 2:6 on ἐν αὐτῷ μένειν).
In this case, however, the subject of μένω is Jesus Christ or God,
rather than the believer.

μένει. Pres act ind 3rd sg μένω. On the unexpressed subject, see
above on ἐν αὐτῷ μένει.

ἐκ τοῦ πνεύματος. Cataphoric pronouns in 1 John are typically
followed by an epexegetical clause introduced by ὅτι (see 1:5;
3:16) or ἵνα (3:8). Here, the instrumental ἐν τούτῳ is picked up
by the preposition ἐκ, probably serving as "a marker of means as
constituting a source" (LN 89.77; contra Brown, 466, who takes
it as partitive). The idea may, however, be that possession of the
Spirit is the grounds (cause; so Strecker, 129) for the conclusion
(γινώσκομεν ὅτι μένει ἐν ἡμῖν) or that the readers' knowledge of
God's continuing relationship with them flows out of (source) the
fact that he has given them the Spirit.

οὗ. Genitive by attraction to τοῦ πνεύματος (see 2:25 on τὴν
ζωὴν τὴν αἰώνιον). Sometimes a relative pronoun takes the case
of its antecedent rather than the case it would bear as a constituent
of the relative clause (in the present instance we would expect the
relative pronoun to be accusative as the direct object of ἔδωκεν).
This phenomenon, known as attraction, occurs a total of more than
50 times throughout the NT. It appears to be a stylistic device or
simply an idiomatic usage with no pragmatic function.

ἡμῖν. Dative indirect object of ἔδωκεν.

ἔδωκεν. Aor act ind 3rd sg δίδωμι. On the unexpressed subject,
see above on ἐν αὐτῷ μένει. In the Fourth Gospel, both the Father
(14:26) and the Son (15:26) are the sender of the Spirit, effectively
highlighting their absolute unity of purpose (see Culy 2010, 119).

1 John 4:1-6

[1]Dear friends, do not trust every spirit, but test the spirits (to determine) whether or not they are from God, since many false prophets
have gone out into the world. [2]This is how you know the Spirit that
comes from God: every spirit that confesses that Jesus Christ has come
as a human being is from God, [3]and every spirit that does not confess
Jesus is not from God. Indeed, this is (a spirit) from the antichrist,
which you have heard is coming and now is already in the world.

⁴You belong to God, dear children, and you have conquered them; for the one who is in you is greater than the one who is in the world. ⁵They belong to the world. This is why they speak from the world's perspective and the world listens to them. ⁶We belong to God. The one who knows God pays attention to us, the one who does not belong to God does not pay attention to us. By this we know the True Spirit and the deceptive spirit.

4:1 Ἀγαπητοί, μὴ παντὶ πνεύματι πιστεύετε, ἀλλὰ δοκιμάζετε τὰ πνεύματα εἰ ἐκ τοῦ θεοῦ ἐστιν, ὅτι πολλοὶ ψευδοπροφῆται ἐξεληλύθασιν εἰς τὸν κόσμον.

Ἀγαπητοί. Vocative (see 2:7). The use of the vocative with an imperative verb following the summary statement that concludes 3:24 provides strong evidence for a paragraph break (so Larsen 1991b, 54; cf. 2:1 on Τεκνία). Longacre (1992, 275) argues that this paragraph (4:1-6) constitutes the doctrinal peak of the main body of the letter (see also "Genre and Structure" in the Introduction).

πνεύματι. Dative complement of πιστεύω.

πιστεύετε. Pres act impv 2nd pl πιστεύω (prohibition). On the significance of the tense and mood, see 2:15 on ἀγαπάτε and "Verbal Aspect and Prominence" in the Introduction.

ἀλλὰ. Introduces a strong contrast to the preceding proposition (see also 2:2).

δοκιμάζετε. Pres act impv 2nd pl δοκιμάζω. On the significance of the tense and mood, see 2:15 on ἀγαπάτε and "Verbal Aspect and Prominence" in the Introduction.

τὰ πνεύματα. Accusative direct object of δοκιμάζετε.

εἰ. Introduces an indirect question.

ἐκ τοῦ θεοῦ. Source.

ἐστιν. Pres act ind 3rd sg εἰμί. Neuter plural subjects characteristically take singular verbs (see Wallace, 399–400). On the loss of accent, see 1:5 on ἐστιν.

ὅτι. Causal.

ψευδοπροφῆται. Nominative (masculine) subject of ἐξεληλύθασιν.

ἐξεληλύθασιν. Prf act ind 3rd pl ἐξέρχομαι.

εἰς τὸν κόσμον. Locative.

4:2 ἐν τούτῳ γινώσκετε τὸ πνεῦμα τοῦ θεοῦ· πᾶν πνεῦμα ὃ ὁμολογεῖ Ἰησοῦν Χριστὸν ἐν σαρκὶ ἐληλυθότα ἐκ τοῦ θεοῦ ἐστιν,

ἐν τούτῳ. Instrumental. The demonstrative pronoun is cataphoric (see 1:5 on αὕτη), pointing forward to the second clause. On the rhetorical function of this expression, see 2:3.
γινώσκετε. Pres act ind 2nd pl γινώσκω.
τὸ πνεῦμα. Accusative direct object of γινώσκετε.
τοῦ θεοῦ. Genitive of source (cf. Smalley, 221). The expression τὸ πνεῦμα τοῦ θεοῦ could also be rendered God's Spirit (possessive genitive). Either way the referent is almost certainly the Holy Spirit, with the context focusing on a contrast between the Spirit that comes from God (ἐκ τοῦ θεοῦ, 4:1) and those that do not. Although the expression, πᾶν πνεῦμα, may imply that there are many spirits that come from God, the use of πᾶν is conditioned by the focus on πολλοὶ ψευδοπροφῆται (4:1), each of whom produce spirit inspired utterances.
πᾶν πνεῦμα. Neuter nominative subject of ἐστιν.
ὃ. Neuter nominative subject of ὁμολογεῖ.
ὁμολογεῖ Ἰησοῦν Χριστὸν ἐν σαρκὶ ἐληλυθότα. The language is very similar to 2 John 7.
ὁμολογεῖ. Pres act ind 3rd sg ὁμολογέω. On the meaning, see 2:23 on ὁ ὁμολογῶν.
Ἰησοῦν Χριστὸν. Accusative direct object of ὁμολογεῖ.
ἐν σαρκὶ. Manner. The term σαρκὶ is an example of synecdoche (see 1:1 on αἱ χεῖρες ἡμῶν), meaning "human body."
ἐληλυθότα. Prf act ptc masc acc sg ἔρχομαι. Accusative complement in an object-complement double accusative construction (see 1:10 on ψεύστην; contra Young, 149; see also 2 John 7 on Ἰησοῦν Χριστὸν). On the distinction between the perfect participle here and the present participle in 2 John, see 2 John 7 on ἐρχόμενον.
ἐκ τοῦ θεοῦ. Source.
ἐστιν. Pres act ind 3rd sg εἰμί. On the loss of accent, see 1:5 on ἐστιν.

4:3 καὶ πᾶν πνεῦμα ὃ μὴ ὁμολογεῖ τὸν Ἰησοῦν ἐκ τοῦ θεοῦ οὐκ ἔστιν· καὶ τοῦτό ἐστιν τὸ τοῦ ἀντιχρίστου, ὃ ἀκηκόατε ὅτι ἔρχεται, καὶ νῦν ἐν τῷ κόσμῳ ἐστὶν ἤδη.

καὶ. The clause-initial καὶ marks thematic continuity (see 1:2 on καὶ).

πᾶν πνεῦμα. Nominative subject of ἔστιν.

ὃ. Neuter nominative subject of ὁμολογεῖ.

μὴ. Although it may simply be a solecism (cf. Porter 1994, 284), according to Law (396) the rare use of μή with the indicative is consistent with "classical correctness, as expressing the subjective conviction of the writer that there are no exceptions to the statement he is making." He goes on, following Westcott (142), to suggest that Polycarp's quotation of this text in *Phil* 7.1 illustrates that this is how he understood the construction: Πᾶς γὰρ ὃς ἂν μὴ ὁμολογῇ Ἰησοῦν Χριστὸν ἐν σαρκὶ ἐληλυθέναι, ἀντιχριστός ἐστιν. While it is questionable whether Polycarp was quoting or even alluding to this particular text, it is not unlikely that he used Πᾶς ὃς ἂν μὴ ὁμολογῇ as an equivalent of ὃ μὴ ὁμολογεῖ.

ὁμολογεῖ. Pres act ind 3rd sg ὁμολογέω. On the meaning, see 2:23 on ὁ ὁμολογῶν.

τὸν Ἰησοῦν. Accusative direct object of ὁμολογεῖ. Although the verb can focus on expressing one's allegiance to either a person or a proposition (LN 33.274), and the use of the direct object without a complement (cf. 4:2) points to confessing allegiance to Jesus as a person, given the context, τὸν Ἰησοῦν may well be an elliptical reference to the participial content of the confession: Ἰησοῦν Χριστὸν ἐν σαρκὶ ἐληλυθότα. This is the way that many scribes appear to have understood the text. The range of textual variants at this point in the text simply reflects a question of whether information is explicit or implicit, with no change in meaning.

ἐκ τοῦ θεοῦ. Source.

ἔστιν. Pres act ind 3rd sg εἰμί. On the movement of the accent, see 1:5 on ἐστιν.

καὶ τοῦτό. The use of καὶ here to mark thematic continuity (see 1:2 on καὶ) suggests that τὸ τοῦ ἀντιχρίστου and πᾶν πνεῦμα ὃ μὴ ὁμολογεῖ τὸν Ἰησοῦν are coreferential.

τοῦτό. Nominative subject (see 1:5 on αὕτη) of ἐστιν. The second accent comes from the enclitic αὕτη (see 1:5 on αὕτη). The antecedent is πᾶν πνεῦμα.

τὸ. The neuter nominative singular article functions as a nominalizer (see 2:13 on τὸν ἀπ᾽ ἀρχῆς), in this case changing the genitive substantive τοῦ ἀντιχρίστου into a predicate nominative substantive.

τοῦ ἀντιχρίστου. Genitive of source. The use of the nominalized expression makes it clear that the writer is not saying that the spirit *is* the antichrist (cf. οὗτός ἐστιν ὁ ἀντίχριστος, 2:22), but rather that such spirits come *from* the antichrist. The construction is probably intended to highlight the contrast between τὸ (πνεῦμα) τοῦ ἀντιχρίστου and τὸ πνεῦμα τοῦ θεοῦ (4:2).

ὅ. If the ὅτι clause serves as a clausal complement of ἀκηκόατε, then the relative pronoun would have to be taken as an accusative of reference. The weaker alternative is to take the relative pronoun as the accusative direct object of ἀκηκόατε and the ὅτι clause as epexegetical.

ἀκηκόατε. Prf act ind 2nd pl ἀκούω.

ὅτι. Introduces the clausal complement (indirect discourse) of ἀκηκόατε (but see above on ὅ).

ἔρχεται. Pres mid ind 3rd sg ἔρχομαι. On the voice, see 2:18 and "Deponency" in the Series Introduction.

ἐν τῷ κόσμῳ. Locative.

ἐστὶν. Pres act ind 3rd sg εἰμί. On the retention of the accent, see 1:5 on ἐστιν.

4:4 ὑμεῖς ἐκ τοῦ θεοῦ ἐστε, τεκνία, καὶ νενικήκατε αὐτούς, ὅτι μείζων ἐστὶν ὁ ἐν ὑμῖν ἢ ὁ ἐν τῷ κόσμῳ.

ὑμεῖς. The explicit nominative subject pronoun sharpens the contrast between the readers and τὸ τοῦ ἀντιχρίστου (4:3).

ἐκ τοῦ θεοῦ ἐστε. On the meaning of this expression, see 3:10 on ἔστιν ἐκ τοῦ θεοῦ.

ἐστε. Pres act ind 2nd pl εἰμί. On the loss of accent, see 1:5 on ἐστιν.

τεκνία. Vocative (cf. 2:1). The use of the vocative here, along with the shift in subject, marks the beginning of a new paragraph.

νενικήκατε. Prf act ind 2nd pl νικάω. As elsewhere in Johannine literature, the reader is left to determine the precise nature of the action associated with νικάω ("to win a victory over"; LN 39.57) through reference to the context of the statement and/or the readers' circumstances. "Conquering" the false prophets (ψευδοπροφῆται, 4:1) and the spirits who inspire them (τὰ πνεύματα, 4:1-3) would apparently involve recognizing their origin and choosing to reject them if they do not "confess (that) Jesus (Christ has come in human form)" (4:2, 3) and are thus not "from God" (ἐκ τοῦ θεοῦ, 4:1, 3).

αὐτούς. Accusative direct object of νενικήκατε. The antecedent is ψευδοπροφῆται, who have been the focus of attention in 4:1-3.

ὅτι. Causal.

μείζων. Predicate adjective.

ἐστὶν. Pres act ind 3rd sg εἰμί. On the retention of the accent, see 1:5 on ἐστιν.

ὁ ἐν ὑμῖν. The article functions as a nominalizer (see 2:13 on τὸν), changing the locative prepositional phrase into the nominative subject of ἐστὶν. It may be possible to read this expression and the one below as relational idioms (see 2:5 on ἐν αὐτῷ).

ὁ ἐν τῷ κόσμῳ. The article functions as a nominalizer (see 2:13 on τὸν), changing the locative prepositional phrase (but see above on ὁ ἐν ὑμῖν) into the nominative subject of an implicit ἐστὶν.

4:5 αὐτοὶ ἐκ τοῦ κόσμου εἰσίν· διὰ τοῦτο ἐκ τοῦ κόσμου λαλοῦσιν καὶ ὁ κόσμος αὐτῶν ἀκούει.

αὐτοὶ. The explicit nominative subject pronoun highlights the contrast between the readers who are ἐκ τοῦ θεοῦ (4:4) and those who are ἐκ τοῦ κόσμου.

ἐκ τοῦ κόσμου. Source/Origin (but see 2:19 on ἦσαν ἐξ; cf. 2:16). Here, the expression strongly associates the referents with the enemy of God (ὁ ἐν τῷ κόσμῳ; 4:4).

εἰσίν. Pres act ind 3rd pl εἰμί. On the retention of the accent, see 1:5 on ἐστιν.

διὰ τοῦτο. Causal. The demonstrative pronoun is anaphoric (contrast 3:1), pointing back to the proposition αὐτοὶ ἐκ τοῦ κόσμου εἰσίν. Their status as those who are of the world has two results, which are introduced by διὰ τοῦτο.

ἐκ τοῦ κόσμου. Lit. "from the world."

λαλοῦσιν. Pres act ind 3rd sg λαλέω.

καὶ. The conjunction is coordinate, introducing a second result of the proposition αὐτοὶ ἐκ τοῦ κόσμου εἰσίν.

ὁ κόσμος. Nominative subject of ἀκούει.

αὐτῶν. Genitive object of ἀκούει.

ἀκούει. Pres act ind 3rd sg ἀκούω. Here, "to believe something and to respond to it on the basis of having heard" (LN 31.56) or "to listen or pay attention to a person, with resulting conformity to what is advised or commanded" (LN 36.14).

4:6 ἡμεῖς ἐκ τοῦ θεοῦ ἐσμεν· ὁ γινώσκων τὸν θεὸν ἀκούει ἡμῶν, ὃς οὐκ ἔστιν ἐκ τοῦ θεοῦ οὐκ ἀκούει ἡμῶν. ἐκ τούτου γινώσκομεν τὸ πνεῦμα τῆς ἀληθείας καὶ τὸ πνεῦμα τῆς πλάνης.

ἡμεῖς. The explicit nominative subject pronoun highlights the contrast between those who are ἐκ τοῦ κόσμου (4:5) and those who are ἐκ τοῦ θεοῦ (perhaps simply the writer in this case; see also 4:4).

ἐκ τοῦ θεοῦ ἐσμεν. On the meaning of this expression, see 3:10 on ἔστιν ἐκ τοῦ θεοῦ. The relational language in this case serves to bolster the authority of the writer by implying that some others are not "of God."

ἐσμεν. Pres act ind 1st pl εἰμί. On the loss of accent, see 1:5 on ἐστιν.

ὁ γινώσκων. Pres act ptc masc nom sg γινώσκω (substantival). The participial construction, ὁ γινώσκων τὸν θεὸν, serves as the nominative subject of ἀκούει.

τὸν θεὸν. Accusative direct object of γινώσκων.

ἀκούει. Pres act ind 3rd sg ἀκούω. On the meaning, see 4:5.

ἡμῶν. Genitive object of ἀκούει.

ὃς οὐκ ἔστιν ἐκ τοῦ θεοῦ. The "headless" relative clause clause (see 1:1 on Ὃ . . . ὃ) functions as the subject of ἀκούει.

ὅς. Nominative subject of ἔστιν.

ἔστιν ἐκ τοῦ θεοῦ. On the meaning of this expression, see 3:10 on ἔστιν ἐκ τοῦ θεοῦ.

ἔστιν. Pres act ind 3rd sg εἰμί. On the movement of the accent, see 1:5 on ἐστιν.

ἀκούει. Pres act ind 3rd sg ἀκούω. On the meaning, see 4:5.

ἡμῶν. Genitive object of ἀκούει.

ἐκ τούτου. The demonstrative pronoun is anaphoric. Here, the preposition is "a marker of means as constituting a source" (LN 89.77).

γινώσκομεν. Pres act ind 1st pl γινώσκω. There is probably a shift from an exclusive "we" in the first part of this verse (ἡμεῖς . . . ἐσμεν) to an inclusive first plural referent here.

τὸ πνεῦμα. Accusative direct object of γινώσκομεν.

τῆς ἀληθείας. Attributive genitive.

τῆς πλάνης. Attributive genitive.

1 John 4:7-10

[7]Dear friends, let us love one another, because love comes from God and everyone who loves has been born of God and knows God. [8]The one who does not love does not know God; for God is love. [9]This is how the love of God was revealed among us: God sent his one and only Son into the world so that we might live through him. [10]This is love: not that we have loved God but that he loved us and sent his Son as the means by which our sins are dealt with.

4:7 Ἀγαπητοί, ἀγαπῶμεν ἀλλήλους, ὅτι ἡ ἀγάπη ἐκ τοῦ θεοῦ ἐστιν, καὶ πᾶς ὁ ἀγαπῶν ἐκ τοῦ θεοῦ γεγέννηται καὶ γινώσκει τὸν θεόν.

Longacre maintains that the second ethical peak of the letter begins here and continues through 4:21. He argues that the second paragraph (4:11-21) is a paraphrase of the first, a phenomenon that is a common feature of peaks (Longacre 1992, 279–80; see also "Genre and Structure" in the Introduction).

Ἀγαπητοί. Vocative (see 2:7).

ἀγαπῶμεν. Pres act subj 1st pl ἀγαπάω. Hortatory subjunctive.

ἀλλήλους. Accusative direct object of ἀγαπῶμεν.

ὅτι. Causal.

ἡ ἀγάπη. Nominative subject of ἐστιν.

ἐκ τοῦ θεοῦ. Source.

ἐστιν. Pres act ind 3rd sg εἰμί. On the loss of accent, see 1:5 on ἐστιν.

πᾶς ὁ ἀγαπῶν. Nominative subject of γεγέννηται. On the rhetorical force of πᾶς with an articular participle, see 2:23 on πᾶς ὁ ἀρνούμενος.

ὁ ἀγαπῶν. Pres act ptc masc nom sg ἀγαπάω (substantival or attributive; see 2:23 on πᾶς ὁ ἀρνούμενος).
ἐκ τοῦ θεοῦ γεγέννηται. See 3:9 on ἐκ τοῦ θεοῦ.
γεγέννηται. Prf pass ind 3rd sg γεννάω.
γινώσκει. Pres act ind 3rd sg γινώσκω.
τὸν θεόν. Accusative direct object of γινώσκει.

4:8 ὁ μὴ ἀγαπῶν οὐκ ἔγνω τὸν θεόν, ὅτι ὁ θεὸς ἀγάπη ἐστίν.

ὁ μὴ ἀγαπῶν. Pres act ptc masc nom sg ἀγαπάω (substantival). Nominative subject of ἔγνω.
ἔγνω. Aor act ind 3rd sg γινώσκω.
τὸν θεόν. Accusative direct object of ἔγνω.
ὅτι. Causal.
ὁ θεὸς. Nominative subject (see 1:5 on ὁ θεὸς) of ἐστίν.
ἀγάπη. Predicate nominative (see 1:5 on ὁ θεὸς).
ἐστίν. Pres act ind 3rd sg εἰμί. On the retention of the accent, see 1:5 on ἐστιν.

4:9 ἐν τούτῳ ἐφανερώθη ἡ ἀγάπη τοῦ θεοῦ ἐν ἡμῖν, ὅτι τὸν υἱὸν αὐτοῦ τὸν μονογενῆ ἀπέσταλκεν ὁ θεὸς εἰς τὸν κόσμον ἵνα ζήσωμεν δι' αὐτοῦ.

ἐν τούτῳ. Instrumental. The demonstrative pronoun is cataphoric (see 1:5 on αὕτη), pointing forward to the ὅτι clause. On the rhetorical function of this expression, see 2:3.
ἐφανερώθη. Aor pass ind 3rd sg φανερόω. The verb could conceivably be viewed as middle here (see "Deponency" in the Series Introduction; cf. BDAG, 1048).
ἡ ἀγάπη. Nominative subject of ἐφανερώθη.
τοῦ θεοῦ. Subjective genitive (see 1:1 on τῆς ζωῆς).
ἐν ἡμῖν. Locative (probably "among us" rather than "within us"; so Burdick, 320; Smalley, 240; contra Brooke, 119; Brown, 516).
ὅτι τὸν υἱὸν αὐτοῦ τὸν μονογενῆ ἀπέσταλκεν ὁ θεὸς εἰς τὸν κόσμον. Several features of the ὅτι clause lend it special prominence: (1) the cataphoric demonstrative pronoun (τούτῳ) focuses attention on the ὅτι clause (cf. Anderson and Anderson, 43); (2) the direct object is fronted (see 1:5 on σκοτία); and (3) the perfect tense is used rather than the aorist.

ὅτι. Introduces a clause that is epexegetical to τούτῳ (see 1:5 on ὅτι).

τὸν υἱὸν . . . τὸν μονογενῆ. Accusative direct object of ἀπέσταλκεν. On its position, see above. The term μονογενής, has frequently been read as "only begotten" under the influence of the KJV, implying that the focus is on being the only son. As many have noted, however, the adjective focuses on unique status rather than unique ancestry ("pertaining to what is unique in the sense of being the only one of the same kind or class"; LN 58.52). Thus Abraham's son Isaac may be described as μονογενής (Heb 11:17), as the unique son of the promise, even though Abraham had another son (Ishmael).

αὐτοῦ. Genitive of relationship.

ἀπέσταλκεν. Prf act ind 3rd sg ἀποστέλλω. On the tense, see above on ὅτι τὸν υἱὸν . . . τὸν κόσμον.

ὁ θεὸς. Nominative subject of ἀπέσταλκεν.

εἰς τὸν κόσμον. Locative.

ἵνα. Introduces a purpose clause.

ζήσωμεν. Aor act subj 1st pl ζάω. Subjunctive with ἵνα.

δι' αὐτοῦ. Intermediate agent. The antecedent is τὸν υἱὸν.

4:10 ἐν τούτῳ ἐστὶν ἡ ἀγάπη, οὐχ ὅτι ἡμεῖς ἠγαπήκαμεν τὸν θεόν, ἀλλ' ὅτι αὐτὸς ἠγάπησεν ἡμᾶς καὶ ἀπέστειλεν τὸν υἱὸν αὐτοῦ ἱλασμὸν περὶ τῶν ἁμαρτιῶν ἡμῶν.

ἐν τούτῳ. Reference. The demonstrative pronoun is cataphoric (see 1:5 on αὕτη), pointing forward to the ὅτι clause. On the rhetorical function of this expression, see 2:3.

ἐστὶν. Pres act ind 3rd sg εἰμί. On the retention of the accent, see 1:5 on ἐστιν.

ἡ ἀγάπη. Nominative subject of ἐστὶν.

ὅτι. Introduces two conjoined clauses that are epexegetical to τούτῳ and provide both negative and positive formulations of love (see 1:5 on ὅτι).

ἡμεῖς. The explicit nominative subject pronoun marks the primary point of contrast between the two clauses (ἡμεῖς vs. αὐτὸς).

ἠγαπήκαμεν. Prf act ind 1st pl ἀγαπάω. Although the external support for the perfect (B Ψ 322 323 945 1241 1739 2298 eth) is

more limited than support for the aorist ἠγαπήκαμεν (‭א‬¹ A 048ᵛⁱᵈ
33 81ᵛⁱᵈ 436 1067 1175 1243 1292 1409 1505 1611 1735 1844
1852 1881 2138 2344 2464 *Byz* [K L] *Lect* arm geo slav Philo-
Carpsia), the aorist can perhaps be accounted for as assimilation to
the following aorist forms (Metzger, 645).

τὸν θεόν. Accusative direct object of ἠγαπήκαμεν.

ἀλλ'. Introduces a proposition that contrasts with the preceding
one (see also 2:2).

αὐτός. Nominative subject of ἠγάπησεν (see also above on
ἡμεῖς).

ἠγάπησεν. Aor act ind 3rd sg ἀγαπάω.

ἡμᾶς. Accusative direct object of ἠγάπησεν.

ἀπέστειλεν. Aor act ind 3rd sg ἀποστέλλω.

τὸν υἱόν. Accusative direct object of ἀπέστειλεν.

αὐτοῦ. Genitive of relationship.

ἱλασμὸν. Accusative complement in an object-complement
double accusative construction (see 1:10 on ψεύστην). On the
meaning, see 2:2.

περὶ τῶν ἁμαρτιῶν. Reference.

ἡμῶν. Subjective genitive (see 1:1 on τῆς ζωῆς).

1 John 4:11-21

¹¹Dear friends, if God has loved us in this way, then we in turn
ought to love one another. ¹²No one has ever seen God. If we love one
another God continues to have a relationship with us and his love has
reached its goal in us. ¹³This is how we know that we continue to have
a relationship with him and he with us: he has given us a portion of
his Spirit.

¹⁴Now, we have seen and testify that the Father sent the Son as
Savior of the world. ¹⁵Whoever confesses that Jesus is the Son of God,
God continues to have a relationship with that person, and he with
God. ¹⁶And we have come to know and to believe the love that God
has for us.

God is love, and the one who continues loving continues to have a
relationship with him, and God continues to have a relationship with
that person. ¹⁷This is how love has reached its goal among us: we will
have confidence on the day of judgment because just as he is (in this
world) so also we are in this world.

110   1 John 4:11-21

¹⁸There is no fear where there is love. On the contrary, perfect love drives out fear, because fear has (anticipated) punishment (in mind). So, the one who has fear has not reached the goal in the matter of love. ¹⁹We love because he first loved us. ²⁰If anyone says, "I love God," and (yet) hates his brother or sister, he is a liar. For the one who does not love his brother or sister, whom he has seen, is not able to love God, whom he has not seen. ²¹And we have this command from him: the one who loves God must also love his brother and sister.

4:11 Ἀγαπητοί, εἰ οὕτως ὁ θεὸς ἠγάπησεν ἡμᾶς, καὶ ἡμεῖς ὀφείλομεν ἀλλήλους ἀγαπᾶν.

Ἀγαπητοί. On the meaning, see 2:7. The use of the vocative suggests a paragraph break (cf. 2:1 on Τεκνία; so Longacre 1992, 275–76).
εἰ. Introduces a first class condition (cf. 3:13).
ὁ θεὸς. Nominative subject of ἠγάπησεν.
ἠγάπησεν. Aor act ind 3rd sg ἀγαπάω.
ἡμᾶς. Accusative direct object of ἠγάπησεν.
ἡμεῖς. The explicit nominative subject pronoun serves to help highlight the necessary connection between the actions of God and the actions of the readers.
ὀφείλομεν. Pres act ind 1st pl ὀφείλω. On the semantics and rhetorical significance of this verb, see 2:6 on ὀφείλει (cf. Longacre 1992, 276).
ἀλλήλους. Accusative direct object of ἠγάπησεν.
ἀγαπᾶν. Pres act inf ἀγαπάω (complementary).

4:12 θεὸν οὐδεὶς πώποτε τεθέαται· ἐὰν ἀγαπῶμεν ἀλλήλους, ὁ θεὸς ἐν ἡμῖν μένει καὶ ἡ ἀγάπη αὐτοῦ ἐν ἡμῖν τετελειωμένη ἐστιν.

θεὸν οὐδεὶς πώποτε τεθέαται. The author does not actually identify the significance of this statement until verse 20.
θεὸς. Accusative direct object of τεθέαται.
οὐδεὶς. Nominative subject of τεθέαται.

τεθέαται. Prf mid ind 3rd sg θεάομαι. On the voice, see 1:1 on ἐθεασάμεθα.

ἐάν. Introduces the protasis of a third class condition (see 1:6 on Ἐάν).

ἀγαπῶμεν. Pres act subj 1st pl ἀγαπάω. Subjunctive with ἐάν.

ἀλλήλους. Accusative direct object of ἀγαπῶμεν.

ὁ θεὸς. Nominative subject of μένει.

ἐν ἡμῖν μένει. See 2:6 on ἐν αὐτῷ μένειν.

μένει. Pres act ind 3rd sg μένω.

ἡ ἀγάπη. Nominative subject of ἐστιν.

αὐτοῦ. The genitive case could be taken as either subjective or objective. Given the semantics of τελειόω and the fact that God is the agent of μένει, the case should most likely be viewed as subjective (so Brooke, 120; Brown, 521; Harris 2003, 190; contra Dodd, 113). Wendland (28), however, argues that this may well be an example of intentional ambiguity, or "semantic density," on the part of the author. Such ambiguity would be a literary rather than syntactic category, and should not be confused with the questionable label "plenary genitive" (see, e.g., Wallace, 119–21).

ἐν ἡμῖν. Locative. Porter (1989, 468) notes the ambiguity in the syntax: If ἐν ἡμῖν "modifies the subject [ἡ ἀγάπη αὐτοῦ], the understanding is that God abides in us and 'his love in us' is in a state of completion. If the locative completes the Participle and the construction is periphrastic, it means that God abides in us and his love is in a state of completion in *us*" (italics mine). The latter is more likely given the parallel construction that precedes.

τετελειωμένη. Prf mid ptc fem nom sg τελειόω (perfect periphrastic; see 1:4 on πεπληρωμένη). On the voice and semantics, see 2:5 on τετελείωται.

ἐστιν. Pres act ind 3rd sg εἰμί. On the retention of the accent, see 1:5 on ἐστιν.

4:13 Ἐν τούτῳ γινώσκομεν ὅτι ἐν αὐτῷ μένομεν καὶ αὐτὸς ἐν ἡμῖν, ὅτι ἐκ τοῦ πνεύματος αὐτοῦ δέδωκεν ἡμῖν.

Ἐν τούτῳ. Instrumental. The demonstrative pronoun is cataphoric (see 1:5 on αὕτη), pointing forward to the second ὅτι clause. On the rhetorical function of this expression, see 2:3.

γινώσκομεν. Pres act ind 1st pl γινώσκω.

ὅτι. Introduces the clausal complement of γινώσκομεν (see also 2:3 on ὅτι).

ἐν αὐτῷ μένομεν. See 2:6 on ἐν αὐτῷ μένειν.

μένομεν. Pres act ind 1st pl μένω.

καὶ. Introduces a clause that is coordinate with the previous clause and in which the verb of the previous clause is implied.

αὐτὸς. Nominative subject of an implicit μένει.

ἐν ἡμῖν. The verb (μένει) is implied. On the meaning, see 2:6 on ἐν αὐτῷ μένειν.

ὅτι. Introduces a clause that is epexegetical to τούτῳ (see 1:5 on ὅτι).

ἐκ τοῦ πνεύματος. The syntax of this verse is similar to but distinct from 3:24 (καὶ ἐν τούτῳ γινώσκομεν ὅτι μένει ἐν ἡμῖν, ἐκ τοῦ πνεύματος οὗ ἡμῖν ἔδωκεν). In 3:24, we had the unusual case of a cataphoric demonstrative pronoun being picked up by the preposition ἐκ rather than the usual epexegetical ὅτι clause. Here, though the choice of words is almost identical, the syntax (and thus semantics) is not. The fact that the verb δίδωμι is not part of a relative clause in this case forces us to take the preposition ἐκ as denoting source or more likely as partitive (so Moule, 72). English readers may tend to react against the rendering "a portion of his Spirit," since our logical minds ask how the Holy Spirit can be divided (but see Num 1:17). Commenting on Pauline pneumatology, however, Fee (864) rightly points out that "Paul does not see life in the Spirit as the result of a single experience of the Spirit at conversion. The Spirit is the key to all of Christian life, and frequently Paul implies there are further, ongoing appropriations of the Spirit's empowering." Such theology probably stands behind John's use of the partitive construction here as well. His point, then, is that his readers' present experience of the Spirit, partial though it may be, provides evidence of their continuing relationship with God.

αὐτοῦ. Possessive genitive.

δέδωκεν. Prf act ind 3rd sg δίδωμι.

ἡμῖν. Dative indirect object of δέδωκεν.

4:14 καὶ ἡμεῖς τεθεάμεθα καὶ μαρτυροῦμεν ὅτι ὁ πατὴρ ἀπέσταλκεν τὸν υἱὸν σωτῆρα τοῦ κόσμου.

καί. If the use of a sentence-initial καί marks thematic continuity (see 1:2 on καί; cf. 4:16), then "remaining" in him also entails continuing to make known the Gospel message: ὁ πατὴρ ἀπέσταλκεν τὸν υἱὸν σωτῆρα τοῦ κόσμου.

ἡμεῖς. The explicit nominative subject pronoun lends further prominence to the statement that follows.

τεθεάμεθα. Prf mid ind 1st pl θεάομαι. On the voice, see 1:1 on ἐθεασάμεθα. The use of the perfect tense lends special prominence, once again, to the eyewitness experience and testimony of the writer. For more on the significance of the tense and number, see 1:1 on ἀκηκόαμεν.

μαρτυροῦμεν. Pres act ind 1st pl μαρτυρέω. For more on the significance of the tense and number, see 1:1 on ἀκηκόαμεν.

ὅτι. Introduces the clausal complement (indirect discourse) of μαρτυροῦμεν.

ὁ πατήρ. Nominative subject of ἀπέσταλκεν.

ἀπέσταλκεν. Prf act ind 3rd sg ἀποστέλλω.

τὸν υἱόν. Accusative direct object of ἀπέσταλκεν.

σωτῆρα. The noun could be viewed as accusative in apposition to τὸν υἱόν, or better as the accusative complement in an object-complement double accusative construction (see 1:10 on ψεύστην; so also Young, 17).

τοῦ κόσμου. Objective genitive (see 1:1 on τῆς ζωῆς).

4:15 ὃς ἐὰν ὁμολογήσῃ ὅτι Ἰησοῦς ἐστιν ὁ υἱὸς τοῦ θεοῦ, ὁ θεὸς ἐν αὐτῷ μένει καὶ αὐτὸς ἐν τῷ θεῷ.

ὃς ἐὰν ὁμολογήσῃ ὅτι Ἰησοῦς ἐστιν ὁ υἱὸς τοῦ θεοῦ. The relative clause functions as the topic (see 1:1) of what follows, which will be picked up with the resumptive demonstrative pronoun αὐτῷ.

ὃς ἐάν. The indefinite relative pronoun (see 2:5 on ὃς ... ἄν) serves as the nominative subject of ὁμολογήσῃ.

ὁμολογήσῃ. Aor act subj 3rd sg ὁμολογέω. On the meaning, see 2:23 on ὁ ὁμολογῶν.

ὅτι. Introduces the clausal complement (direct or indirect discourse) of ὁμολογήσῃ.

Ἰησοῦς. Nominative subject (see 2:22 on Ἰησοῦς).

ἐστιν. Pres act ind 3rd sg εἰμί. On the loss of accent, see 1:5 on ἐστιν.

ὁ υἱὸς. Predicate nominative (see 2:22 on Ἰησοῦς).
τοῦ θεοῦ. Genitive of relationship.
ὁ θεὸς. Nominative subject of μένει.
ἐν αὐτῷ μένει. See 2:6 on ἐν αὐτῷ μένειν.
μένει. Pres act ind 3rd sg μένω.
καὶ. Introduces a clause that is coordinate with the previous clause and in which the verb of the previous clause is implied.
αὐτὸς. Nominative subject of an implicit μένει.
ἐν τῷ θεῷ. The verb (μένει) is implied. On the meaning, see 2:6 on ἐν αὐτῷ μένειν.

4:16 καὶ ἡμεῖς ἐγνώκαμεν καὶ πεπιστεύκαμεν τὴν ἀγάπην ἣν ἔχει ὁ θεὸς ἐν ἡμῖν. Ὁ θεὸς ἀγάπη ἐστίν, καὶ ὁ μένων ἐν τῇ ἀγάπῃ ἐν τῷ θεῷ μένει καὶ ὁ θεὸς ἐν αὐτῷ μένει.

The syntax of the first part of this verse is closely parallel to 4:14.
καὶ. If the use of a sentence-initial καὶ marks thematic continuity (see 1:2 on καὶ; cf. 4:14), then "confessing" Jesus or "remaining" in him also entails bearing witness to and living out the love of God.
ἡμεῖς. The explicit nominative subject pronoun, along with the perfect verbs, lends prominence to this statement (see also "Verbal Aspect and Prominence" in the Introduction).
ἐγνώκαμεν. Prf act ind 1st pl γινώσκω.
πεπιστεύκαμεν. Prf act ind 1st pl πιστεύω.
τὴν ἀγάπην. Accusative direct object of the conjoined verb phrase ἐγνώκαμεν καὶ πεπιστεύκαμεν.
ἣν. Accusative direct object of ἔχει.
ἔχει. Pres act ind 3rd sg ἔχω.
ὁ θεὸς. Nominative subject of ἔχει.
ἐν ἡμῖν. The function of the prepositional phrase is difficult to determine. Most take it as referring to the object of God's love, but this does not conform to any typical use of the preposition. It is probably better to take the preposition as denoting "reference/respect" (though a smooth English translation will probably require "for"). The choice of ἐν was probably dictated by stylistic concerns, in anticipation of the threefold use of the preposition at the end of the verse.

Ὁ θεός. Nominative subject (see 1:5 on ὁ θεὸς) of ἐστίν.

ἀγάπην. Predicate nominative (see 1:5 on ὁ θεὸς).

ἐστίν. Pres act ind 3rd sg εἰμί. On the retention of the accent, see 1:5 on ἐστιν.

ὁ μένων ἐν τῇ ἀγάπῃ. The use of μένει highlights continuity of state (cf. 2:10). Here, where μένειν is used with a non-personal referent (cf. 2:6 on ἐν αὐτῷ μένειν), the sense is to "continue loving." The whole participial construction, headed by the nominative ὁ μένων, serves as the subject of μένει.

ὁ μένων. Pres act ptc masc nom sg μένω (substantival).

ἐν τῷ θεῷ μένει καὶ ὁ θεὸς ἐν αὐτῷ μένει. On the meaning of the idiom, see 2:6 on ἐν αὐτῷ μένειν.

μένει. Pres act ind 3rd sg μένω.

ὁ θεὸς. Nominative subject of μένει.

μένει. Pres act ind 3rd sg μένω.

4:17 ἐν τούτῳ τετελείωται ἡ ἀγάπη μεθ᾽ ἡμῶν, ἵνα παρρησίαν ἔχωμεν ἐν τῇ ἡμέρᾳ τῆς κρίσεως, ὅτι καθὼς ἐκεῖνός ἐστιν καὶ ἡμεῖς ἐσμεν ἐν τῷ κόσμῳ τούτῳ.

ἐν τούτῳ. Instrumental (but see below). The demonstrative pronoun could be either anaphoric or cataphoric (see 1:5 on αὕτη). If it is anaphoric (so Brown, 527; Harris 2003, 196–97; Marshall, 223, n. 17; Westcott, 157), the point would be that through God continuing in relationship with the believer (ὁ θεὸς ἐν αὐτῷ μένει; 4:16), and perhaps through the believer continuing in relationship with God (ἐν αὐτῷ μένει; 4:16) and continuing to live a life of love (ὁ μένων ἐν τῇ ἀγάπῃ; 4:16), love has been brought to maturity among the readers. In favor of this view is the fact that the logic in this reading mirrors the statement made in 4:12: ἐν ἡμῖν μένει καὶ ἡ ἀγάπη αὐτοῦ ἐν ἡμῖν τετελειωμένη ἐστιν. If, on the other hand, the demonstrative pronoun is taken as cataphoric, it could point forward to either the ἵνα clause or the ὅτι clause. The semantics of the verse, however, appear to rule out connecting ἐν τούτῳ to the ἵνα clause (contra Anderson and Anderson, 43; Brooke, 124; Bultmann, 72, n. 1). As Brown (526) notes, it is difficult to unravel the logic of love having reached perfection in something that has not yet occurred. While the logical quandary may be minimized if ἐν τούτῳ means "in this" rather than "by this" (thus, given the fact that the readers have confidence presently, love has been perfected among them), the focus on future (ἐν τῇ ἡμέρᾳ τῆς κρίσεως) rather than present confidence argues against this reading. The final option connects ἐν τούτῳ to the following ὅτι clause (so Schnackenburg, 222), a pattern that occurs frequently in 1 John (e.g., 1:5; 3:16; 4:9, 10, 13). The primary argument against this reading is that the ὅτι clause does not immediately follow the clause of which ἐν τούτῳ is a part. The intervening ἵνα clause is where it is, however, to make clear that confidence on judgment day is closely linked to the perfection in view.

τετελείωται. Prf mid ind 3rd sg τελειόω. On the voice and semantics, see 2:5.

ἡ ἀγάπη. Nominative subject of τετελείωται.

μεθ᾽ ἡμῶν. Association. Harris (2003, 197) may be correct in viewing the statement that love is perfected *with us* as a reference to "our actions in loving our fellow believers."

ἵνα. Likely introduces a result clause but could be epexegetical (see above on ἐν τούτῳ). The relationship between mature or perfect love and freedom from fear of judgment will be fleshed out in 4:18.

παρρησίαν. Accusative direct object of ἔχωμεν. On the meaning, see 2:28.

ἔχωμεν. Pres act subj 1st pl ἔχω. Subjunctive with ἵνα.

ἐν τῇ ἡμέρᾳ. Temporal.

τῆς κρίσεως. "The day *of* judgment" refers to "the day when God judges people."

ὅτι. The function of the ὅτι clause is either epexegetical (with a cataphoric ἐν τούτῳ) or causal (with an anaphoric τούτῳ; see above). The point of the clause is that love has been perfected among the readers through their continuing presence in this world, just as Jesus was present in the world as love incarnate (cf. Larsen 1990a, 4).

καθώς. Introduces a comparison.

ἐκεῖνός. Nominative subject of ἐστιν. The second accent comes from the enclitic ἐστιν (see 1:5 on ἐστιν). The referent is Jesus Christ (see also 2:6).

ἐστιν. Pres act ind 3rd sg εἰμί. On the loss of accent, see 1:5 on ἐστιν. The predicate, ἐν τῷ κόσμῳ τούτῳ, is left implicit until the second part of the comparative construction.

ἡμεῖς. Nominative subject of ἐσμεν. On the loss of accent, see 1:5 on ἐστιν. The explicit subject pronoun helps highlight the contrast that is being drawn between "him" (ἐκεῖνός) and "us."

ἐσμεν. Pres act ind 1st pl εἰμί.

ἐν τῷ κόσμῳ τούτῳ. Locative.

4:18 φόβος οὐκ ἔστιν ἐν τῇ ἀγάπῃ, ἀλλ' ἡ τελεία ἀγάπη ἔξω βάλλει τὸν φόβον, ὅτι ὁ φόβος κόλασιν ἔχει, ὁ δὲ φοβούμενος οὐ τετελείωται ἐν τῇ ἀγάπῃ.

φόβος. Nominative subject of ἔστιν.

ἔστιν. Pres act ind 3rd sg εἰμί. On the movement of the accent, see 1:5 on ἐστιν.

ἐν τῇ ἀγάπῃ. Reference/Respect.

ἀλλ'. Introduces a strong contrast (see also 2:2).

ἡ τελεία ἀγάπη. Nominative subject of βάλλει.

βάλλει. Pres act ind 3rd sg βάλλω.

τὸν φόβον. Accusative direct object of βάλλει.

ὅτι. Causal.

ὁ φόβος κόλασιν ἔχει. Lit. "fear has punishment," i.e., fear stems from an expectation of judgment.

ὁ φόβος. Nominative subject of ἔχει.

κόλασιν. Accusative direct object of ἔχει.

ἔχει. Pres act ind 3rd sg ἔχω.

ὁ . . . φοβούμενος. Pres mid ptc masc nom sg φοβέομαι (substantival). Nominative subject of τετελείωται. Though typically parsed as middle/passive deponent, the form should probably be taken as a true middle (see "Deponency" in the Series Introduction), as is common with verbs that describe an emotional state (cf. Miller, 428).

τετελείωται. Prf mid ind 3rd sg τελειόω. On the voice and semantics, see 2:5.

ἐν τῇ ἀγάπῃ. Reference/Respect.

4:19 ἡμεῖς ἀγαπῶμεν, ὅτι αὐτὸς πρῶτος ἠγάπησεν ἡμᾶς.

ἡμεῖς. The explicit nominative subject pronoun helps highlight the contrast between those who fear (ὁ φοβούμενος, v. 18) and those who have been perfected in love (τετελείωται ἐν τῇ ἀγάπῃ, v. 18).

ἀγαπῶμεν. Pres act ind 1st pl ἀγαπάω. The direct object, which could be God, others, or both, is left implicit.

ὅτι. Causal.

αὐτὸς. Nominative subject of ἠγάπησεν.

ἠγάπησεν. Aor act ind 3rd sg ἀγαπάω.

ἡμᾶς. Accusative direct object of ἠγάπησεν.

4:20 ἐάν τις εἴπῃ ὅτι Ἀγαπῶ τὸν θεόν, καὶ τὸν ἀδελφὸν αὐτοῦ μισῇ, ψεύστης ἐστίν· ὁ γὰρ μὴ ἀγαπῶν τὸν ἀδελφὸν αὐτοῦ ὃν ἑώρακεν, τὸν θεὸν ὃν οὐχ ἑώρακεν οὐ δύναται ἀγαπᾶν.

ἐάν. Introduces the protasis of a third class condition (see 1:6 on Ἐὰν).

τις. Nominative subject of εἴπῃ . . . καὶ . . . μισῇ.

εἴπῃ. Aor act subj 3rd sg λέγω. Subjunctive with ἐάν.

ὅτι. Introduces direct discourse.

Ἀγαπῶ. Pres act ind 1st sg ἀγαπάω.

τὸν θεόν. Accusative direct object of Ἀγαπῶ.

καὶ. Although a smooth English translation may use "but," given the semantic contrast between Ἀγαπῶ τὸν θεόν and τὸν ἀδελφὸν αὐτοῦ μισῇ, the conjunction is coordinate and links μισῇ to the main verb (εἴπῃ).

τὸν ἀδελφὸν. Accusative direct object of μισῇ. On the meaning, see 2:9.

αὐτοῦ. Genitive of relationship.

μισῇ. Pres act subj 3rd sg μισέω. Subjunctive with ἐάν.

ψεύστης. Predicate nominative.

ἐστίν. Pres act ind 3rd sg εἰμί. On the retention of the accent, see 1:5 on ἐστιν.

ὁ γὰρ μὴ ἀγαπῶν τὸν ἀδελφὸν αὐτοῦ ὃν ἑώρακεν. The whole participial construction, headed by the nominative ὁ . . . ἀγαπῶν, serves as the subject of δύναται. On the rhetorical force of the construction, see 2:4 on ὁ λέγων.

γὰρ. Causal (but see 2:19 on γὰρ).

ὁ γὰρ μὴ ἀγαπῶν. Pres act ptc masc nom sg ἀγαπάω (substantival).

τὸν ἀδελφὸν. Accusative direct object of ἀγαπῶν. On the meaning, see 2:9.

αὐτοῦ. Genitive of relationship.

ὃν. Accusative direct object of ἑώρακεν.

ἑώρακεν. Prf act ind 3rd sg ὁράω.
τὸν θεὸν. Accusative direct object of ἀγαπᾶν. This noun phrase, which is part of an infinitival clause, is fronted (see 1:5 on σκοτία) to place it in focus.
ὄν. Accusative direct object of ἑώρακεν.
ἑώρακεν. Prf act ind 3rd sg ὁράω.
δύναται. Pres mid ind 3rd sg δύναμαι. On the voice, see 3:9 and "Deponency" in the Series Introduction.
ἀγαπᾶν. Pres act inf ἀγαπάω (complementary).

4:21 καὶ ταύτην τὴν ἐντολὴν ἔχομεν ἀπ' αὐτοῦ, ἵνα ὁ ἀγαπῶν τὸν θεὸν ἀγαπᾷ καὶ τὸν ἀδελφὸν αὐτοῦ.

καὶ. The sentence-initial καὶ marks thematic continuity (see 1:2 on καὶ) and introduces a further comment on the topic of love.
ταύτην τὴν ἐντολὴν. Accusative direct object of ἔχομεν. The demonstrative pronoun is cataphoric (see 1:5 on αὕτη), pointing forward to the ἵνα clause.
ἔχομεν. Pres act ind 1st pl ἔχω.
ἀπ' αὐτοῦ. Source.
ἵνα. Introduces a clause that is epexegetical to ταύτην τὴν ἐντολὴν.
ὁ ἀγαπῶν. Pres act ptc masc nom sg ἀγαπάω (substantival). The participial construction, ὁ ἀγαπῶν τὸν θεὸν, serves as the subject of ἀγαπῶν.
τὸν θεὸν. Accusative direct object of ἀγαπῶν.
ἀγαπᾷ. Pres act subj 3rd sg ἀγαπῶν. Subjunctive with ἵνα (the indicative form would be the same).
τὸν ἀδελφὸν. Accusative direct object of ἀγαπῶν. On the meaning, see 2:9.
αὐτοῦ. Genitive of relationship.

1 John 5:1-12

[1]Everyone who believes that Jesus is the Christ has been born of God, and everyone who loves the parent [also] loves the one who has been born of him. [2]This is how we know that we love the children of God, when we love God and carry out his commands. [3]For this is the love of God, that we keep his commands; and his commands are not burdensome, [4]since all that is born of God conquers the world.

Now, this is what has conquered the world, our faith. ⁵Who, then, is the one who conquers the world except the one who believes that Jesus is the Son of God? ⁶He, Jesus Christ, is the one who came by water and blood—not with water only but with water and blood. And the Spirit is the one who testifies, since the Spirit is truth ⁷(and) since there are three who testify: ⁸the Spirit, the water, and the blood. And the three are in agreement. ⁹If we accept the testimony of people, the testimony of God is even greater. For this is what God has testified about: he has testified concerning his Son. ¹⁰The one who believes in the Son of God has the testimony in himself. The one who does not believe God has (in effect) branded him a liar, since he has not believed what God has testified concerning his Son. ¹¹And this is the testimony: God has given eternal life to us, and this life is found in his Son. ¹²The one who has the Son has life. The one who does not have the Son of God does not have life.

5:1 Πᾶς ὁ πιστεύων ὅτι Ἰησοῦς ἐστιν ὁ Χριστὸς ἐκ τοῦ θεοῦ γεγέννηται, καὶ πᾶς ὁ ἀγαπῶν τὸν γεννήσαντα ἀγαπᾷ [καὶ] τὸν γεγεννημένον ἐξ αὐτοῦ.

Πᾶς ὁ πιστεύων ὅτι Ἰησοῦς ἐστιν ὁ Χριστὸς. The whole participial construction, headed by the nominative Πᾶς ὁ πιστεύων, functions as the subject of γεγέννηται. On the rhetorical force of πᾶς with an articular participle, see 2:23 on πᾶς ὁ ἀρνούμενος.

ὁ πιστεύων. Pres act ptc masc nom sg πιστεύω (substantival or attributive; see 2:23 on πᾶς ὁ ἀρνούμενος). The present tense, which portrays the action as a process, should not be pressed to imply continual belief (contra Wallace, 621, n. 22).

ὅτι. Introduces the clausal complement of πιστεύων (cf. also 2:3 on ὅτι).

Ἰησοῦς. Nominative subject (see 2:22 on Ἰησοῦς).

ἐστιν. Pres act ind 3rd sg εἰμί. On the loss of accent, see 1:5 on ἐστιν.

ὁ Χριστὸς. Predicate nominative (see 2:22 on Ἰησοῦς).

ἐκ τοῦ θεοῦ γεγέννηται. See 3:9 on ἐκ τοῦ θεοῦ.

γεγέννηται. Prf pass ind 3rd sg γεννάω.

1 John 5:1-2   121

πᾶς ὁ ἀγαπῶν τὸν γεννήσαντα ἀγαπᾷ [καὶ] τὸν γεγεννημένον ἐξ αὐτοῦ. A more idiomatic rendering of this clause
would be: "Everyone who loves the parent/father loves the parent's/father's child."
πᾶς ὁ ἀγαπῶν τὸν γεννήσαντα. The whole participial construction, headed by the nominative πᾶς ὁ ἀγαπῶν, functions as
the subject of ἀγαπῶν. On the rhetorical force of πᾶς with an
articular participle, see 2:23 on πᾶς ὁ ἀρνούμενος.
ὁ ἀγαπῶν. Pres act ptc masc nom sg ἀγαπάω (substantival or
attributive; see 2:23 on πᾶς ὁ ἀρνούμενος).
τὸν γεννήσαντα. Aor act ptc masc acc sg γεννάω (substantival). Accusative direct object of ἀγαπῶν.
ἀγαπᾷ. Pres act ind 3rd sg ἀγαπάω.
[καὶ]. The question of whether or not the conjunction is original
(it is omitted by B Ψ 048ᵛⁱᵈ 33 and a few versions and early fathers)
has little bearing on the meaning of the text.
τὸν γεγεννημένον. Prf pass ptc masc acc sg γεννάω (substantival). Accusative direct object of ἀγαπᾷ.
ἐξ αὐτοῦ. See 3:9 on ἐκ τοῦ θεοῦ.

5:2 ἐν τούτῳ γινώσκομεν ὅτι ἀγαπῶμεν τὰ τέκνα τοῦ θεοῦ,
ὅταν τὸν θεὸν ἀγαπῶμεν καὶ τὰς ἐντολὰς αὐτοῦ ποιῶμεν.

ἐν τούτῳ. Instrumental. The demonstrative pronoun is cataphoric (see 1:5 on αὕτη), pointing forward to the ὅταν clause. On
the rhetorical function of this expression, see 2:3.
γινώσκομεν. Pres act ind 1st pl γινώσκω.
ὅτι. Introduces the clausal complement of γινώσκομεν (see also
2:3 on ὅτι).
ἀγαπῶμεν. Pres act ind 1st pl ἀγαπάω.
τὰ τέκνα. Accusative direct object of ἀγαπῶμεν.
τοῦ θεοῦ. Genitive of relationship.
ὅταν. Introduces a clause that is epexegetical to τούτῳ (see 1:5
on ὅτι).
τὸν θεὸν. Accusative direct object of ἀγαπῶμεν.
ἀγαπῶμεν. Pres act subj 1st pl ἀγαπάω. Subjunctive with ὅταν.

τὰς ἐντολάς. Accusative direct object of ποιῶμεν.

αὐτοῦ. Subjective genitive (see 1:1 on τῆς ζωῆς).

ποιῶμεν. Pres act subj 1st pl ποιέω. Subjunctive with ὅταν. It is not surprising that some scribes (probably unintentionally) substituted τηρῶμεν for ποιῶμεν. The verb τηρέω is typically used with τὰς ἐντολάς, while ποιέω is not (except in the Majority Text reading for Rev 22:14). The former verb occurs in ℵ 1175 1241 1243 1735 1846 1881 *Byz* [K L P] *Lect* vg^mss slav, while ποιῶμεν is found in B Ψ 81 322 323 436 945 1067 1292 1409 1505 1611 1739 1844 1852 2138 2298 2344 2464 it^ar, q vg syr^p, h cop^sa, bo arm eth geo Lucifer Augustine. Given the fact that ποιῶμεν is the harder reading and τηρῶμεν is used in the next verse with τὰς ἐντολάς, it is more likely that scribes changed the original ποιῶμεν to τηρῶμεν.

5:3 αὕτη γάρ ἐστιν ἡ ἀγάπη τοῦ θεοῦ, ἵνα τὰς ἐντολὰς αὐτοῦ τηρῶμεν· καὶ αἱ ἐντολαὶ αὐτοῦ βαρεῖαι οὐκ εἰσίν.

αὕτη. Predicate nominative (see 1:5 on αὕτη). The demonstrative is cataphoric (see 1:5 on αὕτη), pointing forward to the ἵνα clause.

γάρ. See 2:19.

ἐστιν. Pres act ind 3rd sg εἰμί. On the loss of accent, see 1:5 on ἐστιν.

ἡ ἀγάπη. Nominative subject of ἐστιν.

τοῦ θεοῦ. Given the ἵνα clause that follows, the genitive must be objective (see 1:1 on τῆς ζωῆς).

ἵνα. Introduces a clause that is epexegetical to αὕτη (see 1:5 on ὅτι).

τὰς ἐντολάς. Accusative direct object of τηρῶμεν.

αὐτοῦ. Subjective genitive (see 1:1 on τῆς ζωῆς).

τηρῶμεν. Pres act subj 1st pl τηρέω. Subjunctive with ἵνα.

καί. The sentence-initial καὶ marks thematic continuity (see 1:2 on καί) and introduces a further comment on τὰς ἐντολὰς αὐτοῦ (see 1:2 on καί).

αἱ ἐντολαί. Nominative subject of εἰσίν.

αὐτοῦ. Subjective genitive (see 1:1 on τῆς ζωῆς).

βαρεῖαι. Predicate adjective.

εἰσίν. Pres act ind 3rd pl εἰμί. On the retention of the accent, see 1:5 on ἐστιν.

1 John 5:2-4

5:4 ὅτι πᾶν τὸ γεγεννημένον ἐκ τοῦ θεοῦ νικᾷ τὸν κόσμον· καὶ αὕτη ἐστὶν ἡ νίκη ἡ νικήσασα τὸν κόσμον, ἡ πίστις ἡμῶν.

ὅτι. Causal. The ὅτι introduces a clause that provides the reason why God's commands are not burdensome.

πᾶν τὸ γεγεννημένον ἐκ τοῦ θεοῦ. The whole participial construction, headed by the nominative πᾶν τὸ γεγεννημένον, functions as the subject of νικᾷ. On the rhetorical force of πᾶς with an articular participle, see 2:23 on πᾶς.

πᾶν. Although the masculine πᾶς may have been expected, the writer uses the neuter form instead. BDF §138(1) notes that "the neuter is sometimes used with respect to persons if it is not the individuals but a general quality that is to be emphasized." Or, as Brown (542) suggests, the choice of the neuter may reflect "the author's desire to set up a category of what God has begotten over against another category, 'the world.'"

τὸ γεγεννημένον. Prf pass ptc neut nom sg γεννάω (substantival or attributive; see 2:23 on πᾶς ὁ ἀρνούμενος).

γεγεννημένον ἐκ τοῦ θεοῦ. See 3:9 on ἐκ τοῦ θεοῦ.

νικᾷ. Pres act ind 3rd sg νικάω.

τὸν κόσμον. Accusative direct object of νικᾷ.

καὶ. The clause-initial καὶ marks thematic continuity (see 1:2 on καὶ) and introduces a further comment on νικᾷ.

αὕτη. Predicate nominative (see 1:5 on αὕτη). The demonstrative is cataphoric (see 1:5 on αὕτη), pointing forward to ἡ πίστις ἡμῶν.

ἐστὶν. Pres act ind 3rd sg εἰμί. On the retention of the accent, see 1:5 on ἐστιν.

ἡ νίκη ἡ νικήσασα τὸν κόσμον. Lit. "The victory that has conquered the world."

ἡ νίκη. Nominative subject of ἐστὶν.

νικήσασα. Aor act ptc fem nom sg νικάω (attributive). The writer adds extra rhetorical force through the use of a verb that is cognate to the noun it modifies (cf. 2:25; Anderson and Anderson, 44).

τὸν κόσμον. Accusative direct object of νικήσασα.

ἡ πίστις. Nominative in apposition to αὕτη.

ἡμῶν. Subjective genitive (see 1:1 on τῆς ζωῆς).

5:5 τίς [δέ] ἐστιν ὁ νικῶν τὸν κόσμον εἰ μὴ ὁ πιστεύων ὅτι Ἰησοῦς ἐστιν ὁ υἱὸς τοῦ θεοῦ;

τίς. Predicate nominative. On the force of the rhetorical question that follows, see 2:22 on Τίς.

ἐστιν. Pres act ind 3rd sg εἰμί. On the loss of accent, see 1:5 on ἐστιν.

ὁ νικῶν. Pres act ptc masc nom sg νικάω (substantival).

τὸν κόσμον. Accusative direct object of νικῶν.

εἰ μὴ. Louw and Nida (89.131) describe this expression as "a marker of contrast by designating an exception—'except that, but, however, instead, but only.'"

ὁ πιστεύων ὅτι Ἰησοῦς ἐστιν ὁ υἱὸς τοῦ θεοῦ. Constructions introduced by εἰ μὴ should probably be viewed as elliptical. In this case, the whole participial construction, headed by the nominative ὁ πιστεύων, would then serve as the subject of an implied ἐστιν (ὁ νικῶν τὸν κόσμον).

ὁ πιστεύων. Pres act ptc masc nom sg πιστεύω (substantival).

ὅτι. Introduces the clausal complement of πιστεύων (cf. also 2:3 on ὅτι).

Ἰησοῦς. Nominative subject (see 2:22 on Ἰησοῦς).

ἐστιν. Pres act ind 3rd sg εἰμί. On the loss of accent, see 1:5 on ἐστιν.

ὁ υἱὸς. Predicate nominative (see 2:22 on Ἰησοῦς).

τοῦ θεοῦ. Genitive of relationship.

5:6 Οὗτός ἐστιν ὁ ἐλθὼν δι' ὕδατος καὶ αἵματος, Ἰησοῦς Χριστός· οὐκ ἐν τῷ ὕδατι μόνον ἀλλ' ἐν τῷ ὕδατι καὶ ἐν τῷ αἵματι· καὶ τὸ πνεῦμά ἐστιν τὸ μαρτυροῦν, ὅτι τὸ πνεῦμά ἐστιν ἡ ἀλήθεια.

Οὗτός. Although the referent of the demonstrative is reiterated in what follows (Ἰησοῦς Χριστός), the semantics of 5:5-6 still point to an anaphoric usage here (the antecedent is Ἰησοῦς, v. 5). It is thus the nominative subject of ἐστιν (see 1:5 on αὕτη).

ἐστιν. Pres act ind 3rd sg εἰμί. On the loss of accent, see 1:5 on ἐστιν.

ὁ ἐλθὼν. Aor act ptc masc nom sg ἔρχομαι (substantival). Predicate nominative (see 1:5 on αὕτη).

δι' ὕδατος καὶ αἵματος. Means. There are a number of variant readings at this point. The UBS⁴ text is supported by B Ψ 322 323 1175 1739* 1881 2298 Byz [K L] Lect itᵃʳ vg syrᵖ geo Clementˡᵃᵗ Cyril²ᐟ⁴ Tertullian. A number of witnesses substitute πνεύματος for αἵματος (945 1241 / 165 / 170 / 422 / 593 / 617 / 1441 Cyril¹ᐟ⁴ Ambrose). Others add καὶ πνεύματος (ℵ A 436 1067 1292 1409 1505 1611 1735 2138 2344 / 598 vgᵐˢˢ syrʰ copˢᵃ, ᵇᵒ eth slav Cyril¹ᐟ⁴), while still others read ὕδατος καὶ πνεύματος καὶ αἵματος (P 81 1243 1844 1846 1852 2464 / 884 itˡ vgᵐˢˢ arm). The UBS⁴ has upgraded the rating for δι' ὕδατος καὶ αἵματος from a "B" to an "A." As Metzger (646) notes, scribes familiar with John 3:5 likely "introduced πνεύματος either (a) as a substitution for αἵματος . . . or as an addition (b) before αἵματος . . . or (c) after αἵματος . . . occasionally appending ἁγίου after πνεύματος." The referent of the two nouns poses an even more difficult challenge than the textual issue. Some take both elements as a reference to John 19:34 (καὶ ἐξῆλθεν εὐθὺς αἷμα καὶ ὕδωρ). Although there is certainly a conceptual link between the two texts, the difference in word order and contexts argues against an intentional echo. The majority of commentators take ὕδατος and αἵματος as metonymies (see 2:2 on τοῦ κόσμου) for Jesus' baptism and death. Taking the two terms as referring to two events rather than one is supported by the following verse, which groups them with τὸ πνεῦμά as three distinct witnesses. A number of factors, however, suggest that Jesus' baptism is not one of the events in view. First, the language of "coming" associated with Jesus (ὁ ἐλθών) refers to his incarnation. Indeed, a central focus of 1 John, apparently designed to counter "progressive" teachings that were threatening the readers, is the theme of Jesus "coming in the flesh." This proposition serves as the obligatory confession of every true believer. Larsen (1990b) argues that ὕδατος should be viewed as a metonymy not for Jesus' baptism but for his birth. To support this view, he turns to the only other context in the NT where ὕδωρ is used figuratively and not qualified by another term (such as a term for cleansing): John 3:5. Larsen maintains that the statement in John 3:5, ἐὰν μή τις γεννηθῇ ἐξ ὕδατος καὶ πνεύματος, is fleshed out in the structurally parallel statements that follow. The proposition, τις γεννηθῇ ἐξ ὕδατος (v. 5), is parallel with τὸ γεγεννημένον ἐκ τῆς σαρκὸς σάρξ ἐστιν (v. 6). Similarly, the proposition τις γεννηθῇ ἐξ . . . πνεύματος

(v. 5) is parallel with τὸ γεγεννημένον ἐκ τοῦ πνεύματος πνεῦμά ἐστιν (v. 6). Larsen thus maintains that ὕδατος in both John 3 and 1 John 5 is a metonymy (see 2:2 on τοῦ κόσμου) for natural birth built on the breaking of the water that precedes childbirth. The point, then, which is consistent with the overall message of 1 John, is that not only was Jesus born as a normal human being but his death also bore witness to his humanness, as his blood was spilled.

Ἰησοῦς Χριστός. Nominative in apposition to Οὗτός. The second accent comes from the enclitic ἐστιν (see 1:5 on ἐστιν).

ἐν τῷ ὕδατι . . . ἐν τῷ ὕδατι . . . ἐν τῷ αἵματι. Louw and Nida (89.76) note that both διά and ἐν may function instrumentally, i.e., as "markers of the means by which one event makes another event possible." Where there is such semantic overlap, the choice of preposition is frequently determined by collocation, i.e., a particular preposition is chosen simply because it is conventionally used with a particular word. Here, however, the author has shifted from διά to ἐν even though he is still talking about ὕδωρ and αἷμα. Unfortunately, as Louw and Nida note (89.76, n. 12), "There are probably certain subtle distinctions between the use of διά in contrast with εἰς or ἐν as markers of means, but this cannot be clearly determined from existing contexts." Consequently, many scholars argue that there is no difference in meaning involved (see, e.g., Bultmann, 79, n. 1; Marshall, 232, n. 6; Smalley, 280; cf. Brooke, 135). It may be appropriate, however, to maintain that διά focuses on the actual vehicle or instrument by which the event was carried out, while ἐν focuses more on the circumstances in which the event took place (cf. BDAG, 329; BDF §198; but Moule, 57, links διά with the notion of circumstance).

ἀλλ'. See 2:2.

καί. The clause-initial καί marks thematic continuity (see 1:2 on καί) and suggests that what precedes is the focal point of the Spirit's testimony.

τὸ πνεῦμά. Neuter nominative subject of ἐστιν. The second accent comes from the enclitic ἐστιν (see 1:5 on ἐστιν).

ἐστιν. Pres act ind 3rd sg εἰμί. On the loss of accent, see 1:5 on ἐστιν.

τὸ μαρτυροῦν. Pres act ptc neut nom sg μαρτυρέω (substantival). Predicate nominative. Here, both the subject and predicate of the equative verb are articular, since the predicate requires the article to nominalize (see 2:13 on τὸν) the participle (cf. 1:5 on ὁ θεὸς).

ὅτι. Causal. Given the fact that τὸ πνεῦμά is the subject of both the main clause and the ὅτι clause, it is unlikely that the ὅτι would introduce a clausal complement of μαρτυροῦν.

τὸ πνεῦμά. Neuter nominative subject of ἐστιν. The second accent comes from the enclitic ἐστιν (see 1:5 on ἐστιν).

ἐστιν. Pres act ind 3rd sg εἰμί. On the loss of accent, see 1:5 on ἐστιν.

ἡ ἀλήθεια. Predicate nominative. Where an equative clause has a nominative personal referent and a nominative abstract referent, the personal referent will be the subject.

5:7 ὅτι τρεῖς εἰσιν οἱ μαρτυροῦντες,

ὅτι. The ὅτι is used to introduce a second causal clause, which either (a) stands in apposition to the previous ὅτι clause (see the translation), or (b) provides a reason why τὸ πνεῦμά ἐστιν ἡ ἀλήθεια.

τρεῖς. Predicate adjective.

εἰσιν. Pres act ind 3rd pl εἰμί. On the loss of accent, see 1:5 on ἐστιν.

οἱ μαρτυροῦντες. Pres act ptc masc nom pl μαρτυρέω (substantival). Nominative subject of εἰσιν (lit. "the ones who testify are three"). The writer chooses a masculine form of both the participle and the numeral even though the ultimate referents are all neuter (τὸ πνεῦμα καὶ τὸ ὕδωρ καὶ τὸ αἷμα), perhaps due to the fact that the three are personified as "witnesses." The masculine gender should not be viewed as an oblique reference to the Spirit's personality (Wallace 1996, 332, n. 44).

A few late manuscripts add what is known as the "Johannine Comma": ἐν τῷ οὐρανῷ, ὁ Πατήρ, ὁ Λόγος, καὶ τὸ Ἅγιον Πνεῦμα· καὶ οὗτοι οἱ τρεῖς ἕν εἰσι. ⁸καὶ τρεῖς εἰσιν οἱ μαρτυροῦντες ἐν τῇ γῇ ("in heaven: the Father, the Word, and the Holy Spirit. And these three are one. And there are three who testify on the earth"). While the KJV popularized this reading among English speakers, it appears in only eight Greek manuscripts (four times as a marginal reading), none of which dates earlier than 1400 C.E. (Strecker, 189). It "is quoted by none of the Greek Fathers," "The passage is absent from the manuscripts of all ancient versions . . . except the Latin," and "no good reason can be found to account for its omission" (Metzger, 648).

5:8 τὸ πνεῦμα καὶ τὸ ὕδωρ καὶ τὸ αἷμα, καὶ οἱ τρεῖς εἰς τὸ ἕν εἰσιν.

τὸ πνεῦμα καὶ τὸ ὕδωρ καὶ τὸ αἷμα. Nominative in apposition to τρεῖς (verse 7).

καὶ. The clause-initial καὶ marks thematic continuity (see 1:2 on καὶ).

οἱ τρεῖς. Nominative subject of εἰσιν.

εἰς τὸ ἕν. Scholars point out that the preposition εἰς with an accusative noun is frequently used as a substitute for a predicate modifier to indicate equivalence, i.e., "X is Y" (cf. Acts 5:36; 7:5, 21; 8:20; 11:29; 13:22, 47; 19:47). The construction usually occurs in Old Testament quotations, and thus is said to typically reflect a Semitic influence (see Wallace, 47). If such is the case here, the verse should be rendered "And these three are one." It may be better, however, to take the preposition as denoting "goal" in such constructions. The point here would then be that the three lead to the same conclusion or "are in agreement" (NIV, NASB, REB; cf. CEV, GW, NCV, NLT).

εἰσιν. Pres act ind 3rd pl εἰμί. On the loss of accent, see 1:5 on ἐστιν.

5:9 εἰ τὴν μαρτυρίαν τῶν ἀνθρώπων λαμβάνομεν, ἡ μαρτυρία τοῦ θεοῦ μείζων ἐστίν, ὅτι αὕτη ἐστὶν ἡ μαρτυρία τοῦ θεοῦ, ὅτι μεμαρτύρηκεν περὶ τοῦ υἱοῦ αὐτοῦ.

εἰ. Introduces a first class condition (cf. 3:13).

τὴν μαρτυρίαν. Accusative direct object of λαμβάνομεν.

τῶν ἀνθρώπων. Subjective genitive (see 1:1 on τῆς ζωῆς).

λαμβάνομεν. Pres act ind 1st pl λαμβάνω.

ἡ μαρτυρία. Nominative subject of ἐστίν.

τοῦ θεοῦ. Subjective genitive (see 1:1 on τῆς ζωῆς).

μείζων. Predicate adjective. The proposition, "we should therefore accept God's testimony," is left implicit.

ἐστίν. Pres act ind 3rd sg εἰμί. On the retention of the accent, see 1:5 on ἐστιν.

ὅτι. Causal.

αὕτη. Predicate nominative (see 1:5 on αὕτη). The demonstrative is cataphoric (see 1:5 on αὕτη), pointing forward to the ὅτι clause.

ἐστὶν. Pres act ind 3rd sg εἰμί. On the retention of the accent, see 1:5 on ἐστιν.

ἡ μαρτυρία. Nominative subject of ἐστὶν.

τοῦ θεοῦ. Subjective genitive (see 1:1 on τῆς ζωῆς).

ὅτι. Introduces a clause that is epexegetical to αὕτη (see 1:5 on ὅτι).

μεμαρτύρηκεν. Prf act ind 3rd sg μαρτυρέω.

περὶ τοῦ υἱοῦ. Reference/Respect.

αὐτοῦ. Genitive of relationship.

5:10 ὁ πιστεύων εἰς τὸν υἱὸν τοῦ θεοῦ ἔχει τὴν μαρτυρίαν ἐν ἑαυτῷ· ὁ μὴ πιστεύων τῷ θεῷ ψεύστην πεποίηκεν αὐτόν, ὅτι οὐ πεπίστευκεν εἰς τὴν μαρτυρίαν ἣν μεμαρτύρηκεν ὁ θεὸς περὶ τοῦ υἱοῦ αὐτοῦ.

ὁ πιστεύων εἰς τὸν υἱὸν τοῦ θεοῦ. The whole participial construction, headed by the nominative ὁ πιστεύων, serves as the subject of ἔχει. On the rhetorical force of the construction, see 2:4 on ὁ λέγων.

ὁ πιστεύων. Pres act ptc masc nom sg πιστεύω (substantival).

εἰς τὸν υἱὸν. The preposition introduces the object of belief.

τοῦ θεοῦ. Genitive of relationship.

ἔχει. Pres act ind 3rd sg ἔχω.

τὴν μαρτυρίαν. Accusative direct object of ἔχει.

ἐν ἑαυτῷ. Locative. The variation in the text's history illustrates the fact that personal pronouns were frequently used in a reflexive sense. The UBS⁴ text is read by ℵ Ψ et al., while ἐν αὐτῷ is read by B² *Byz* et al., and εν αυτω, which could either be accented ἐν αὐτῷ or ἐν αὑτῷ, is found in A B* L P. The meaning is the same in each case (see also 2:8 on ὃ ἐστιν ἀληθὲς ἐν αὐτῷ καὶ ἐν ὑμῖν).

ὁ μὴ πιστεύων τῷ θεῷ. The whole participial construction, headed by the nominative ὁ . . . πιστεύων, serves as the subject of πεποίηκεν. On the rhetorical force of the construction, see 2:4 on ὁ λέγων.

ὁ . . . πιστεύων. Pres act ptc masc nom sg πιστεύω (substantival).

τῷ θεῷ. Dative complement of πιστεύων. The dative case may have been chosen here rather than εἰς (see above) because the author is now talking about believing something that God has said, rather than believing "in him." Such a subtle distinction, however, should not be pressed given the use of εἰς below with πιστεύω along with τὴν μαρτυρίαν as the object of belief.

ψεύστην. Accusative complement in an object-complement double accusative construction (see 1:10 on ψεύστην).

πεποίηκεν. Prf act ind 3rd sg ποιέω.

αὐτόν. Accusative direct object of πεποίηκεν. The antecedent is τῷ θεῷ rather than ὁ μὴ πιστεύων. Thus, the clause should not be interpreted "the one who does not believe in God makes *himself* a liar."

ὅτι. Causal.

πεπίστευκεν. Prf act ind 3rd sg πιστεύω.

εἰς τὴν μαρτυρίαν. The preposition introduces the object of belief.

τὴν μαρτυρίαν ἣν μεμαρτύρηκεν ὁ θεός. Lit. "the testimony that God has testified."

ἣν. Accusative direct object of μεμαρτύρηκεν.

μεμαρτύρηκεν. Prf act ind 3rd sg μαρτυρέω.

ὁ θεὸς. Nominative subject of μεμαρτύρηκεν.

περὶ τοῦ υἱοῦ. Reference/Respect.

αὐτοῦ. Genitive of relationship.

5:11 καὶ αὕτη ἐστὶν ἡ μαρτυρία, ὅτι ζωὴν αἰώνιον ἔδωκεν ἡμῖν ὁ θεός, καὶ αὕτη ἡ ζωὴ ἐν τῷ υἱῷ αὐτοῦ ἐστιν.

καὶ. The sentence-initial καὶ marks thematic continuity (see 1:2 on καὶ) and introduces a further comment on τὴν μαρτυρίαν.

αὕτη. Predicate nominative (see 1:5 on αὕτη). The demonstrative is cataphoric (see 1:5 on αὕτη), pointing forward to the ὅτι clause.

ἐστὶν. Pres act ind 3rd sg εἰμί. On the retention of the accent, see 1:5 on ἐστιν.

ἡ μαρτυρία. Nominative subject of ἐστὶν.

ὅτι. Introduces a clause that is epexegetical to αὕτη (see 1:5 on ὅτι).

ζωὴν αἰώνιον. Accusative direct object of ἔδωκεν.
ἔδωκεν. Aor act ind 3rd sg δίδωμι.
ἡμῖν. Dative indirect object of ἔδωκεν.
ὁ θεός. Nominative subject of ἔδωκεν.
αὕτη ἡ ζωὴ. Nominative subject of ἐστιν.
ἐν τῷ υἱῷ. Here, the prepositional phrase probably functions as a locative idiom ("something is found in someone") rather than a relational idiom (see 2:5 on ἐν αὐτῷ).
αὐτοῦ. Genitive of relationship.
ἐστιν. Pres act ind 3rd sg εἰμί. On the loss of accent, see 1:5 on ἐστιν.

5:12 ὁ ἔχων τὸν υἱὸν ἔχει τὴν ζωήν· ὁ μὴ ἔχων τὸν υἱὸν τοῦ θεοῦ τὴν ζωὴν οὐκ ἔχει.

ὁ ἔχων τὸν υἱὸν. On the meaning of the idiom, ἔχων τὸν υἱὸν, see 2:23 on τὸν πατέρα ἔχει.
ὁ ἔχων. Pres act ptc masc nom sg ἔχω (substantival). The participial construction, ὁ ἔχων τὸν υἱὸν, serves as the subject of ἔχει.
τὸν υἱὸν. Accusative direct object of ἔχων.
ἔχει. Pres act ind 3rd sg ἔχω.
τὴν ζωήν. Accusative direct object of ἔχει.
ὁ . . . ἔχων. Pres act ptc masc nom sg ἔχω (substantival). The participial construction, ὁ μὴ ἔχων τὸν υἱὸν τοῦ θεοῦ, serves as the subject of ἔχει.
τὸν υἱὸν. Accusative direct object of ἔχων.
τοῦ θεοῦ. Genitive of relationship.
τὴν ζωὴν. Accusative direct object of ἔχει. The fronting (see 1:5 on σκοτία) lends prominence to the statement.

1 John 5:13-21

[13]I have written these things to you—those who believe in the name of the Son of God—in order that you may know that you have eternal life. [14]And this is the confidence that we have before him: if we ask for anything according to his will, he hears us. [15]And if we know that he hears us—that is, whatever we ask—we know that we have the things that we have asked for from him. [16]If anyone sees his brother or sister committing a sin that does not lead to death, he should ask, and (God)

will give him life, that is, to those committing sins that do not lead to death. There is sin that leads to death. I am not saying that he should ask about that. ¹⁷All wrongdoing is sin. And there is sin that does not lead to death. ¹⁸We know that everyone who has been born of God does not sin. Instead, the one born of God guards himself (from sin) and the Evil One does not touch him. ¹⁹We know that we are from God and the whole world is under the control of the Evil One. ²⁰And we know that the Son of God has come and has given us understanding so that we (might) know the One who is true. And we have a relationship with the One who is true, that is, with his Son Jesus Christ. He is the True God and Eternal Life. ²¹Dear children, guard yourselves from idols.

5:13 Ταῦτα ἔγραψα ὑμῖν ἵνα εἰδῆτε ὅτι ζωὴν ἔχετε αἰώνιον, τοῖς πιστεύουσιν εἰς τὸ ὄνομα τοῦ υἱοῦ τοῦ θεοῦ.

The language in this verse is reminiscent of John 20:31—ταῦτα δὲ γέγραπται ἵνα πιστεύ[σ]ητε ὅτι Ἰησοῦς ἐστιν ὁ Χριστὸς ὁ υἱὸς τοῦ θεοῦ, καὶ ἵνα πιστεύοντες ζωὴν ἔχητε ἐν τῷ ὀνόματι αὐτοῦ.

Ταῦτα. Neuter accusative direct object of ἔγραψα. The demonstrative pronoun is anaphoric and probably refers to the entire letter.

ἔγραψα. Aor act ind 1st sg γράφω. On the tense, see 2:14 on ἔγραψα. In this case, the new paragraph is introduced by a shift in topic introduced by Ταῦτα ἔγραψα (cf. 3 John 9).

ὑμῖν. Dative indirect object of ἔγραψα.

ἵνα. Introduces a purpose clause.

εἰδῆτε. Prf act subj 2nd pl οἶδα. Subjunctive with ἵνα.

ὅτι. Introduces the clausal complement of εἰδῆτε (see also 2:3 on ὅτι).

ζωὴν . . . αἰώνιον. The discontinuous accusative noun phrase serves as the direct object of ἔχετε. The fronting (see 1:5 on σκοτία) of ζωὴν, particularly without its modifier, helps lend prominence to this clause (see 2:2 on αὐτὸς).

ἔχετε. Pres act ind 2nd pl ἔχω.

τοῖς πιστεύουσιν. Dative in apposition to ὑμῖν.

εἰς τὸ ὄνομα. The preposition introduces the object of belief.
τοῦ υἱοῦ. The genitive could be viewed as either possessive (but see 2:5 on αὐτοῦ) or objective (see 1:1 on τῆς ζωῆς).
τοῦ θεοῦ. Genitive of relationship.

5:14 καὶ αὕτη ἐστὶν ἡ παρρησία ἣν ἔχομεν πρὸς αὐτόν, ὅτι ἐάν τι αἰτώμεθα κατὰ τὸ θέλημα αὐτοῦ ἀκούει ἡμῶν.

καὶ. The sentence-initial καὶ generally marks thematic continuity (see 1:2 on καὶ). While the progression of thought is more difficult to see here, the conjunction probably suggests that the παρρησία in view is linked to the possession of ζωὴν αἰώνιον (v. 13).
αὕτη. Predicate nominative (see 1:5 on αὕτη). The demonstrative is cataphoric (see 1:5 on αὕτη), pointing forward to the ὅτι clause.
ἐστὶν. Pres act ind 3rd sg εἰμί. On the retention of the accent, see 1:5 on ἐστιν.
ἡ παρρησία. Nominative subject of ἐστὶν. See 2:28 on παρρησίαν.
ἣν. Accusative direct object of ἔχομεν.
ἔχομεν. Pres act ind 1st pl ἔχω.
πρὸς αὐτόν. Locative, in a metaphorical sense (see also 3:21).
ὅτι. Introduces a clause that is epexegetical to αὕτη (see 1:5 on ὅτι).
ἐάν. Introduces the protasis of a third class condition (see 1:6 on Ἐάν).
τι. Accusative direct object of αἰτώμεθα.
αἰτώμεθα. Pres mid subj 1st pl αἰτέω. Subjunctive with ἐάν. The fact that the writer used the same verb with the active voice earlier (3:22) suggests that the force of the middle voice, highlighting the benefit to the subject, should not be ignored (cf. Moulton, 160; contra Brooke, 144; Law, 406).
κατὰ τὸ θέλημα. Standard.
αὐτοῦ. Subjective genitive (see 1:1 on τῆς ζωῆς).
ἀκούει. Pres act ind 3rd sg ἀκούω.
ἡμῶν. Genitive object of ἀκούει.

5:15 καὶ ἐὰν οἴδαμεν ὅτι ἀκούει ἡμῶν ὃ ἐὰν αἰτώμεθα, οἴδαμεν ὅτι ἔχομεν τὰ αἰτήματα ἃ ᾐτήκαμεν ἀπ' αὐτοῦ.

καὶ. The sentence-initial καὶ marks thematic continuity (see 1:2 on καὶ).

ἐὰν. Introduces the protasis of a third class condition (see 1:6 on Ἐὰν). The use of the third class condition rather than a first class condition may serve as a mild rebuke by portraying something as hypothetical (οἴδαμεν ὅτι ἀκούει ἡμῶν) that has just been established as true (cf. 2:28, 29 on ἐὰν). The fact that it has just been established as true may have led the writer to weaken the third class condition by using an indicative rather than the expected subjunctive verb with ἐάν. Alternatively, the presence of the same form in the apodosis "and the author's desire to show the connection between the two" (Brown, 610) may have led to the solecistic use of the indicative form here.

οἴδαμεν. Prf act ind 1st pl οἶδα.

ὅτι. Introduces the clausal complement of οἴδαμεν (see also 2:3 on ὅτι).

ἀκούει. Pres act ind 3rd sg ἀκούω.

ἡμῶν. Genitive object of ἀκούει.

ὃ ἐὰν αἰτώμεθα. The headless relative clause (see 1:1 on Ὃ ... ὃ) should probably be viewed as a direct object of an implied ἀκούει. The clause of which it is a part would thus stand in apposition to ἀκούει ἡμῶν and be epexegetical in nature: "he hears us, that is, he hears whatever we ask."

ὃ ἐὰν. The indefinite relative pronoun (see 2:5 on ὃς ... ἂν) serves as the accusative direct object of αἰτώμεθα.

αἰτώμεθα. Pres mid subj 1st pl αἰτέω. Subjunctive with ἐάν. On the significance of the middle voice, see 5:14.

οἴδαμεν ὅτι. See above.

ἔχομεν. Pres act ind 1st pl ἔχω.

τὰ αἰτήματα. Accusative direct object of ἔχομεν.

ἃ. Accusative direct object of ᾐτήκαμεν.

ᾐτήκαμεν. Prf act ind 1st pl αἰτέω.

ἀπ' αὐτοῦ. Source.

5:16 Ἐάν τις ἴδῃ τὸν ἀδελφὸν αὐτοῦ ἁμαρτάνοντα ἁμαρτίαν μὴ πρὸς θάνατον, αἰτήσει, καὶ δώσει αὐτῷ ζωήν, τοῖς ἁμαρτάνουσιν μὴ πρὸς θάνατον. ἔστιν ἁμαρτία πρὸς θάνατον· οὐ περὶ ἐκείνης λέγω ἵνα ἐρωτήσῃ.

Ἐάν. Introduces the protasis of a third class condition (see 1:6 on Ἐὰν).

τις. Nominative subject of ἴδῃ.

ἴδῃ. Aor act subj 3rd sg ὁράω/εἶδον. Subjunctive with ἐάν.

τὸν ἀδελφὸν. Accusative direct object of ἴδῃ. On the meaning, see 2:9.

αὐτοῦ. Genitive of relationship.

ἁμαρτάνοντα. Pres act ptc masc acc sg ἁμαρτάνω. Accusative complement in an object-complement double accusative construction (see 1:10 on ψεύστην).

ἁμαρτίαν. Accusative direct object of ἁμαρτάνοντα. Some reference works will identify ἁμαρτίαν as a "cognate accusative," since the noun shares the same root with the verb. Given the fact that there is no clear semantic significance associated with such a construction, it may be better to avoid this label.

πρὸς θάνατον. Louw and Nida (89.44) note that πρὸς with the accusative can serve as "a marker of result, with focus upon the end point."

αἰτήσει. Fut act ind 3rd sg αἰτέω. Imperatival future. The subject is τις. According to Louw and Nida, αἰτέω carries a nuance of urgency (33.163), while ἐρωτάω, which the writer uses below, focuses more on asking for information (33.180) or asking "with the implication of an underlying question" (33.161). Whether or not this writer intended such a distinction is debatable.

δώσει. Fut act ind 3rd sg δίδωμι. The implied subject is God.

αὐτῷ. Dative indirect object of δώσει.

ζωήν. Accusative direct object of δώσει.

τοῖς ἁμαρτάνουσιν. Pres act ptc masc dat pl ἁμαρτάνω (substantival). Dative in apposition to αὐτῷ. The discontinuity within the syntax—αὐτῷ and τοῖς ἁμαρτάνουσιν are separated by ζωήν— functions like a rhetorical pause that highlights the importance of the writer's clarification (τοῖς ἁμαρτάνουσιν μὴ πρὸς θάνατον).

πρὸς θάνατον. See above.

ἔστιν. Pres act ind 3rd sg εἰμί. On the movement of the accent, see 1:5 on ἐστιν.

ἁμαρτία. Nominative subject of ἔστιν.

πρὸς θάνατον. See above.

περὶ ἐκείνης. Reference. The antecedent of ἐκείνης is ἁμαρτία.

λέγω. Pres act ind 1st sg λέγω.

ἵνα. Introduces indirect discourse.

ἐρωτήσῃ. Aor act subj 3rd sg ἐρωτάω. Subjunctive with ἵνα.

5:17 πᾶσα ἀδικία ἁμαρτία ἐστίν, καὶ ἔστιν ἁμαρτία οὐ πρὸς θάνατον.

πᾶσα ἀδικία. Nominative subject of ἐστίν. Although both nouns are anarthrous, the use of the quantifier πᾶσα with ἀδικία makes it clear that it must be the subject ("Sin is all wrongdoing" would not make sense).

ἁμαρτία. Predicate nominative of ἐστίν.

ἐστίν. Pres act ind 3rd sg εἰμί. On the retention of the accent, see 1:5 on ἐστιν.

ἔστιν. Pres act ind 3rd sg εἰμί. On the movement of the accent, see 1:5 on ἐστιν.

ἁμαρτία. Nominative subject of ἔστιν.

πρὸς θάνατον. See 5:16.

5:18 Οἴδαμεν ὅτι πᾶς ὁ γεγεννημένος ἐκ τοῦ θεοῦ οὐχ ἁμαρτάνει, ἀλλ' ὁ γεννηθεὶς ἐκ τοῦ θεοῦ τηρεῖ αὐτόν, καὶ ὁ πονηρὸς οὐχ ἅπτεται αὐτοῦ.

Οἴδαμεν. Prf act ind 1st pl οἶδα.

ὅτι. Introduces the clausal complement of Οἴδαμεν (see also 2:3 on ὅτι).

πᾶς ὁ γεγεννημένος ἐκ τοῦ θεοῦ. The whole participial construction, headed by the nominative πᾶς ὁ γεγεννημένος, functions as the subject of ἁμαρτάνει. On the rhetorical force of πᾶς with an articular participle, see 2:23 on πᾶς ὁ ἀρνούμενος.

ὁ γεγεννημένος. Prf pass ptc masc nom sg γεννάω (substantival or attributive; see 2:23 on πᾶς ὁ ἀρνούμενος).

ἐκ τοῦ θεοῦ. See 3:9 on ἐκ τοῦ θεοῦ.

ἁμαρτάνει. Pres act ind 3rd sg ἁμαρτάνω.

ἀλλ'. Introduces a clause that strongly contrasts with the notion of one who is born of God committing sin (see also 2:2).

ὁ γεννηθεὶς. Aor pass ptc masc nom sg γεννάω (substantival). The referent is likely the Christian (see below on αὐτόν).

ἐκ τοῦ θεοῦ. See 3:9 on ἐκ τοῦ θεοῦ.

τηρεῖ. Pres act ind 3rd sg τηρέω.

αὐτόν. Accusative direct object of τηρεῖ. There is a textual variant at this point that has a significant bearing on how the passage is understood. The editors of the UBS[4] give the reading αὐτόν a "B" rating (upgraded from a "C" in earlier editions), even though it is only found in B[2] 1505 1852 2138 it[ar, l, t] vg Chromatius Jerome Vigilius. Most manuscripts read ἑαυτόν (ℵ A[c] Ψ 33 81 322 323 436 945 1067 1175 1241 1243 1292 1409 1611 1735 1739 1844 1846 1881 2298 2344 2464 Byz [K L P] Lect arm eth geo slav Origen). The editorial committee based their choice primarily on their view that the referent of ὁ γεννηθεὶς is Christ (Metzger, 650). As we examine the textual tradition of codex A and codex B, we find that later scribes working with these manuscripts made different decisions regarding whether the form was reflexive (A[c]) or not (B[2]). Although αὐτόν is clearly the harder reading, given the fact that the variation almost certainly reflects an unintentional error on the part of scribes working with an unaccented original, the harder reading principle does not apply. In light of the strong external support for the full reflexive form ἑαυτόν, the unaccented reading found in A* and B* (αυτον) should either be taken as αὐτόν functioning reflexively or be read αὑτόν (see also the discussion at 2:8 on ὅ ἐστιν ἀληθὲς ἐν αὐτῷ καὶ ἐν ὑμῖν). The referent of ὁ γεννηθεὶς would then be the Christian (so Brown, 622; contra most scholars). In this reading, τηρεῖ αὐτόν is closely linked in meaning to οὐχ ἁμαρτάνει. The fact that John elsewhere always uses the perfect rather than aorist participle to refer to the believer does not preclude this reading.

ὁ πονηρὸς. Nominative subject of ἅπτεται.

ἅπτεται. Pres mid ind 3rd sg ἅπτω.

αὐτοῦ. Genitive object of ἅπτεται.

5:19 οἴδαμεν ὅτι ἐκ τοῦ θεοῦ ἐσμεν, καὶ ὁ κόσμος ὅλος ἐν τῷ πονηρῷ κεῖται.

οἴδαμεν. Prf act ind 1st pl οἶδα.

ὅτι. Introduces the clausal complement of οἴδαμεν (see also 2:3 on ὅτι).

ἐκ τοῦ θεοῦ ἐσμεν. On the meaning of this expression, see 3:10 on ἔστιν ἐκ τοῦ θεοῦ.

ἐσμεν. Pres act ind 1st pl εἰμί. On the loss of accent, see 1:5 on ἐστιν.

ὁ κόσμος ὅλος. Nominative subject of κεῖται.

ἐν τῷ πονηρῷ κεῖται. Lit. "lies in the Evil One." It is possible that the prepositional phrase points to an intimate relationship (see 2:5 on ἐν αὐτῷ), with the verb highlighting the fact that the relationship has been firmly established (cf. LN 13.73).

ἐν τῷ πονηρῷ. Locative, in a metaphorical sense (but see above). The noun phrase should be taken in a personal ("the Evil One") rather than impersonal ("wickedness") sense given the clear personal usage in verse 18 (ὁ πονηρὸς).

κεῖται. Pres mid ind 3rd sg κεῖμαι. Miller (429) describes the use of the middle form with this verb as indicating a state in which the subject is the "center of gravity." For more on the voice, see "Deponency" in the Series Introduction.

5:20 οἴδαμεν δὲ ὅτι ὁ υἱὸς τοῦ θεοῦ ἥκει, καὶ δέδωκεν ἡμῖν διάνοιαν ἵνα γινώσκωμεν τὸν ἀληθινόν· καὶ ἐσμὲν ἐν τῷ ἀληθινῷ, ἐν τῷ υἱῷ αὐτοῦ Ἰησοῦ Χριστῷ. οὗτός ἐστιν ὁ ἀληθινὸς θεὸς καὶ ζωὴ αἰώνιος.

οἴδαμεν. Prf act ind 1st pl οἶδα.

ὅτι. Introduces the clausal complement of οἴδαμεν (see also 2:3 on ὅτι).

ὁ υἱὸς. Nominative subject of ἥκει.

τοῦ θεοῦ. Genitive of relationship

δέδωκεν. Prf act ind 3rd sg δίδωμι.

ἡμῖν. Dative indirect object of δέδωκεν.

διάνοιαν. Accusative direct object of δέδωκεν.

ἵνα. Introduces either a purpose or result clause.

γινώσκωμεν. Pres act subj 1st pl γινώσκω. Subjunctive with ἵνα.

τὸν ἀληθινόν. Given both the preceding and following context, the referent of the substantival adjective must be God the Father, as a significant number of scribes (A Ψ 33 et al.) attest by adding θεόν, though the addition could also be conditioned by the following reference to ὁ ἀληθινὸς θεός. Here, the sense "genuine" is in view, setting up the contrast with τῶν εἰδώλων in the following verse (cf. 1 Thess 1:9—ἐπεστρέψατε πρὸς τὸν θεὸν ἀπὸ τῶν εἰδώλων δουλεύειν θεῷ ζῶντι καὶ ἀληθινῷ).

καί. The clause-initial καὶ marks thematic continuity (see 1:2 on καί), and introduces a further comment on what it means to "know the True One."

ἐσμὲν ἐν τῷ ἀληθινῷ. On the meaning of the idiom, see 2:5 on ἐν αὐτῷ. On the referent of τῷ ἀληθινῷ, see below.

ἐσμὲν. Pres act ind 1st pl εἰμί. On the retention of the accent, see 1:5 on ἐστιν.

ἐν τῷ υἱῷ αὐτοῦ Ἰησοῦ Χριστῷ. On the surface, it seems natural to take this prepositional phrase as standing in apposition to ἐν τῷ ἀληθινῷ (see the translation). Most scholars (see, e.g., Brooke, 152; Law, 412), however, argue that since the referent of τὸν ἀληθινόν must be the Father, it is unlikely that a writer would use the same title (τῷ ἀληθινῷ) to refer to a new referent without warning. They, therefore, prefer to read the text something like: "And we have a relationship with the One who is true, in/through our relationship with his Son Jesus Christ." On the contrary, this prepositional phrase likely is included to clarify that the writer did intend to switch referents in his use of τῷ ἀληθινῷ (see also "Trinitarian Ambiguity" in the Introduction).

αὐτοῦ. Genitive of relationship.

Ἰησοῦ Χριστῷ. Dative in apposition to τῷ υἱῷ.

οὗτός. Nominative subject of ἐστιν (see 1:5 on αὕτη). The demonstrative pronoun is anaphoric and the most natural antecedent, given its proximity, is τῷ υἱῷ αὐτοῦ Ἰησοῦ Χριστῷ (for

140   1 John 5:13-21

additional arguments for this view, see Wallace 1996, 326–27).
Ultimately, determining the antecedent of οὗτός is closely linked
to the interpretation of ἐν τῷ υἱῷ αὐτοῦ Ἰησοῦ Χριστῷ above. If
the prepositional phrase is taken appositionally, then the focus
shifts to Jesus Christ, and he must be the referent of οὗτός. If, on
the other hand, the prepositional phrase simply contextualizes the
readers' relationship with the Father as being "in his Son Jesus
Christ," then the focus remains on the Father and he should be
viewed as the antecedent of οὗτός.
ἐστιν. Pres act ind 3rd sg εἰμί. On the loss of accent, see 1:5 on
ἐστιν.
ὁ ἀληθινὸς θεὸς καὶ ζωὴ αἰώνιος. Predicate nominative.

5:21 Τεκνία, φυλάξατε ἑαυτὰ ἀπὸ τῶν εἰδώλων.

Τεκνία. Vocative (cf. 2:1). As in 3:18, this sentence, rhetorically set off by a vocative, provides a summary of what has pre-
ceded. Although it may encompass the entire letter, it is probably
better to view it as a summary of the two peaks (see "Genre and
Structure" in the Introduction) in chapter 4: "the doctrinal peak
(don't be deceived by false teachers) and the ethical peak (love one
another)" (see Larsen 1991b, 54).
φυλάξατε. Aor act impv 2nd pl φυλάσσω. On the significance
of the tense and mood, see 2:15 on ἀγαξᾶτε and "Verbal Aspect
and Prominence" in the Introduction.
ἑαυτὰ. Accusative direct object of φυλάξατε. The neuter plural
form provides gender concord with Τεκνία.
ἀπὸ τῶν εἰδώλων. Separation.

2 JOHN

2 John 1-3

¹The Elder, to the Elect Lady and her children, whom I truly love, and not only I but also all those who have known the truth, ²because of the truth that remains in us and will be with us forever. ³Grace, mercy, and peace will be with us from God the Father and Jesus Christ, the Father's Son, in truth and love.

1 Ὁ πρεσβύτερος ἐκλεκτῇ κυρίᾳ καὶ τοῖς τέκνοις αὐτῆς, οὓς ἐγὼ ἀγαπῶ ἐν ἀληθείᾳ, καὶ οὐκ ἐγὼ μόνος ἀλλὰ καὶ πάντες οἱ ἐγνωκότες τὴν ἀλήθειαν,

Ὁ πρεσβύτερος. Nominative absolute. The nominative absolute is used with introductory material that is not part of a complete sentence, such as titles, headings, salutations, and addresses (Wallace, 49). It is uncertain whether the term, πρεσβύτερος, should be understood simply as "an adult male advanced in years" (LN 9.31), with a connotation of respected individual, or as a title of office (cf. LN 53.77). As Brown (647) notes, the use of Ὁ πρεσβύτερος as a nominative absolute in 2 and 3 John are the only Christian examples of this term from the period where it is not accompanied by a personal name. This usage suggests that the writer is using it as a title of some sort, and the context of the letter makes it likely that the title reflects a set office within the early church.

ἐκλεκτῇ κυρίᾳ καὶ τοῖς τέκνοις. Dative of recipient.

ἐκλεκτῇ κυρίᾳ. As Westcott (223) notes, "the rendering of this phrase is beset by the greatest difficulties." Brown (652–54) points out that either the first or second term may be construed as a proper name ("the lady Electa" or "the elect Kyria," though the former is highly unlikely given the use of τῆς ἀδελφῆς σου τῆς ἐκλεκτῆς at the end of the letter); the expression may be viewed as a courteous way of greeting a female addressee ("dear lady"); or "Elect Lady" may be viewed as a figurative way of referring to the church. The context of the letter itself favors the final option, with the greeting at the end of the letter coming from a "sister" church (τῆς ἀδελφῆς σου τῆς ἐκλεκτῆς, v. 13). The greeting from τὰ τέκνα τῆς ἀδελφῆς σου τῆς ἐκλεκτῆς makes it clear that ἐκλεκτῇ κυρίᾳ cannot be a metaphor for the universal church (Brown, 653). Brown (654) thus posits that the lack of article with ἐκλεκτῇ κυρίᾳ marks this as "a circular letter meant to be read in several communities."

αὐτῆς. Genitive of relationship.

οὓς. Accusative direct object of ἀγαπῶ. The masculine gender is used with the compound antecedent, ἐκλεκτῇ κυρίᾳ καὶ τοῖς τέκνοις, which has both feminine and neuter elements.

ἐγώ. Although the explicit nominative subject pronoun may appear to provide a springboard for the writer to broaden the referent in what follows (οὐκ ἐγὼ μόνος ἀλλὰ καὶ πάντες), its use in 3 John 1 suggests that it is used to emphasize the writer's love.

ἀγαπῶ. Pres act ind 1st sg ἀγαπάω.

ἐν ἀληθείᾳ. The prepositional phrase could either indicate reference ("with reference to the truth/the Gospel") or manner ("truly").

οὐκ . . . μόνος ἀλλὰ καὶ. "Not only . . . but also . . ."

ἐγώ. Nominative subject of an implied ἀγαπῶ.

ἀλλά. On the semantics, see 1 John 2:2.

πάντες οἱ ἐγνωκότες τὴν ἀλήθειαν. The whole participial construction, headed by the nominative πάντες οἱ ἐγνωκότες, functions as the subject of an implied ἀγαπῶσιν.

οἱ ἐγνωκότες. Prf act ptc masc nom pl γινώσκω (substantival or attributive; see 1 John 2:23 on πᾶς ὁ ἀρνούμενος).

τὴν ἀλήθειαν. Accusative direct object of ἐγνωκότες.

2 διὰ τὴν ἀλήθειαν τὴν μένουσαν ἐν ἡμῖν, καὶ μεθ' ἡμῶν ἔσται εἰς τὸν αἰῶνα.

διὰ τὴν ἀλήθειαν. Causal, introducing the reason why the writer and others love "the elect lady" and her children.

μένουσαν ἐν ἡμῖν. See 1 John 2:6 on ἐν αὐτῷ μένειν.

μένουσαν. Pres act ptc fem acc sg μένω (attributive).

μεθ' ἡμῶν. Association.

ἔσται. Fut ind 3rd sg εἰμί.

εἰς τὸν αἰῶνα. A temporal idiom (see 1 John 1:6 on ἐν τῷ σκότει περιπατῶμεν) denoting "unlimited duration of time, with particular focus upon the future" (LN 67.95).

3 ἔσται μεθ' ἡμῶν χάρις ἔλεος εἰρήνη παρὰ θεοῦ πατρός, καὶ παρὰ Ἰησοῦ Χριστοῦ τοῦ υἱοῦ τοῦ πατρός, ἐν ἀληθείᾳ καὶ ἀγάπῃ.

ἔσται. Fut ind 3rd sg εἰμί.
μεθ' ἡμῶν. Association.
χάρις ἔλεος εἰρήνη. Nominative subject of ἔσται.
παρὰ θεοῦ. Source.
πατρός. Genitive in apposition to θεοῦ.
παρὰ Ἰησοῦ Χριστοῦ. Source.
τοῦ υἱοῦ. Genitive in apposition to Ἰησοῦ Χριστοῦ.
τοῦ πατρός. Genitive of relationship.
ἐν ἀληθείᾳ καὶ ἀγάπῃ. The function of the preposition is difficult to label. It appears to point to the context or circumstances in which grace, mercy, and peace will be experienced: clinging to the truth and loving one another. Brown (660) argues that ἐν ἀληθείᾳ καὶ ἀγάπῃ works together with ἐγὼ ἀγαπῶ ἐν ἀληθείᾳ (v. 1) to form an inclusio (see 1 John 1:6), marking the end of the opening formula.

2 John 4-7
⁴I was overjoyed because I have found some of your children living in the truth, just as we received the command from the Father. ⁵And now, I ask you, Lady, not as one writing a new command to you, but one which we have had from the beginning: let us love one another. ⁶And this is love: that we live in accord with his commands. This is the command—just as you have heard from the beginning—live in (love), ⁷because many deceivers have gone out into the world, who do not confess that Jesus Christ came as a human being. Such a person is a deceiver and an antichrist.

4Ἐχάρην λίαν ὅτι εὕρηκα ἐκ τῶν τέκνων σου περιπατοῦντας ἐν ἀληθείᾳ, καθὼς ἐντολὴν ἐλάβομεν παρὰ τοῦ πατρός.

Ἐχάρην. Aor mid ind 3rd sg χαίρω. The verb χαίρω occurs in the active in the present tense, in the middle in the future tense, and in the "passive" in the aorist tense. Historically, the variation may be accounted for by noting that the volitional nature of the future tense frequently led to the use of middle morphology (Cooper, 594; cited by Conrad, 8, n. 18), while -θη- forms (and the less common -η- forms) were originally aorist *intransitive* markers, which eventually came to be used to identify the aorist middle/passive (Conrad, 5; see also "Deponency" in the Series Introduction).

ὅτι. With the verb χαίρω, the ὅτι can introduce either a causal clause or a clausal complement that provides the content of the rejoicing. Given the tense of this verb and εὕρηκα, the clausal complement analysis is unlikely ("I rejoiced greatly that I have found . . .").

εὕρηκα. Prf act ind 1st sg εὑρίσκω.

ἐκ τῶν τέκνων. Partitive. BDF §164(2) notes that partitive constructions sometimes function (substantivally) as the subject or object of a verb (as here). They also point out that such expressions are rare in classical Greek but common in Semitic languages (cf. John 16:17). Given the use of the participle that follows (see below), it is likely that the writer viewed τινας as implicit. The partitive expression could imply that some among the readers were not walking in the truth and thus serve as a subtle rebuke. Alternatively, the writer may simply be saying that he has found those among the readers' group that he has had contact with to be walking in the truth, without any implications regarding the rest of τῶν τέκνων.

σου. Genitive of relationship.

περιπατοῦντας. Pres act ptc masc acc pl περιπατέω. Accusative complement in an object-complement double accusative construction (see 1 John 1:10 on ψεύστην), in which the direct object (τινας) is unstated (see above on ἐκ τῶν τέκνων).

ἐν ἀληθείᾳ. Manner.

καθὼς. Introduces a comparison.

ἐντολὴν. Accusative direct object of ἐλάβομεν.

ἐλάβομεν. Aor act ind 1st pl λαμβάνω.

παρὰ τοῦ πατρός. Source.

5 καὶ νῦν ἐρωτῶ σε, κυρία, οὐχ ὡς ἐντολὴν καινὴν γράφων σοι ἀλλὰ ἣν εἴχομεν ἀπ' ἀρχῆς, ἵνα ἀγαπῶμεν ἀλλήλους.

2 John 4-5   145

καὶ νῦν. The conjunction and adverb together here point to a transition to the hortatory heart of the letter (cf. Culy and Parsons, 78, on Acts 4:29).

ἐρωτῶ. Pres act ind 1st sg ἐρωτάω.

σε. Accusative direct object of ἐρωτῶ.

κυρία. Vocative (cf. 1 John 2:1 on Τεκνία). On the meaning, see verse 1. Here, the vocative does not occur until the second sentence in the paragraph.

ὡς. Introduces a comparison. Many have taken the comparative clause as a parenthetical comment that precedes a clausal complement (ἵνα ἀγαπῶμεν ἀλλήλους) providing the content of ἐρωτῶ: "And now, I ask you, lady, (not as one writing a new command to you, but one which you have had from the beginning) that we love one another." For the weaknesses of such an analysis, see below.

ἐντολὴν καινὴν. Accusative direct object of γράφων.

γράφων. Pres act ptc masc nom sg γράφω. In comparative constructions such as this, the participle is best viewed as substantival: Lit. "I ask . . . not as one writing a new command. . . ."

σοι. Dative indirect object of γράφων.

ἀλλὰ. On the semantics, see 1 John 2:2. In the following clause, ὡς γράφων ἐντολὴν is left implicit.

ἣν εἴχομεν ἀπ' ἀρχῆς. The headless relative clause (see 1 John 1:1 on Ὅ . . . ὅ) serves as the direct object of an implied γράφων.

ἣν. Accusative direct object of εἴχομεν.

εἴχομεν. Impf act ind 1st pl ἔχω.

ἀπ' ἀρχῆς. Temporal (see 1 John 2:7).

ἵνα. The ἵνα could introduce a clause that is epexegetical to the relative clause: "And now, I urge you, lady, not as one writing a new command to you, but one which we have had from the beginning, *namely, we should love one another.*" This view is supported by the use of the first person ἀγαπῶμεν rather than a second person form, since we would expect, "I ask you that you love one another" (but see the parallel syntax in 1 John 3:11). In this reading, the parenthetical ὡς clause resulted in the writer never syntactically identifying his request, though it is clear in the semantics. Since, however, such a reading leaves ἐρωτῶ without a clause that provides the content of the request (cf. Mark 7:26; Luke 16:27; John 4:47; 17:15; 19:31, 38; 1 Thess 4:1) and requires that ἐρωτῶ be rendered something like "urge," most scholars prefer to

take the ἵνα as introducing the clausal complement of ἐρωτῶ (see,
e.g., Brown, 664).
ἀγαπῶμεν. Pres act subj 1st pl ἀγαπάω. Subjunctive with ἵνα.
ἀλλήλους. Accusative direct object of ἀγαπῶμεν.

**6 καὶ αὕτη ἐστὶν ἡ ἀγάπη, ἵνα περιπατῶμεν κατὰ τὰς ἐντολὰς
αὐτοῦ· αὕτη ἡ ἐντολή ἐστιν, καθὼς ἠκούσατε ἀπ' ἀρχῆς, ἵνα
ἐν αὐτῇ περιπατῆτε.**

καὶ. The sentence-initial καὶ marks thematic continuity (see 1
John 1:2 on καὶ) and introduces a further comment on love.
αὕτη. Predicate nominative. The demonstrative pronoun is cataphoric (see 1 John 1:5 on αὕτη), pointing forward to the ἵνα clause.
ἐστὶν. Pres act ind 3rd sg εἰμί. On the retention of the accent, see
1 John 1:5 on ἐστιν.
ἡ ἀγάπη. Nominative subject (see 1 John 1:5 on αὕτη) of ἐστὶν.
ἵνα. Introduces a clause that is epexegetical to αὕτη (see 1 John
1:5 on ὅτι).
περιπατῶμεν. Pres act subj 1st pl περιπατέω. Subjunctive with
ἵνα.
κατὰ τὰς ἐντολάς. Standard.
αὐτοῦ. Subjective genitive (see 1 John 1:1 on τῆς ζωῆς).
αὕτη. See above.
ἡ ἐντολή. Nominative subject (see 1 John 1:5 on αὕτη) of ἐστιν.
ἐστιν. Pres act ind 3rd sg εἰμί. On the loss of accent, see 1 John
1:5 on ἐστιν.
καθὼς. Introduces a comparison that is parenthetical.
ἠκούσατε. Aor act ind 2nd pl ἀκούω.
ἀπ' ἀρχῆς. Temporal (see 1 John 2:7).
ἵνα. Introduces a clause that is epexegetical to αὕτη (see 1 John
1:5 on ὅτι).
ἐν αὐτῇ περιπατῆτε. The idiom (see 1 John 1:6 on ἐν τῷ σκότει
περιπατῶμεν) here means to live in accordance with the command
to love one another or the truth more broadly (see verse 4). The
most obvious antecedent of αὐτῇ is ἡ ἐντολή. The content of the
command, however, relates to ἀγάπη ("Let us love one another")
and comes under the broad label ἀληθείᾳ, which was used with
περιπατέω in verse 4. Wendland (32–33), may be correct in seeing
intentional ambiguity here (or "semantic density") that encom-
passes all three of these closely related notions.

περιπατῆτε. Pres act subj 2nd pl περιπατέω. Subjunctive with ἵνα.

7 ὅτι πολλοὶ πλάνοι ἐξῆλθον εἰς τὸν κόσμον, οἱ μὴ ὁμολογοῦντες Ἰησοῦν Χριστὸν ἐρχόμενον ἐν σαρκί· οὗτός ἐστιν ὁ πλάνος καὶ ὁ ἀντίχριστος.

ὅτι. Causal, introducing the grounds for the previous exhortation. Wendland (41–42) places a paragraph break between verses 6 and 7, apparently due to the "sudden shift from a positive to a negative tone" at this point (cf. NA²⁷). The use of the ὅτι at the beginning of verse 7, however, argues against such a division (see also 1 John 3:11).

πολλοὶ πλάνοι. Nominative subject of ἐξῆλθον.

ἐξῆλθον. Aor act ind 3rd pl ἐξέρχομαι.

εἰς τὸν κόσμον. Locative.

οἱ μὴ ὁμολογοῦντες Ἰησοῦν Χριστὸν ἐρχόμενον ἐν σαρκί. The language is very similar to 1 John 4:2.

ὁμολογοῦντες. Pres act ptc masc nom pl ὁμολογέω (attributive).

Ἰησοῦν Χριστὸν. Accusative direct object of ὁμολογοῦντες.

ἐρχόμενον. Pres mid ptc masc acc sg ἔρχομαι. On the voice, see 1 John 2:18. Wallace (645–46) lists this passage as an example where "An anarthrous participle in the accusative case, in conjunction with an accusative noun or pronoun, sometimes indicates indirect discourse after a verb of perception or communication." In terms of syntax, however, it is probably more appropriate simply to maintain that the participle functions as the complement in an object-complement double accusative construction (see 1 John 1:10 on ψεύστην; cf. 2:6 on μένειν). Moule (101) simply describes the present participle as equivalent to the perfect participle in 1 John 4:2. Following Porter, however, it is more likely that the different tenses point to different focal semantic elements. Porter (1989, 273–81) argues that the perfect tense serves in part, with transitive verbs, to place the emphasis on the subject rather than the object. With intransitive verbs, as here, it is likely that the perfect focuses more attention on the subject (who came; 1 John 4:2), while the present tense keeps the focus on the action of "coming." This distinction is best captured in English through the use of "has come" and "came" respectively.

ἐν σαρκί. Manner. The term σαρκί is an example of synecdoche (see 1 John 1:1 on αἱ χεῖρες ἡμῶν), meaning "human body."

οὗτός. Nominative subject of ἐστιν (see 1 John 1:5 on αὕτη). The second accent comes from the enclitic ἐστιν (see 1 John 1:5 on ἐστιν). The demonstrative is anaphoric, referring back to πολλοὶ πλάνοι. The use of the singular form serves to narrow the focus to any member of the larger group of πλάνοι.

ἐστιν. Pres act ind 3rd sg εἰμί. On the loss of accent, see 1 John 1:5 on ἐστιν.

ὁ πλάνος καὶ ὁ ἀντίχριστος. Predicate nominative. On the meaning of ἀντίχριστος, see 1 John 2:18.

2 John 8-11

⁸Watch yourselves so that you do not lose what all of us have worked for, but receive (your) full reward. ⁹Everyone who "goes ahead" and does not continue to hold to the teaching of Christ does not have God. The one who continues to hold to the teaching—this one has both the Father and the Son. ¹⁰If anyone comes to you and does not bring this teaching, do not receive him into (your) home and do not greet him. ¹¹For the one who greets him participates in his evil deeds.

8 βλέπετε ἑαυτούς, ἵνα μὴ ἀπολέσητε ἃ εἰργασάμεθα ἀλλὰ μισθὸν πλήρη ἀπολάβητε.

βλέπετε ἑαυτούς. Lit. "Look at yourselves!" The idiom (see 1 John 1:6 on ἐν τῷ σκότει περιπατῶμεν) points to self-vigilance: "to be ready to learn about future dangers or needs, with the implication of preparedness to respond appropriately" (LN 27.58).

βλέπετε. Pres act impv 2nd pl βλέπω. The use of this imperative, along with the two in verse 10 (the only imperatives in the whole letter), mark this paragraph as the "peak" of the letter (see "Genre and Structure" in the Introduction).

ἑαυτούς. Accusative direct object of βλέπετε.

ἵνα. Introduces both negative and positive purpose clauses.

ἀπολέσητε. Aor act subj 2nd pl ἀπόλλυμι. Subjunctive with ἵνα. Although a number of manuscripts (945 1175 1844 *Byz* [K L P] *Lect* slav) use first plural forms of the verbs here (ἀπολέσωμεν . . . ἀπολάβωμεν), the weight of external evidence (ℵ⁽*⁾ A B Ψ 81 322 323 et al.) strongly favors the 2nd plural form found in the UBS⁴. Assuming that εἰργασάμεθα is original, it is easy to see how

scribes could accidentally change the second plural form to first
plural under the influence of εἰργασάμεθα (see also below).
ἃ εἰργασάμεθα. The headless relative clause (see 1 John 1:1 on
Ὅ . . . ὅ) functions as the direct object of ἀπολέσητε.
ἃ. Accusative direct object of εἰργασάμεθα.
εἰργασάμεθα. Aor mid ind 1st pl ἐργάζομαι. The aorist form of
the verb is sometimes spelled with ει as here and sometimes with
η. Miller (429) describes the use of the middle form with this verb
as indicating that "the subject is acting in his own interest." For
more on the voice, see "Deponency" in the Series Introduction.
It is unclear whether the original text read εἰργασάμεθα (B 945
1175 1844 *Byz* [K L P] *Lect* syr^hmg cop^sams geo slav) or εἰργάσασθε
(א A Ψ 33 81 322 323 436 *al* it^ar, l vg syr^ph, h cop^bo, sams arm eth
Irenaeus^lat Isidore Lucifer). The UBS⁴ editorial committee "was
persuaded that the delicate nuance (". . . that you do not destroy
things which we, apostles and teachers, wrought in you") is more
likely to be due to the author than to copyists. On transcriptional
grounds also this reading best explains the origin of the second
person verb, which arose through a levelling process" (Metzger,
652–53). Given the context and the scribal understanding revealed
in the variant reading, the first plural form should likely be viewed
as inclusive ("we including you") rather than exclusive ("we
apostles/leaders").
ἀλλὰ. On the semantics, see 1 John 2:2.
μισθὸν πλήρη. Accusative direct object of ἀπολάβητε.
ἀπολάβητε. Aor act subj 2nd pl ἀπολαμβάνω. Subjunctive
with ἵνα.

**9 πᾶς ὁ προάγων καὶ μὴ μένων ἐν τῇ διδαχῇ τοῦ Χριστοῦ θεὸν
οὐκ ἔχει· ὁ μένων ἐν τῇ διδαχῇ, οὗτος καὶ τὸν πατέρα καὶ τὸν
υἱὸν ἔχει.**

πᾶς ὁ προάγων καὶ μὴ μένων ἐν τῇ διδαχῇ τοῦ Χριστοῦ.
The whole participial construction, headed by the nominative πᾶς
ὁ προάγων καὶ μὴ μένων, functions as the subject of ἔχει. On the
rhetorical force of πᾶς with an articular participle, see 1 John 2:23
on πᾶς.
ὁ προάγων. Pres act ptc masc nom sg προάγω (substantival or
attributive; see 1 John 2:23 on πᾶς ὁ ἀρνούμενος). Here, linked
with μὴ μένων ἐν τῇ διδαχῇ τοῦ Χριστοῦ, the verb carries a

negative connotation of not simply "going ahead" but "going too far." There is thus irony involved. Brown (673) is probably correct in seeing a reference to "progressive" teachings here.

μένων ἐν τῇ διδαχῇ. The use of μένω highlights continuity of state (cf. 1 John 2:10). Used with an inanimate object of the preposition ἐν (τῇ διδαχῇ), the idiom refers to continued adherence to that object.

μένων. Pres act ptc masc nom sg μένω (substantival or attributive; see 1 John 2:23 on πᾶς ὁ ἀρνούμενος).

τοῦ Χριστοῦ. The genitive could be either subjective ("what Christ taught"; so Brooke, 177; Brown, 675; Schnackenburg, 286; Westcott, 230) or objective ("the teaching about Christ"; so Bultmann, 113; Burdick, 427–28; Marshall, 72–73, n. 13; Smalley, 332). Given the fact that the concern is with aspects of Jesus' incarnation, e.g., he "came in the flesh," rather than his own teachings per se, the objective genitive view is more likely, though Wendland (33), may be correct in seeing intentional ambiguity (or "semantic density") here. Such ambiguity would be a literary rather than syntactic category, and should not be confused with the questionable label "plenary genitive" (see, e.g., Wallace, 119–21).

θεὸν. Accusative direct object of ἔχει.

ἔχει. Pres act ind 3rd sg ἔχω.

ὁ μένων ἐν τῇ διδαχῇ. The whole substantival construction serves as the topic (see 1 John 1:1) of what follows and will be picked up with the resumptive demonstrative pronoun οὗτος. On its internal syntax and meaning, see above.

οὗτος. Nominative subject of ἔχει. The antecedent is ὁ μένων ἐν τῇ διδαχῇ.

καὶ ... καὶ. "Both ... and."

τὸν πατέρα καὶ τὸν υἱὸν. Accusative direct object of ἔχει.

ἔχει. Pres act ind 3rd sg ἔχω.

10 εἴ τις ἔρχεται πρὸς ὑμᾶς καὶ ταύτην τὴν διδαχὴν οὐ φέρει, μὴ λαμβάνετε αὐτὸν εἰς οἰκίαν καὶ χαίρειν αὐτῷ μὴ λέγετε·

εἴ. Introduces a first class condition (cf. 1 John 3:13). The accent comes from the enclitic τις (see 1:5 on ἐστιν).

τις. Nominative subject of ἔρχεται.

ἔρχεται. Pres mid ind 3rd sg ἔρχομαι. On the voice, see 1 John 2:18 and "Deponency" in the Series Introduction.

πρὸς ὑμᾶς. Locative.

ταύτην τὴν διδαχὴν. Accusative direct object of φέρει.

φέρει. Pres act ind 3rd sg φέρω.

λαμβάνετε. Pres act impv 2nd pl λαμβάνω (prohibition). On the significance of the imperative, see verse 8 on βλέπετε.

αὐτὸν. Accusative direct object of λαμβάνετε.

εἰς οἰκίαν. Locative. While lexical analysis cannot solve the question of whether the reference is to a personal residence or house church, Brown (676) points out that unambiguous references to house churches elsewhere in the NT always use οἶκος rather than οἰκία.

χαίρειν αὐτῷ μὴ λέγετε. Lit. "Do not say 'Greetings' to him."

χαίρειν. Pres act inf χαίρω. Although this form typically occurs as an infinitive absolute, here the infinitive functions as the syntactic direct object of λέγετε (see also verse 11). The greeting in view could either be connected with inviting someone into one's home ("Hello") or wishing him well when he leaves ("Goodbye," "Farewell"). Brown (676) is probably correct in arguing that "the rhythm of the verse where the two verbs in the protasis (10ab) constitute the one action of coming to teach suggests that the two verbs in the apodosis also constitute the one action of receiving and initial greeting."

αὐτῷ. Dative indirect object of λέγετε.

λέγετε. Pres act impv 2nd pl λέγω (prohibition). The use of μὴ rather than οὐ makes it clear that this form is imperative rather than indicative. On the significance of the imperative, see verse 8 on βλέπετε.

11 ὁ λέγων γὰρ αὐτῷ χαίρειν κοινωνεῖ τοῖς ἔργοις αὐτοῦ τοῖς πονηροῖς.

ὁ λέγων γὰρ αὐτῷ χαίρειν. The whole participial construction, headed by the nominative ὁ λέγων, serves as the subject of κοινωνεῖ. On the rhetorical force of the construction, see 1 John 2:4 on ὁ λέγων.

ὁ λέγων. Pres act ptc masc nom sg λέγω (substantival).

γὰρ. Introduces the grounds for the prohibitions in verse 10 (but see 1 John 2:19 on γὰρ).

αὐτῷ. Dative indirect object of λέγων.

χαίρειν. Pres act inf χαίρω. On the syntax of the infinitive, see verse 10.

κοινωνεῖ. Pres act ind 3rd sg κοινωνέω.

τοῖς ἔργοις ... τοῖς πονηροῖς. Dative complement of κοινωνεῖ. As BDAG (552) notes, "To share, participate in the deeds of others means to be equally responsible for them."

αὐτοῦ. Subjective genitive (see 1 John 1:1 on τῆς ζωῆς).

2 John 12-13

¹²Although I could write much (more) to you, I do not want (to communicate) with paper and ink. Instead, I hope to be with you and speak face to face so that our joy might be full. ¹³The children of your Elect Sister greet you.

12 Πολλὰ ἔχων ὑμῖν γράφειν οὐκ ἐβουλήθην διὰ χάρτου καὶ μέλανος, ἀλλὰ ἐλπίζω γενέσθαι πρὸς ὑμᾶς καὶ στόμα πρὸς στόμα λαλῆσαι, ἵνα ἡ χαρὰ ἡμῶν πεπληρωμένη ᾖ.

Πολλὰ. Accusative direct object of γράφειν (see below).

ἔχων. Pres act ptc masc nom sg ἔχω (concessive).

ὑμῖν. Dative indirect object of γράφειν.

γράφειν. Pres act inf γράφω. Superficially, the expression Πολλὰ ἔχων ὑμῖν γράφειν appears to involve an infinitive (γράφειν) that is epexegetical to the direct object of ἔχων (i.e., Πολλὰ): "I have much, namely, to write to you." The analogous construction in Acts 25:26 is analyzed this way in Culy and Parsons (486). It is preferable, however, to view ἔχω plus an infinitive as a verb phrase that means "be in a position to do something" (see BDAG, 421). The infinitive is thus complementary with Πολλὰ as its direct object.

ἐβουλήθην. Aor mid ind 1st sg βούλομαι. This form is typically parsed "aorist passive deponent" (cf. verse 4 on Ἐχάρην). Given the fact, however, that (1) βούλομαι *only* occurs in middle and passive forms in all tenses; and (2) the -θη- morpheme should likely be viewed as middle/passive rather than simply passive (see Conrad), ἐβουλήθην should probably be treated as a true *middle* (see also "Deponency" in the Series Introduction). Miller (428)

2 John 11-12   153

argues that "some verbs involve the self in the processes going on within the action," and places this verb under the sub-category of "volitional activities."

διὰ χάρτου καὶ μέλανος. Means. An idiom meaning, "by letter" (cf. διὰ μέλανος καὶ καλάμου, 3 John 13).

ἀλλὰ. On the semantics, see 1 John 2:2.

ἐλπίζω. Pres act ind 1st sg ἐλπίζω.

γενέσθαι. Aor mid inf γίνομαι (complementary). The voice should be read as a true middle (see "Deponency" in the Series Introduction). Conrad (17, n. 34) argues that γίνομαι, when used with πρός plus an accusative noun phrase, involves "conscious and deliberate participation of the agent in the movement."

πρὸς ὑμᾶς. Locative.

καὶ. The conjunction links a second complementary infinitival clause to γενέσθαι πρὸς ὑμᾶς.

στόμα πρὸς στόμα. This idiom (lit. "mouth to mouth") denotes "in person."

λαλῆσαι. Aor act inf λαλέω (complementary to ἐλπίζω).

ἵνα ἡ χαρὰ ἡμῶν πεπληρωμένη. The same clause appears in 1 John 1:4, with the participle following the verb ᾖ (but note the textual issue below on ἡμῶν).

ἵνα. Introduces a purpose clause.

ἡ χαρὰ. Nominative subject of ᾖ.

ἡμῶν. Subjective genitive (see 1 John 1:1 on τῆς ζωῆς). As in 1 John 1:4, the textual tradition varies between ἡμῶν and ὑμῶν and the external evidence is not heavily weighted in either direction. Here, the first plural form ἡμῶν occurs in א Ψ 945 1175 1292 1505 1611 1735 1844 1846 1852 2138 *Byz* [K L P] *Lect* vg^mss syr^ph, h arm geo, while the second person form ὑμῶν occurs in A B 33 81 322 323 436 1067 1243 1409 1739 1881 2298 2344 2464 *l* 422 *l* 596 *l* 921 it^ar, l vg cop^bo eth slav. In this case, the first person pronoun fits the context more naturally and scribes may have changed it to second person through either faulty hearing or to harmonize it (probably unintentionally) with what I have argued was likely the original reading for 1 John 1:4 (see that discussion). If the first person pronoun is read, it should be taken as inclusive, referring to both the writer and readers.

πεπληρωμένη. Prf ptc fem nom sg πληρόω (perfect periphrastic;

see 1 John 1:4). The verb could be viewed as either middle or passive voice. Porter (1989, 486) *may* be correct in arguing that "the periphrasis [here] draws attention to the state of completeness of such a joy."

ᾖ. Pres act subj 3rd sg εἰμί. Subjunctive with ἵνα.

13 Ἀσπάζεταί σε τὰ τέκνα τῆς ἀδελφῆς σου τῆς ἐκλεκτῆς.

Ἀσπάζεταί. Pres mid ind 3rd sg ἀσπάζομαι. Neuter plural subjects characteristically take singular verbs (see Wallace, 399–400). The second accent comes from the enclitic σε (see 1 John 1:5 on ἐστιν). The form is typically parsed "middle/passive deponent" but is most likely a true middle (see "Deponency" in the Series Introduction). Miller (427) maintains that verbs that by their nature involve two parties, or a sense of reciprocity, tend to utilize the middle voice. She places this verb under the subcategory of "positive communication."

σε. Accusative direct object of Ἀσπάζεταί.

τὰ τέκνα. Nominative subject of Ἀσπάζεταί.

τῆς ἀδελφῆς. Genitive of relationship.

τῆς ἐκλεκτῆς. On the meaning of this attributive modifier of τῆς ἀδελφῆς, see verse 1.

σου. Genitive of relationship. Although many manuscripts add ἀμήν (945 1175 1292 1505 1611 1844 1852 2138 *Byz* [K L] *Lect* vg^mss slav), it is not found in an impressive set of witnesses (ℵ A B P Ψ 33 81 322 323 1243 1409 1735 1739 1846 1881 2298 2344 2464 it^ar, l vg cop^sa, bo geo) and it reflects a common liturgical addition (Metzger, 654).

3 JOHN

3 John 1-4

[1]The Elder, to (my) dear friend Gaius, whom I truly love.
[2]Dear friend, I hope that all is well with you and that you are in good health, just as it is well with your soul. [3]For I was overjoyed when the brothers and sisters came and confirmed your (message of) truth, even as you are living in the truth. [4]I have no greater joy than this: I hear that my children are living in the truth.

1 Ὁ πρεσβύτερος Γαΐῳ τῷ ἀγαπητῷ, ὃν ἐγὼ ἀγαπῶ ἐν ἀληθείᾳ.

Ὁ πρεσβύτερος. On the use of the nominative absolute and meaning of πρεσβύτερος, see 2 John 1.

Γαΐῳ τῷ ἀγαπητῷ. Dative of recipient. On the diaeresis over the *iota*, see 1 John 3:12 on Κάϊν.

ὅν. Accusative direct object of ἀγαπῶ.

ἐγώ. Nominative subject of ἀγαπῶ. The explicit subject pronoun probably emphasizes the writer's love rather than being merely stylistic.

ἀγαπῶ. Pres act ind 1st sg ἀγαπάω.

ἐν ἀληθείᾳ. The prepositional phrase could either indicate reference ("with reference to the truth/the Gospel") or manner ("truly").

2 Ἀγαπητέ, περὶ πάντων εὔχομαί σε εὐοδοῦσθαι καὶ ὑγιαίνειν, καθὼς εὐοδοῦταί σου ἡ ψυχή.

Ἀγαπητέ. On the meaning, see 1 John 2:7. As in 1 John (see 1 John 2:1 on Τεκνία), the use of the vocative in 3 John tends to mark, or at least occur, at the beginning of a new paragraph (so Floor, 6; see also "Genre and Structure" in the Introduction).

περὶ πάντων. Reference. BDF §229(2) argues that the phrase is synonymous with πρὸ μὲν πάντων ("above all"), an expression that frequently appears in the salutation of letters in the papyri (cf. Moule, 63). Such a sense, however, is otherwise unattested for περὶ πάντων. The prepositional phrase most likely modifies εὐοδοῦσθαι and has been fronted (see 1:5 on σκοτία) for emphasis.

εὔχομαί. Pres mid ind 1st sg εὔμοχαι. The second accent comes from the enclitic σε (see 1 John 1:5 on ἐστιν). Kemmer labels the use of the middle form with this verb as an "indirect middle, self-benefactive," i.e., the subject of the verb acts for himself or in his own interest (see Conrad, 9). For more on the voice, see "Deponency" in the Series Introduction. Louw and Nida argue that this term may either denote "to speak to or to make requests of God" (33.178) or "to desire something, with the implication of a pious wish" (25.6), but they list Romans 9:3 as the only probable example of the latter usage. BDAG (417) cites the same two senses of the verb and lists Acts 27:29 and the present passage as examples of the meaning "wish." Brown (703) argues that "The use of the verb in secular letters as a polite wish for good health means that receivers of a NT letter would interpret it the same way unless there was a contextual indication of more profound intent, and that is lacking here." Indeed, while in none of the cases where εὔχομαι supposedly denotes "wish" can the notion of prayer be ruled out (cf. Culy and Parsons, 523), the use of εὔχομαι with εὐοδοῦσθαι and ὑγιαίνειν does suggest that the conventional expression of desire for the well being of the recipient is in view.

σε. The accusative pronoun is an example of what has traditionally been called either the "accusative subject of the infinitive" or the "accusative of general reference." Neither label is fully satisfactory. The former has in its favor the fact that the accusative noun is the conceptual "subject" of the infinitive verb. The latter has in its favor the fact that, strictly speaking, only finite verbs can take a subject. Some linguists have argued that in infinitive constructions that are not part of a prepositional phrase "raising" has occurred. The noun that we expect to be the subject of the infinitive has been raised from the infinitive (or lower/subordinate) clause to the main (or upper) clause where it functions syntactically as the direct object of the verb. It is, therefore, placed in the accusative case. While such an analysis may account for most infinitival constructions, it cannot explain the accusative case marking where the infinitive clause is part of a prepositional phrase, such as ἐν τῷ σπείρειν αὐτὸν (Matt 13:4). It cannot be said that the "subject of the infinitive" takes its case from the preposition since it always bears accusative case even when used with a preposition that takes a noun in a different case. We have thus retained the label "accusative subject of the infinitive," since conceptual subjects of infinitives always bear accusative case marking.

εὐοδοῦσθαι. Pres mid inf εὐοδόω (complementary or "indirect discourse," depending on whether the main verb means "wish" or "pray"). Louw and Nida (22.47) provide the following definition: "to experience and enjoy favorable circumstances." This definition suggests that the form should be viewed as middle (intransitive) rather than passive (contra BDAG, 410).

ὑγιαίνειν. Pres act inf ὑγιαίνω (complementary or "indirect discourse," depending on whether the main verb means "wish" or "pray").

καθώς. Introduces a comparison.

εὐοδοῦταί. Pres mid ind 3rd sg εὐοδόω. On the meaning and voice, see above. The second accent comes from the enclitic σου (see 1 John 1:5 on ἐστιν).

σου. Genitive of possession.

ἡ ψυχή. Nominative subject of εὐοδοῦσθαι. The use of this term as part of a comparison set against περὶ πάντων . . . σε εὐοδοῦσθαι καὶ ὑγιαίνειν points to a wish for well-being and health to extend beyond the spiritual (εὐοδοῦταί σου ἡ ψυχή) to encompass all areas of life (περὶ πάντων). The expression σου ἡ ψυχή should thus be viewed as a metonymy (see 1 John 2:2 on τοῦ κόσμου) for "your spiritual life."

3 ἐχάρην γὰρ λίαν ἐρχομένων ἀδελφῶν καὶ μαρτυρούντων σου τῇ ἀληθείᾳ, καθὼς σὺ ἐν ἀληθείᾳ περιπατεῖς.

ἐχάρην. Aor mid ind 3rd sg χαίρω. On the voice, see 2 John 4 and "Deponency" in the Series Introduction.

γάρ. Introduces a reason for the previous statement, εὐοδοῦταί σου ἡ ψυχή (but see 1 John 2:19 on γάρ).

ἐρχομένων. Pres mid ptc masc gen pl ἔρχομαι. On the voice, see 1 John 2:18 and "Deponency" in the Series Introduction. Genitive absolute, temporal. The genitive absolute is used when the subject of the participle (which must also be in the genitive case) is different from the subject of the main clause (see Healey and Healey). Although genitive absolute constructions typically occur prior to the finite clause they modify, here the genitive absolute follows the finite clause. Although the syntax certainly allows for a reference to multiple arrivals, an examination of the use of this verb as a present participle in the NT should quickly dispel the notion that the present tense "almost precludes the reference of the words to a single occasion" (contra Brooke, 183; cf. Smalley 347, Westcott, 236).

ἀδελφῶν. Genitive subject (see above on ἐρχομένων). On the meaning, see 1 John 2:9.

μαρτυρούντων. Pres act ptc masc gen pl μαρτυρέω. Genitive absolute, temporal (see above on ἐρχομένων).

σου τῇ ἀληθείᾳ. It is difficult to determine how these words relate to μαρτυρούντων and each other. Testifying "about" something requires the use of the preposition περί rather than the simple genitive of reference (see, e.g., 1 John 5:9, 10; John 1:7, 8, 15; 2:25; 5:32, 36, 37, 39; 7:7). This, along with the parallel expression in verse 6, where σου clearly modifies τῇ ἀγάπῃ rather than ἐμαρτύρησάν, suggests that the pronoun modifies τῇ ἀληθείᾳ rather than μαρτυρούντων. When μαρτυρέω is modified by a dative noun phrase (dative of advantage), it often carries the sense of providing confirming or affirming testimony (cf. LN 33.263—"to speak well of, to approve of"). The sense here would then be that other believers have come to the writer and confirmed/affirmed the truth/message that Gaius was proclaiming (but see below on καθώς). For other examples of this construction, see, e.g., Luke 4:22; Acts 14:3 (variant); 15:8; 22:5; Romans 10:2; Galatians 4:15; and Colossians 4:13.

σου. Subjective genitive ("you are truthful" or "you speak the truth"; see also 1 John 1:1 on τῆς ζωῆς).

τῇ ἀληθείᾳ. Dative of advantage (see above; see also verse 12 on μεμαρτύρηται).

καθώς. The conjunction could either introduce a comparison or indirect discourse ("indicating how something took place"; see LN 89.86). The latter would be awkward given the fact that μαρτυρούντων is already modified by σου τῇ ἀληθείᾳ. A comparative use of καθώς, on the other hand, would yield a structure parallel to the previous verse. If σου τῇ ἀληθείᾳ refers to the nature of Gaius' message (see above), then a clause comparing the nature of his conduct would be quite natural.

σύ. Nominative subject of περιπατεῖς.

ἐν ἀληθείᾳ. Manner. Used with περιπατέω, the prepositional phrase points to conduct that is consistent with the Gospel.

περιπατεῖς. Pres act ind 2nd sg περιπατέω.

4 μειζοτέραν τούτων οὐκ ἔχω χαράν, ἵνα ἀκούω τὰ ἐμὰ τέκνα ἐν τῇ ἀληθείᾳ περιπατοῦντα.

μειζοτέραν. Attributive modifier of χαράν. The fronting of this element and consequent splitting of the noun phrase, μειζοτέραν χαράν, lend prominence to the mitigated exhortation that follows (Floor, 14; cf. BDF §473).

τούτων. Genitive of comparison. The use of the plural may suggest at first glance that the pronoun is anaphoric and refers to multiple reports of Gaius' piety. The fact that the demonstrative is followed by a ἵνα clause, however, suggests that the demonstrative is cataphoric (see 1 John 1:5 on αὕτη). The use of the plural form may simply be idiomatic (cf. John 1:50; Wallace, 332–33).

ἔχω. Pres act ind 1st sg ἔχω.

χαράν. Accusative direct object of ἔχω. Although some manuscripts read χάριν (B 1243 1844 2298 it^{ar*, 1} vg cop^{bo} Hilary), the external evidence strongly favors χαράν (א A Ψ K L P et al.).

ἵνα. Introduces a clause that is epexegetical to τούτων, and serves as a mitigated exhortation: "Continue to give me joy by walking in the truth" (Floor, 9; see also "Mitigated Exhortations" in the Introduction).

ἀκούω. Pres act subj 1st sg ἀκούω. Subjunctive with ἵνα.

τὰ ἐμὰ τέκνα. Accusative direct object of ἀκούω. The expression is used figuratively of those under the spiritual care of the elder and/or those who converted through his ministry.

ἐν τῇ ἀληθείᾳ. On the meaning, see verse 3. There is no apparent distinction between ἐν τῇ ἀληθείᾳ and ἐν ἀληθείᾳ. John freely shifts from ἐν τῇ ἀληθείᾳ in John 17:17 to ἐν ἀληθείᾳ in the analogous context of John 17:19, and many scribes (א C² P Ψ Byz) apparently omitted the article here with no change in meaning (for a fuller discussion of the variation between articular and anarthrous forms, see Moule, 112).

περιπατοῦντα. Pres act ptc neut acc pl περιπατέω. Accusative complement in an object-complement double accusative construction (see 1 John 1:10 on ψεύστην; see also 2 John 7 on ἐρχόμενον).

3 John 5-8

⁵Dear friend, you act faithfully in whatever you have done for the brothers and sisters, and (you do) this (for) strangers, ⁶who have confirmed your love before the church, (and) whom you will do well to send on in a manner worthy of God. ⁷For they went out on behalf of the Name, not taking anything from the Gentiles. ⁸Therefore, we ought to support such people as these, in order that we might become fellow-workers (with them) in (the spreading of) the truth.

5 Ἀγαπητέ, πιστὸν ποιεῖς ὃ ἐὰν ἐργάσῃ εἰς τοὺς ἀδελφοὺς καὶ τοῦτο ξένους,

Ἀγαπητέ. On the meaning, see 1 John 2:7. As in 1 John (see 1 John 2:1 on Τεκνία), the use of the vocative in 3 John tends to mark, or at least occur, at the beginning of a new paragraph (so Floor, 6; see also "Genre and Structure" in the Introduction). Here, the new paragraph is also signaled by the fact that verse 4 serves as a summary statement of the previous paragraph.

πιστὸν. The neuter singular form of an adjective is frequently used to form an adverb, as here (cf. Robertson, 294–95).

ποιεῖς. Pres act ind 2nd sg ποιέω.

ὃ ἐὰν ἐργάσῃ εἰς τοὺς ἀδελφοὺς. The headless relative clause (see 1 John 1:1 on Ὅ . . . ὅ) serves as the direct object of ποιεῖς.

ὃ ἐὰν. The indefinite relative pronoun (see 1 John 2:5 on ὅς . . . ἄν) serves as the accusative direct object of ἐργάσῃ.

ἐργάσῃ. Aor mid subj 2nd sg ἐργάζομαι. Subjunctive with ἐάν. Miller (429) describes the use of the middle form with this verb as indicating that "the subject is acting in his own interest." For more on the voice, see "Deponency" in the Series Introduction.

εἰς τοὺς ἀδελφοὺς. Advantage.

καὶ τοῦτο ξένους. In this highly elliptical construction, the accusative singular τοῦτο serves as the direct object of an implied ἐργάσῃ or ποιεῖς and the accusative plural ξένους serves as the accusative object of an implied εἰς (denoting advantage): καὶ ἐργάσῃ τοῦτο εἰς ξένους (cf. P *Byz*, which read εἰς τοὺς ξένους).

6 οἳ ἐμαρτύρησάν σου τῇ ἀγάπῃ ἐνώπιον ἐκκλησίας, οὓς καλῶς ποιήσεις προπέμψας ἀξίως τοῦ θεοῦ·

οἵ. Nominative subject of ἐμαρτύρησάν. The antecedent is τοὺς ἀδελφοὺς/ξένους.

ἐμαρτύρησάν. Aor act ind 3rd pl μαρτυρέω. The second accent comes from the enclitic σου (see 1 John 1:5 on ἐστιν). On the meaning of the verb with a dative complement, see verse 3 on σου τῇ ἀληθείᾳ.

σου. Subjective genitive (see 1 John 1:1 on τῆς ζωῆς).

τῇ ἀγάπῃ. Dative complement of ἐμαρτύρησάν.

ἐνώπιον ἐκκλησίας. Locative.

οὓς. Accusative direct object of προπέμψας.

καλῶς ποιήσεις. Rhetorically, this expression introduces a mitigated exhortation: "Help the brothers on their journey" (see "Mitigated Exhortations" in the Introduction). The fact that it occurs within a relative clause—a rhetorical device that marks foregrounding or thematic material (see Larson, 413)—adds further prominence to the implied exhortation (see Floor, 9, 14).

ποιήσεις. Fut act ind 2nd sg ποιέω.

προπέμψας. Aor act ptc masc nom sg προπέμψας (means). The verb means "to send someone on in the direction in which he has already been moving, with the probable implication of providing help" (LN 15.72).

τοῦ θεοῦ. Genitive complement of ἀξίως.

7 ὑπὲρ γὰρ τοῦ ὀνόματος ἐξῆλθον μηδὲν λαμβάνοντες ἀπὸ τῶν ἐθνικῶν.

ὑπὲρ γὰρ τοῦ ὀνόματος. Representation/advantage.

γὰρ. Introduces the grounds for the request that Gaius send them on their way in an appropriate manner (but see 1 John 2:19 on γὰρ).

τοῦ ὀνόματος. Metonymy (see 1 John 2:2 on τοῦ κόσμου) for "God" or "Jesus Christ."

ἐξῆλθον. Aor act ind 3rd pl ἐξέρχομαι. The implied starting point from which they "went out" is probably the church.

μηδὲν. Accusative direct object of λαμβάνοντες. When used with a non-indicative verb, Greek writers characteristically chose μηδείς rather than οὐδείς.

λαμβάνοντες. Pres act ptc masc nom pl λαμβάνω (manner).

ἀπὸ τῶν ἐθνικῶν. Source.

8 ἡμεῖς οὖν ὀφείλομεν ὑπολαμβάνειν τοὺς τοιούτους, ἵνα συνεργοὶ γινώμεθα τῇ ἀληθείᾳ.

ἡμεῖς. The explicit subject pronoun shifts the focus from τοὺς ἀδελφοὺς (v. 5) to the elder and his readers.

ὀφείλομεν. Pres act ind 1st pl ὀφείλω. On the semantics and rhetorical significance of this verb, see 1 John 2:6 on ὀφείλει.

ὑπολαμβάνειν. Pres act inf ὑπολαμβάνω (complementary). Here, "to assist in supplying what may be needed" (LN 35.1).

τοὺς τοιούτους. Accusative direct object of ὑπολαμβάνειν.

ἵνα. Introduces a purpose clause.

συνεργοὶ. Predicate nominative.

γινώμεθα. Pres mid subj 1st pl γίνομαι. Subjunctive with ἵνα. On the middle voice, see 2 John 12 and "Deponency" in the Series Introduction.

τῇ ἀληθείᾳ. The dative noun phrase could either be (1) a complement of a συν- word (thus, "fellow-workers with the truth"), or (2) dative of reference, with the complement of συνεργοί being an implied αὐτοῖς (thus, "fellow-workers with them in the truth"). The term ἀληθείᾳ is likely another word for the "true message" or "Gospel." The fact that (a) συνεργοί more naturally would take a personal complement; (b) "Neither the LXX nor the New Testament uses the dative with this noun, which normally governs the genitive or *eis* with the accusative" (Brown, 714); and (c) συνεργοί is not contiguous with τῇ ἀληθείᾳ makes the second interpretation slightly more likely (for a defense of the alternative view, see Brown, 714). The ambiguity, which led to the potential dissonance of the notion "fellow-workers with the truth," probably led two early scribes (א* A) to substitute τῇ ἐκκλησίᾳ.

3 John 9-12

⁹I wrote something to the church, but that one who loves to be first among them, Diotrephes, does not pay attention to us. ¹⁰For this reason, if I come, I will bring up his works, which he is doing by disparaging us with wicked words. And since he is not satisfied with that, he also does not welcome the brothers and sisters. Indeed, he hinders those who want to (welcome them) and throws them out of the church. ¹¹Dear friend, do not imitate (such) bad behavior but (imitate) good behavior. The one who does good belongs to God. The one who does

evil has not seen God. ¹²Demetrius has been affirmed by everyone and by the truth itself. And we also affirm (him), and you know that our testimony is true.

9 Ἔγραψά τι τῇ ἐκκλησίᾳ· ἀλλ' ὁ φιλοπρωτεύων αὐτῶν Διοτρέφης οὐκ ἐπιδέχεται ἡμᾶς.

Ἔγραψά τι. There is a great deal of textual variation here. The UBS⁴ reading is supported by ℵ* A et al.; Codex B reads Ἔγραψάς τι (so also copˢᵃ, ᵇᵒ); the second corrector of ℵ reads Ἔγραψα ἄν (so also 33 et al.); a number of witnesses (C Ψ *Byz* et al.) simply read Ἔγραψα; and a few late manuscripts read Ἔγραψα ἄν τι, with one reading Ἔγραψα αὐτῇ. As Metzger notes (655), the UBS⁴ text is the reading that best explains the origin of the other readings, though it is appropriately given a "B" or "C" (UBS³) rating. The reading of Codex B is probably simply a scribal error. Although Metzger (655) claims that the reading Ἔγραψα was intended to avoid undue deprecation of apostolic authority, it is unclear how this reading would accomplish this. Some of the variants likely arose from the fact that the connection between the first clause and the ἀλλ' clause is not readily apparent in the UBS⁴ reading. Certain information has been left implicit, i.e., the Elder expected the letter to be recognized as authoritative by the recipients, making this conceptually a difficult reading. This led some scribes to alter the text so that the Elder claimed a desire to write but was deterred by Diotrophes' opposition: "I would have written [something] to the church . . ." (Ἔγραψα ἄν [τι]).

Ἔγραψά. Aor act ind 1st sg γράφω. The second accent comes from the enclitic τι (see 1 John 1:5 on ἐστιν). In this case, the new paragraph is introduced by a shift in topic introduced by Ἔγραψά τι (cf. 1 John 5:13) and by the fact that verse 8 serves as a summary statement of the previous paragraph.

τι. Accusative direct object of τι.

τῇ ἐκκλησίᾳ. Dative indirect object of Ἔγραψά.

ἀλλ'. The conjunction introduces a proposition that runs contrary to the implied expectation that the letter would be recognized as authoritative. For more on the semantics of ἀλλά, see 1 John 2:2.

ὁ φιλοπρωτεύων. Pres act ptc masc nom sg φιλοπρωτεύω (substantival). Nominative subject of ἐπιδέχεται. The verb, which occurs only here in the NT and only rarely elsewhere, means, "to like or love to be first in rank or position" (LN 25.110).

αὐτῶν. Genitive of subordination.

Διοτρέφης. Nominative in apposition to ὁ φιλοπρωτεύων.

ἐπιδέχεται. Pres mid ind 3rd sg ἐπιδέχομαι. The verb, which occurs only here and in verse 10 in the NT, could simply mean, "welcome" or "receive," as Mitchell strongly argues. Given the context, however, the "reception" appears to relate more to being confronted with what was written in a letter than a personal encounter with a visitor, suggesting a sense like, "to listen or pay attention to a person, with resulting conformity to what is advised or commanded" (LN 36.14).

ἡμᾶς. Accusative direct object of ἐπιδέχεται.

10 διὰ τοῦτο, ἐὰν ἔλθω, ὑπομνήσω αὐτοῦ τὰ ἔργα ἃ ποιεῖ, λόγοις πονηροῖς φλυαρῶν ἡμᾶς· καὶ μὴ ἀρκούμενος ἐπὶ τούτοις οὔτε αὐτὸς ἐπιδέχεται τοὺς ἀδελφοὺς καὶ τοὺς βουλομένους κωλύει καὶ ἐκ τῆς ἐκκλησίας ἐκβάλλει.

διὰ τοῦτο. Causal. The demonstrative pronoun is anaphoric (contrast 1 John 3:1), pointing back to the proposition Διοτρέφης οὐκ ἐπιδέχεται ἡμᾶς as the reason for the following result.

ἐὰν. Introduces the protasis of a third class condition (see 1 John 1:6 on Ἐὰν). The conditional construction should probably be taken as indicating genuine doubt regarding whether or not the writer will be able to come (cf. v. 14: ἐλπίζω δὲ εὐθέως σε ἰδεῖν).

ἔλθω. Aor act subj 1st sg ἔρχομαι. Subjunctive with ἐάν.

ὑπομνήσω. Fut act ind 1st sg ὑπομιμνήσκω. Here, the sense is "call to mind, bring up" (BDAG, 1039).

αὐτοῦ. Subjective genitive (see 1 John 1:1 on τῆς ζωῆς).

τὰ ἔργα. Accusative direct object of ὑπομνήσω.

ἃ. Accusative direct object of ποιεῖ.

ποιεῖ. Pres act ind 3rd sg ποιέω.

λόγοις πονηροῖς. Dative of instrument.

φλυαρῶν. Pres act ptc masc nom sg φλυαρέω (means). The verb, which occurs only here in the NT, means, "to indulge in utterance that makes no sense, *talk nonsense (about), disparage*" (BDAG, 1060). BDAG goes on to note that the expression φλυαρῶν ἡμᾶς may be captured in modern English through the rendering, "bad-mouthing us."

ἡμᾶς. Accusative direct object of φλυαρῶν.

ἀρκούμενος. Pres ptc masc nom sg ἀρκέω (causal). The voice should probably be viewed as middle rather than passive (contra BDAG, 132).

ἐπὶ τούτοις. The thing with which the person is satisfied is typically placed in the dative case. This is the only use of ἀρκέω with ἐπί in the NT and the construction is rare elsewhere. It may be a stylistic variant for the simple dative (cf. BDAG, 132), or ἐπί may carry a causal nuance ("a marker of cause or reason as the basis for a subsequent event or state"; LN 89.27).

αὐτός. Nominative subject of ἐπιδέχεται. The explicit subject pronoun focuses attention on Diotrephes and his behavior.

ἐπιδέχεται. Pres mid ind 3rd sg ἐπιδέχομαι. On the voice and meaning, see verse 9.

τοὺς ἀδελφούς. Accusative direct object of ἐπιδέχεται.

τοὺς βουλομένους. Pres mid ptc masc acc pl βούλομαι (substantival). Accusative direct object of κωλύει. On the middle voice, see 2 John 12 and "Deponency" in the Series Introduction. The complementary infinitival clause modifying βουλομένους is left implicit: ἐπιδέξασθαι αὐτούς ("to welcome them").

κωλύει. Pres act ind 3rd sg κωλύω.

ἐκ τῆς ἐκκλησίας. Separation.

ἐκβάλλει. Pres act ind 3rd sg ἐκβάλλω. In Greek, whether or not one is successful in his or her efforts to do something generally must be determined by the context. Where the action is unsuccessful, scholars typically label the verb tense "conative" (but see "Verbal Aspect and Prominence" in the Introduction) and render the expression, "X tried to Y." Here, the context does not tell us whether or not Diotrephes was successful in expelling such hospitable members of the congregation. Given the lack of contextual markers, we should probably read ἐκβάλλει as what he actually accomplished.

11 Ἀγαπητέ, μὴ μιμοῦ τὸ κακὸν ἀλλὰ τὸ ἀγαθόν. ὁ ἀγαθοποιῶν ἐκ τοῦ θεοῦ ἐστιν· ὁ κακοποιῶν οὐχ ἑώρακεν τὸν θεόν.

Ἀγαπητέ. As in 1 John (see 1 John 2:1 on Τεκνία), the use of the vocative in 3 John tends to mark, or at least occur, at the beginning of a new paragraph (so Floor, 6; see also "Genre and Structure" in the Introduction). While such a boundary may be made more likely by the use of the imperative mood (μιμοῦ), the referential link between verse 11 and verses 9-10 should not be overlooked.

μιμοῦ. Pres mid impv 2nd sg μιμέομαι. Miller (427) classifies this as a reflexive verb with the underlying semantics, "to pattern oneself after." This first and only imperative verb in the body of the letter marks the "peak" of the letter (Floor, 16).

τὸ κακὸν. Accusative direct object of μιμοῦ. The referent is likely the wicked actions of Diotrephes.

ἀλλὰ. On the semantics, see 1 John 2:2.

τὸ ἀγαθόν. Accusative direct object of an implied μιμοῦ. The referent is likely the godly actions of those who sought to welcome the visiting brothers.

ὁ ἀγαθοποιῶν. Pres act ptc masc nom sg ἀγαθοποιέω (substantival). Nominative subject of ἐστιν.

ἐκ τοῦ θεοῦ ἐστιν. On the meaning of this expression, see 1 John 3:10 on ἔστιν ἐκ τοῦ θεοῦ.

ἐστιν. Pres act ind 3rd sg εἰμί. On the loss of accent, see 1 John 1:5 on ἐστιν.

ὁ κακοποιῶν. Pres act ptc masc nom sg κακοποιέω (substantival). Nominative subject of ἑώρακεν.

ἑώρακεν. Prf act ind 3rd sg ὁράω. On the meaning, see 1 John 3:6.

τὸν θεόν. Accusative direct object of ἑώρακεν.

12 Δημητρίῳ μεμαρτύρηται ὑπὸ πάντων καὶ ὑπὸ αὐτῆς τῆς ἀληθείας· καὶ ἡμεῖς δὲ μαρτυροῦμεν, καὶ οἶδας ὅτι ἡ μαρτυρία ἡμῶν ἀληθής ἐστιν.

Δημητρίῳ. Dative of advantage (see note on μεμαρτύρηται) or perhaps dative of reference.

μεμαρτύρηται. Prf pass ind 3rd sg μαρτυρέω. When μαρτυρέω is modified by a dative noun phrase, it often carries the sense of providing confirming or affirming testimony (cf. LN 33.263—"to speak well of, to approve of"; see also verse 3 on σου τῇ ἀληθείᾳ). The construction here, μαρτυρέω with a dative modifier, can be confusing, since the verb is passive and its syntactic subject is unclear. With an active form of μαρτυρέω, someone (nominative case) affirms something (the unstated direct object of the verb) for someone else (dative case). When the verb is passivized, the one doing the affirming is introduced by ὑπό, and the one being affirmed remains in the dative case. The unstated content of the affirmation becomes the subject of the passive verb. Thus, "Everyone affirms (something) for Demetrius" becomes literally, "It is affirmed by everyone for Demetrius."

ὑπὸ πάντων. Ultimate agent.

ὑπὸ αὐτῆς τῆς ἀληθείας. Ultimate agent.

ἡμεῖς. Nominative subject of μαρτυροῦμεν. The explicit subject pronoun shifts the focus to the writer's testimony.

μαρτυροῦμεν. Pres act ind 1st pl μαρτυρέω.

οἶδας. Prf act ind 2nd sg οἶδα.

ὅτι. Introduces the clausal complement of οἶδας (see also 1 John 2:3 on ὅτι).

ἡ μαρτυρία. Nominative subject of ἐστιν.

ἡμῶν. Subjective genitive (see 1:1 on τῆς ζωῆς).

ἀληθής. Predicate adjective.

ἐστιν. Pres act ind 3rd sg εἰμί. On the loss of accent, see 1 John 1:5 on ἐστιν.

3 John 13-15

¹³I could have written much (more) to you, but I do not want to communicate with you using pen and ink. ¹⁴I hope to see you very soon, and we will speak face to face (then). ¹⁵Peace to you. The friends (here) greet you. Greet the friends (there) by name.

13 Πολλὰ εἶχον γράψαι σοι, ἀλλ᾽ οὐ θέλω διὰ μέλανος καὶ καλάμου σοι γράφειν·

Πολλά. Accusative direct object of γράψαι (see 2 John 12).

εἶχον. Impf act ind 1st sg ἔχω.

γράψαι. Aor act inf γράφω (complementary; see 2 John 12).

σοι. Dative indirect object of γράψαι.

ἀλλ᾽. On the semantics, see 1 John 2:2.

θέλω. Pres act ind 1st sg θέλω.

διὰ μέλανος καὶ καλάμου. Means. Another idiom meaning, "by letter" (cf. διὰ χάρτου καὶ μέλανος, 2 John 12).

σοι. Dative indirect object of γράφειν.

γράφειν. Pres act inf γράφω (complementary).

**14 ἐλπίζω δὲ εὐθέως σε ἰδεῖν, καὶ στόμα πρὸς στόμα
λαλήσομεν.**

ἐλπίζω. Pres act ind 1st sg ἐλπίζω.

σε. Accusative direct object of ἰδεῖν.

ἰδεῖν. Aor act inf ὁράω/εἶδον (complementary).

στόμα πρὸς στόμα. This idiom (lit. "mouth to mouth") denotes
"in person."

λαλήσομεν. Fut act ind 1st pl λαλέω.

**15 εἰρήνη σοι. ἀσπάζονταί σε οἱ φίλοι. ἀσπάζου τοὺς φίλους
κατ᾽ ὄνομα.**

εἰρήνη. Nominative absolute (see 2 John 1 on πρεσβύτερος).

σοι. The dative element is used to mark the recipient of the
wish prayer. It could be viewed as dative of advantage ("Peace
[*is wished*] for you") or dative indirect object ("[May] peace [be
given] to you").

ἀσπάζονταί. Pres mid ind 3rd pl ἀσπάζομαι. The second accent
comes from the enclitic σε (see 1 John 1:5 on ἐστιν). On the voice,
see 2 John 13 on Ἀσπάζεταί.

σε. Accusative direct object of ἀσπάζονταί.

οἱ φίλοι. Nominative subject of ἀσπάζονταί. The use of this
term, rather than οἱ ἀδελφοί, may highlight a strong personal
affinity, which goes beyond simple brotherhood in Christ, between
those in the Elder's church and the group to which he is writing.
The following use (τοὺς φίλους) may also serve as a means of dis-
tinguishing supporters of Diotrephes from supporters of the Elder.

ἀσπάζου. Pres mid impv 2nd sg ἀσπάζομαι. On the voice, see 2
John 13 on Ἀσπάζεταί.

τοὺς φίλους. Accusative direct object of ἀσπάζου (see also
above).

κατ᾽ ὄνομα. The expression, generally rendered "by name,"
probably reflects the distributive use of κατά with the accusative:
lit. "name by name." The focus would then be on greeting each and
every one of them individually, rather than as a group.

GLOSSARY

Adjectivizer – In Greek syntax, this term refers to an article that is used to change a non-adjective into an adjectival modifier. Thus, in the phrase, ἀπὸ παντὸς ἔθνους τῶν ὑπὸ τὸν οὐρανόν, the article τῶν changes the prepositional phrase, ὑπὸ τὸν οὐρανόν, into an attributive modifier of παντὸς ἔθνους.

Anaphoric – Referring back to, i.e., coreferential with, a preceding word or group of words. Thus, pronouns are anaphoric references to participants that have already been introduced into the discourse.

Anarthrous – Lacking an article.

Antecedent – An element that is referred to by another expression that follows it. Thus, the antecedent of a relative pronoun is that element in the preceding context to which the relative clause provides additional information.

Apodosis – The second part ("then" clause) in a conditional construction.

Arthrous/Articular – Including an article.

Aspect – This term is used in relation to verb tense and refers to the writer's/speaker's subjective choice of how to portray the verbal action, e.g., perfective or imperfective.

Attraction – Relative pronouns at times take on or "attract" to the case of their antecedent. For example, in the text, Πάντων δὲ θαυμαζόντων ἐπὶ πᾶσιν οἷς ἐποίει εἶπεν πρὸς τοὺς μαθητὰς αὐτοῦ ("While everyone was marveling at all that he was doing, he said to his disciples"), the expected case for the relative pronoun would be accusative (οὕς), since it functions as the direct object of ἐποίει. Instead, it has been attracted to the case of its antecedent (πᾶσιν).

Background – This term is used to refer to information that is off the event line, or storyline, i.e., those events or material that do not move the narrative forward. Instead, background information comments on, amplifies, or otherwise supports the narration.

Cataphoric – Referring forward to, i.e., coreferential with, a following word or group of words. The demonstrative οὗτος is frequently used in this manner.

Clausal complement – This type of complement is structurally a direct object, but since it is a clause rather than a noun phrase scholars often use the language of "complement" rather than "direct object." For example, ὅτι is often used to introduce complement clauses with verbs of speech that represent what was said: λέγω γὰρ ὑμῖν ὅτι δύναται ὁ θεὸς ἐκ τῶν λίθων τούτων ἐγεῖραι τέκνα τῷ Ἀβραάμ ("For I tell you that God is able to raise up children for Abraham from these stones.")

Cognition – A verb of cognition is a verb that refers to some sort of mental process.

Complement – In the handbook, this term is used in two ways in addition to its use in the phrase, "clausal complement": (1) A constituent, other than an accusative direct object, that is required to complete a verb phrase. Verbs that include a prepositional prefix often take a complement whose case is determined by the prefix. For example, verbs with the prefix συν- characteristically take a dative complement. (2) The second element in a double accusative construction, which completes the verbal idea. In the sentence, "I call my son Superman," Superman would be the complement.

Doublet – Two near synonyms that are joined by a καί and used to express a single idea (often also referred to as hendiadys). Doublets in Greek, such as τέρατα καὶ σημεῖα, tend to serve as a way of intensifying the semantics of the conjoined terms.

Enclitic – A clitic is a word that appears as a discreet word in the syntax but is pronounced as if it were part of another word. Enclitics "give" their accent to the *preceding* word.

Equative verb/clause – An equative verb, like εἰμί, γίνομαι, or ὑπάρχω, is a verb that joins a subject and predicate to form an equative clause ("something is something"), e.g., Ἡ γενεὰ αὕτη γενεὰ πονηρά ἐστιν ("This generation is a wicked generation").

Foreground – This term is used to refer to information that is on the event line, or storyline, i.e., those events that move the narrative forward.

Fronting – Placing a constituent earlier in the sentence than its default order, most commonly in a pre-verbal position.

Genitive of relationship – Wallace (83) prefers to limit this label to *familial* relationships, but we have followed Young (25-26) in applying it to a variety of *social* relationships as well, including slaves, friends, and enemies.

Headless relative clause – A relative clause with no expressed antecedent, e.g., "He is doing *that which is not lawful.*"

Inclusio – An "envelope" or "bookend" structure in which the same or similar language is used to begin and end a unit of discourse.

Litotes – A figure of speech in which a statement is made by negating the opposite idea. For example, "she is *not* a *bad* tennis player" means "she is a *good* tennis player."

Marked – Departing from the normal or neutral pattern, or having additive features. At various levels of grammar, speakers/ writers have a choice between various options. One option will typically be viewed as the "default" or "unmarked" member of the set. The other members are "marked." Something that is "marked" may be more prominent, in focus, emphatic, etc.

Metonymy/Metonym – Metonymy is a figure of speech in which one term is used in place of another with which it is associated. In the expression, "he was reading the prophet Isaiah," the writer ("the prophet Isaiah") is used as a metonym for his writings ("the book that the prophet Isaiah wrote").

Nominal (clause) – A nominal is a noun or something that functions like a noun. In a nominal clause, a nominative noun stands alone in the clause without a verb, and sometimes without any other elements.

Nominalizer – In Greek syntax, this term refers to an article that is used to change a word, phrase, or clause into a substantive. Most commonly, nominalizers are used to make an adjective or participle substantival.

Prominence – The "semantic and grammatical elements of discourse that serve to set aside certain subjects, ideas or motifs of the author as more or less semantically or pragmatically significant than others" (Reed, 75-76).

Protasis – The first part ("if" clause) in a conditional construction.

Synecdoche – A figure of speech in which one term is used in place of another with which it is associated, specifically involving a part-whole relationship. In the sentence, "Do you have your own wheels?" the word "wheels" stands for the entire "vehicle" of which it is a part.

Topic construction – In the handbook, this term is used in relation to the phenomenon that linguists refer to as left-dislocation. This literary device introduces "the next primary topic of the discourse" (Runge §14.2) by placing it at the beginning of the sentence and then picking it up with a resumptive pronoun in the actual sentence. For example, "The struggling student in my Greek class, he passed his mid-term exam with flying colors."

Unmarked – The unmarked or default choice between two or more options refers to a writer choosing not to signal the presence of some feature (Runge §9.2).

BIBLIOGRAPHY

Anderson, Jay, and Joy Anderson. "Cataphora in 1 John." *Notes on Translation* 7.2 (1993): 41–46.

Anderson, John L. *An Exegetical Summary of 1, 2, and 3 John.* Dallas: Summer Institute of Linguistics, 1992.

Avishur, Yitzhak. *Stylistic Studies of Word-Pairs in Biblical and Ancient Semitic.* Neukirchen-Vluyn: Neukirchener, 1984.

Bakker, Egbert J. "Voice, Aspect and Aktionsart: Middle and Passive in Ancient Greek." Pages 23–47 in *Voice: Form and Function. Typological Studies in Language* 27. Edited by Barbara A. Fox and Paul J. Hopper. Amsterdam/Philadelphia: John Benjamins, 1994.

Bauer, Johannes. "ΠΩΣ in der Griechischen Bibel." *Novum Testamentum* 2 (1958): 81–91.

Bauer, Walter, William F. Arndt, and F. Wilbur Gingrich. *A Greek-English Lexicon of the New Testament and Other Early Christian Literature.* Translated and adapted by W. F. Arndt, and F. W. Gingrich. 2d ed. revised and augmented by F. W. Gingrich and F. W. Danker. Chicago: University of Chicago Press, 1979.

Beekman, John, and John Callow. *Translating the Word of God.* Dallas: Summer Institute of Linguistics, 1974.

Beekman, John, John Callow, and Michael Kopesec. *The Semantic Structure of Written Communication.* Dallas: Summer Institute of Linguistics, 1981.

Behm, Johannes. "παράκλητος." Pages 800–14 in vol. 5 of *Theological Dictionary of the New Testament.* Edited by G. Kittel and G. Friedrich. Translated by G. Bromiley. 10 vols. Grand Rapids: Eerdmans, 1964–1976.

Boyer, James L. "A Classification of Imperatives: A Statistical Study." *Grace Theological Journal* 8 (1987): 35–54.

Brooke, A. E. *The Johannine Epistles. International Critical Commentary*. Edinburgh: T&T Clark, 1912.

Brown, Gillian, and George Yule. *Discourse Analysis*. Cambridge: Cambridge University Press, 1983.

Brown, Raymond E. *The Epistles of John*. Anchor Bible. New York: Doubleday, 1982.

Büchsel, Friedrich. "ἱλασμός." Pages 317–18 in vol. 3 of *Theological Dictionary of the New Testament*. Edited by G. Kittel and G. Friedrich. Translated by G. Bromiley. 10 vols. Grand Rapids: Eerdmans, 1964–1976.

Bultmann, Rudolf. *The Johannine Epistles*. Translated by R. Philip O'Hara, Lane C. McGaughy and Robert W. Funk. Hermeneia. Philadelphia: Fortress, 1973.

Burdick, Donald W. *The Letters of John the Apostle*. Chicago: Moody, 1985.

Callow, John. "Where Does 1 John 1 End?" Pages 392–406 in *Discourse Analysis and the New Testament: Approaches and Results*. Edited by Stanley E. Porter and Jeffrey T. Reed. Journal for the Study of the New Testament: Supplement Series 170. Sheffield: Sheffield Academic Press, 1999.

Campbell, J. Y. "*Koinonia* and its Cognates in the New Testament." *Journal of Biblical Literature* 51 (1932): 352–80.

Caragounis, Chrys C. *The Development of Greek and the New Testament: Morphology, Syntax, Phonology, and Textual Transmission*. Grand Rapids, Baker Academic, 2006.

Carson, D. A. "The Purpose of the Fourth Gospel: John 20:21 Reconsidered." *Journal of Biblical Literature* 106 (1987): 639–51.

————. *Greek Accents: A Student's Manual*. Grand Rapids: Baker, 1985.

Clarke, Kent D. *Textual Optimism: A Critique of the United Bible Societies' Greek New Testament*. Journal for the Study of the New Testament: Supplement Series 138. Sheffield: Sheffield Academic Press, 1997.

Conrad, Carl W. "New Observations on Voice in the Ancient Greek Verb. November 19, 2002." Online: http://www.ioa.com/~cwconrad/Docs/NewObsAncGrkVc.pdf. Accessed April, 22, 2004.

Cooper, Guy L. III. *Attic Greek Prose Syntax*. 2 vols. Ann Arbor: University of Michigan Press, 1998–2002.

Culy, Martin M. *Echoes of Friendship in the Gospel of John*. New Testament Monographs 30. Sheffield: Sheffield Phoenix, 2010.

———. "Relative Clauses in Koine Greek: A Transformational Approach." M.A. thesis, University of North Dakota, 1989.

Culy, Martin M., and Mikeal C. Parsons. *Acts: A Handbook on the Greek Text*. Waco, Tex.: Baylor University Press, 2003.

Dana, H. E., and Julius R. Mantey. *A Manual Grammar of the Greek New Testament*. Upper Saddle River, NJ: Prentice Hall, 1957.

Danker, Frederick W., ed. *A Greek-English Lexicon of the New Testament and Other Early Christian Literature*, 3d ed. Based on Walter Bauer's *Griechisch-Deutsches Wörterbuch zu den Schriften des Neuen Testaments und der Frühchristlichen Literatur*, 6th ed., and on previous English editions by William F. Arndt, F. Wilbur Gingrich, and F. W. Danker. Chicago: University of Chicago, 2000.

Dodd, C. H. *The Johannine Epistles*. London: Hodder and Stoughton, 1946.

Floor, Sebastiaan. "A Discourse Analysis of 3 John." *Notes on Translation* 4.4 (1990): 1–17.

Foerster, Werner. "διαβάλλω διάβολος." Pages 71–81 in vol. 2 of *Theological Dictionary of the New Testament*. Edited by G. Kittel and G. Friedrich. Translated by G. Bromiley. 10 vols. Grand Rapids: Eerdmans, 1964–1976.

Francis, Fred O. "The Form and Function of the Opening and Closing Paragraphs of James and 1 John." *Zeitschrift für die neutestamentliche Wissenschaft und die Kunde der älteren Kirche* 61 (1970): 110–26.

Freed, E. D. "Variations in the Language and Thought of John." *Zeitschrift für die neutestamentliche Wissenschaft und die Kunde der älteren Kirche* 55 (1964): 167–97.

Friberg, Timothy. "New Testament Greek Word Order in the Light of Discourse Considerations." Ph.D. diss., University of Minnesota, 1982.

Grayston, Kenneth. *The Johannine Epistles*. New Century Bible Commentary. Grand Rapids: Eerdmans, 1984.

———. "The Meaning of *Parakletos*." *Journal for the Study of the New Testament* 13 (1981): 67–82.

Greenlee, J. Harold. "1 John 3:2—'If It/He is Manifested.'" *Notes on Translation* 14.1 (2000): 47–48.

Haas, C., M. de Jonge, and J. L. Swellengrebel. *A Translator's Handbook on the Letters of John.* New York: United Bible Societies, 1972.

Harris, Murray J. "Appendix: Prepositions and Theology in the Greek New Testament." Pages 1171–1215 in vol. 3 of *The New International Dictionary of New Testament Theology.* 3 vols. Edited by Colin Brown. Grand Rapids: Zondervan, 1975–1978.

Harris, W. Hall III. *1, 2, 3 John: Comfort and Counsel for a Church in Crisis.* Biblical Studies Press, 2003.

Healey, Phillis, and Alan Healey. "Greek Circumstantial Participles: Tracking Participants with Participles in the Greek New Testament." *Occasional Papers in Translation and Textlinguistics* 4.3 (1990): 177–257.

Houlden, James L. *A Commentary on the Johannine Epistles.* Harper's New Testament Commentary. New York: Harper & Row, 1973.

Kemmer, Suzanne. *The Middle Voice.* Philadelphia: John Benjamins, 1993.

Kruse, Colin G. *The Letters of John.* Pillar New Testament Commentary. Grand Rapids: Eerdmans, 2000.

Larsen, Iver. "Word Order and Relative Prominence in New Testament Greek: A New Look." *Notes on Translation* 15.2 (2001): 13–27.

———. "Notes on the Function of γάρ, οὖν, μέν, δέ, and τέ in the Greek New Testament." *Notes on Translation* 5.1 (1991a): 35–47.

———. "Boundary Features in the Greek New Testament." *Notes on Translation* 5.1 (1991b): 48–54.

———. "The Phrase ἐν τούτῳ in 1 John." *Notes on Translation* 4.4 (1990a): 27–34.

———. "Jesus Came through Water and Blood: 1 John 5.6." *Notes on Translation* 4.4 (1990b): 35–38.

Larson, Mildred L. *Meaning-based Translation: A Guide to Cross-Language Equivalence.* New York: University Press of America, 1984.

Law, Robert. *The Tests of Life: A Study of the First Epistle of St. John.* 3d ed. Edinburgh: T&T Clark, 1914.

Levinsohn, Stephen H. *Discourse Features of New Testament Greek*. Dallas: Summer Institute of Linguistics, 1992.

———. *Textual Connections in Acts*. Atlanta: Scholars Press, 1987.

Longacre, Robert E. "Towards an Exegesis of 1 John Based on the Discourse Analysis of the Greek Text." Pages 271–86 in *Linguistics and New Testament Interpretation: Essays on Discourse Analysis*. Edited by David Alan Black. Dallas: Summer Institute of Linguistics, 1992.

———. "Exhortation and Mitigation in First John." *Selected Technical Articles Related to Translation* 9 (1983): 3–44.

Louw, Johannes P. "Verbal Aspect in the First Letter of John." *Neotestamentica* 9 (1975): 98–104.

Louw, Johannes P., and Eugene A. Nida, eds. *Greek-English Lexicon of the New Testament Based on Semantic Domains*. 2 vols. New York: United Bible Societies, 1988.

Marshall, I. Howard. *The Epistles of John*. New International Commentary on the New Testament. Grand Rapids: Eerdmans, 1978.

McKay, K. L. *A New Syntax of the Verb in New Testament Greek: An Aspectual Approach*. Studies in Biblical Greek 5. New York: Peter Lang, 1994.

Metzger, Bruce M. *A Textual Commentary on the Greek New Testament*. 2d ed. Stuttgart: German Bible Society, 1994.

Miehle, Helen L. "Theme in Greek Hortatory Discourse: Van Dijk and Beekman-Callow Approaches Applied to 1 John." Ph.D. diss., University of Texas at Arlington, 1981.

Miller, Neva F. "Appendix 2: A Theory of Deponent Verbs." Pages 423–30 in *Analytical Lexicon of the Greek New Testament*. Edited by Timothy Friberg, Barbara Friberg, and Neva Miller. Grand Rapids: Baker, 2000.

Mitchell, Margaret M. "'Diotrephes Does not Receive Us': The Lexicographical and Social Context of 3 John 9-10." *Journal of Biblical Literature* 117 (1998): 299–320.

Moule, C. F. D. *An Idiom Book of New Testament Greek*. Cambridge: University Press, 1959.

Moulton, James Hope. *A Grammar of New Testament Greek*. Volume 1: *Prolegomena*. 3d ed. Edinburgh: T&T Clark, 1908.

Olsson, Birger. "First John: Discourse Analyses and Interpretations." Pages 369–91 in *Discourse Analysis and the*

New Testament: Approaches and Results. Edited by Stanley
   E. Porter and Jeffrey T. Reed. Journal for the Study of the
   New Testament: Supplement Series 170. Sheffield: Sheffield
   Academic Press, 1999.

Pennington, Jonathan T. "Deponency in Koine Greek: The
   Grammatical Question and the Lexicographical Dilemma."
   Trinity Journal 24 (2003): 55–76.

Persson, Andrew. "Some Exegetical Problems in 1 John." *Notes
   on Translation* 4.4 (1990): 18–26.

Porter, Stanley E. *Idioms of the Greek New Testament.* 2d ed.
   Sheffield: Sheffield Academic Press, 1994.

————. *Verbal Aspect in the Greek of the New Testament, with
   Reference to Tense and Mood.* New York: Peter Lang, 1989.

Robertson, A. T. *A Grammar of the Greek New Testament in the
   Light of Historical Research.* Nashville: Broadman, 1934.

Rogers, Cleon L. Jr., and Cleon L. Rogers III. *The New Linguistic
   and Exegetical Key to the Greek New Testament.* Grand Rapids:
   Zondervan, 1998.

Rogers, Elinor. "Vocatives and Boundaries." *Selected Technical
   Articles Related to Translation* 11 (1984): 24–29.

Ross, Alexander. *The Epistles of James and John.* New
   International Commentary on the New Testament. Grand
   Rapids: Eerdmans, 1954.

Schnackenburg, Rudolf. *The Johannine Epistles: A Commentary.*
   Translated by Reginald and Ilse Fuller. New York: Crossroad,
   1992.

Sherman, Grace E., and John C. Tuggy. *A Semantic and Structural
   Analysis of the Johannine Epistles.* Dallas: Summer Institute of
   Linguistics, 1994.

Smalley, Stephen S. *1, 2, 3 John.* Word Biblical Commentary.
   Dallas: Word Books, 1984.

Stälin, Gustav. "σκάνδαλον, σκαδαλίζω." Pages 339–58 in vol.
   7 of *Theological Dictionary of the New Testament.* Edited by
   G. Kittel and G. Friedrich. Translated by G. Bromiley. 10 vols.
   Grand Rapids: Eerdmans, 1964–1976.

Stott, John R.W. *The Epistles of John.* Tyndale New Testament
   Commentaries. Grand Rapids: Eerdmans, 1983.

Strecker, Georg. *The Johannine Letters.* Hermeneia. Minneapolis:
   Fortress, 1996.

Talbert, Charles H. *Reading John: A Literary and Theological Commentary on the Fourth Gospel and the Johannine Epistles.* New York: Crossroad, 1992.

Tarelli, C. C. "Johannine Synonyms." *Journal of Theological Studies* 47 (1946): 175–77.

Taylor, Bernard A. "Deponency and Greek Lexicography." Pages 167–76 in *Biblical Greek Language and Lexicography: Essays in Honor of Frederick W. Danker.* Edited by B. A. Taylor, et al. Grand Rapids: Eerdmans, 2004.

Tiller, Patrick A. "Reflexive Pronouns in the New Testament." *Filologia Neotestamentaria* 14 (2001): 43–63.

Titrud, Kermit. "The Function of καί in the Greek New Testament and an Application to 2 Peter." Pages 240–70 in *Linguistics and New Testament Interpretation: Essays on Discourse Analysis.* Edited by David Alan Black. Dallas: Summer Institute of Linguistics, 1992.

Wallace, Daniel B. *Greek Grammar Beyond the Basics: An Exegetical Syntax of the New Testament.* Grand Rapids: Zondervan, 1996.

————. "The Semantics and Exegetical Significance of the Object-Complement Construction in the New Testament." *Grace Theological Journal* 6 (1985): 91–112.

Wendland, Ernst R. "What is Truth? Semantic Density and the Language of the Johannine Epistles with Special Reference to 2 John." *Notes on Translation* 5.1 (1991): 21–60.

Wenham, Gordon J. *Genesis 1–15.* Word Bibical Commentary. Dallas: Word, 1987.

Westcott, Brooke Foss. *Epistles of St. John: The Greek Text.* London: Macmillan, 1909.

Young, Richard A. *Intermediate New Testament Greek: A Linguistic and Exegetical Approach.* Nashville: Broadman and Holman, 1994.

GRAMMAR INDEX

182 Grammar Index

εἰς (advantage), 3 John 5
εἰς (goal), 5:8
εἰς (locative), 3:14; 4:1, 9; 2 John 7, 10
εἰς (purpose), 3:8
εἰς (temporal), 2:17; 2 John 2
ἐκ (means), 3:24; 4:6
ἐκ (partitive), 4:19; 2 John 4
ἐκ (separation), 2:19; 3:14; 3 John 10
ἐκ (source/origin), 2:16, 19, 21; 3:8, 9, 10, 24; 4:1, 2, 3, 5, 6, 7, 13
ἐν (instrumental), 2:3, 5; 3:10, 16, 18, 19, 24; 4:2, 9, 13, 17; 5:2, 6
ἐν (locative), 1:5, 6, 7; 2:5, 15², 16; 3:5, 15; 4:3, 4², 9, 12, 17; 5:10, 11, 19
ἐν (manner), 4:2; 2 John 1, 4, 7; 3 John 1, 3
ἐν (means), 5:6
ἐν (reference/respect), 2:5, 8²; 4:10, 18; 2 John 1; 3 John 1
ἐν (temporal), 2:28; 4:17
ἐπί (cause), 3 John 10

fronting, 1:5, 6, 7, 8, 9, 10; 2:3, 4, 7, 8, 19, 24, 27; 3:9; 4:9, 20; 5:12, 13; 3 John 2, 4

γάρ (causal), 2:19; 4:20
γάρ (explanatory), 2:19
genitive absolute (temporal), 3 John 3²
genitive in apposition, 1:3, 7; 3:23; 2 John 3²
genitive of comparison, 3:20; 3 John 4
genitive of reference, 3 John 3
genitive of relationship, 1:3, 7;

2:1, 9, 10, 11; 3:1, 2, 8, 10², 12, 15, 17, 23; 4:9, 10, 15, 20², 21; 5:2, 5, 9, 10², 11, 12, 13, 16, 20²; 2 John 1, 3, 4, 13²
genitive of source, 1:10; 2:14, 16³, 4:2
genitive of subordination, 3 John 9
genitive subject, 3 John 3

headless relative clause, 1:1, 3; 2:5, 24²; 4:6; 5:15; 2 John 5, 8; 3 John 5
hendiadys, 3:18²
hortatory subjunctive, 3:18; 4:7
hyperbole, 3:15

ἵνα (clausal complement), 2 John 5
ἵνα (conclusion), 1:9
ἵνα (epexegetical), 2:27; 3:8; 4:17; 2 John 5
ἵνα (indirect discourse), 5:16
ἵνα (purpose), 1:3, 4, 2:1, 19, 28; 3:5; 4:9; 5:13, 20; 2 John 8, 12; 3 John 8
ἵνα (result), 4:17; 5:20
inclusio, 1:6, 10; 2 John 3
infinitive (complementary), 2:6; 3:9, 16; 4:12, 20; 2 John 12³; 3 John 2², 8, 13², 14
infinitive (direct object), 2 John 10, 11
infinitive (indirect discourse), 2:6, 9; 3 John 2²

καθώς (comparative), 2:6, 18, 27; 3:2, 3, 7, 12, 23; 4:17; 2 John 4, 6; 3 John 2, 3
κατά (distributive), 3 John 15
κατά (standard), 5:14; 2 John 6

AUTHOR INDEX